Outlook®

for dummies®
A Wiley Brand

Outlook®

By Faithe Wempen, M.A.

for dummies®

A Wiley Brand

Outlook® For Dummies®

Published by: **John Wiley & Sons, Inc.,** 111 River Street, Hoboken, NJ 07030-5774, www.wiley.com

Copyright © 2022 by John Wiley & Sons, Inc., Hoboken, New Jersey

Published simultaneously in Canada

For general information on our other products and services, please contact our Customer Care Department within the U.S. at 877-762-2974, outside the U.S. at 317-572-3993, or fax 317-572-4002. For technical support, please visit https://hub.wiley.com/community/support/dummies.

Wiley publishes in a variety of print and electronic formats and by print-on-demand. Some material included with standard print versions of this book may not be included in e-books or in print-on-demand. If this book refers to media such as a CD or DVD that is not included in the version you purchased, you may download this material at http://booksupport.wiley.com. For more information about Wiley products, visit www.wiley.com.

Library of Congress Control Number: 2021950179

ISBN 978-1-119-82911-9 (pbk); ISBN 978-1-119-82912-6 (ebk); ISBN 978-1-119-82913-3 (ebk)

Contents at a Glance

Table of Contents

Introduction

Microsoft Outlook has become an essential business tool in the years since it was first released in the 1990s. If you work in a company that employs more than a dozen people, it's a pretty good bet that you'll be using Microsoft Outlook to manage your email and calendar. Whether you're giving or taking directions, organizing meetings, collaborating on important projects, or just keeping up with business, Outlook is what you'll use to get it done fast. Outlook has become even more important to businesses in recent years, with more companies encouraging telecommuting and hiring employees who work from home.

Outlook is not just for business use, though — far from it. Outlook is also the application of choice for millions of people who use it for their own personal communication needs. Students use it to communicate with their teachers and fellow students about academic projects. Parents use it to manage the family calendar so that everyone knows where they need to be. Hobbyists use it to communicate with other people who share their passion for whatever makes them smile, whether it's birdwatching, woodworking, or role-playing games.

Outlook: What Is It Good For?

Outlook is a personal information manager that can act as your assistant in dealing with the flurry of small but important details that stand between you and the work (or play) you do. It sends and receives email, maintains your address book, schedules meetings and appointments, tracks your to-do list, and more, all in one place.

Here are just a few of the cool things it can do for you:

» Send email messages to individuals or groups, including attachments, graphics, text formatting, signature blocks, and more.

» Keep an address book of all your contacts with consistently up-to-date information.

>> Manage multiple calendars (such as for work and for home) and overlay their appointments in a single view so you can make sure there aren't any conflicts.

>> Schedule a meeting and reserve a conference room in your workplace, then send out meeting invitations and track who has accepted or declined.

>> Organize hundreds of little pieces of data with digital "sticky notes" that you can search, sort, and color-code.

About This Book

Outlook For Dummies Office 2021 Edition is your one-stop guide to all things Outlook. Whether you're brand-new to Outlook or a long-time casual user looking to go deeper, you'll find the help you need here. The book is organized in six parts, each with a specific theme:

Part 1: Getting Started with Outlook. Start here if you're not already familiar with Outlook at a basic level. Here you'll get an overview of what Outlook does, take a guided tour of the interface, and learn some handy shortcuts for getting around.

Part 2: Taming the Email Beast. If you're mostly interested in Outlook's email capabilities, start here. You'll learn how to send and receive messages with all kinds of different options, like attachments, special formatting, signature lines, and read receipts. You'll also learn how to organize your messages into folders, create mail-handling rules that automatically move incoming messages into certain folders, and set up multiple email accounts to work with Outlook.

Part 3: Keeping Track of Contacts, Dates, Tasks, and More. In this part you'll learn about several of Outlook's tools for organizing your busy life and schedule. You'll see how to set up your address book (which Outlook calls *Contacts*), how to schedule meetings and appointments on your calendar(s), and how to manage your to-do list.

Part 4: Taking Outlook to the Next Level. This part tackles some less common topics that may be of interest to you. You'll find out how to integrate Outlook with other Office applications and with Google and iCloud services, for example. You'll also learn how to use Outlook on mobile devices that run iOS or Android, and how to customize Outlook to better serve you.

Part 5: Outlook at Work. Some Outlook features only work if your office uses an Exchange mail server (and a lot of offices do). You'll learn about those features in this part, and you'll find out how to use Outlook.com and the Outlook Web app for telecommuting.

Part 6: The Part of Tens. As is customary in a Dummies book, I wrap things up by providing some Top 10 lists that you can skim at your leisure. You'll learn about ten time-saving shortcuts, ten things that Outlook actually *can't* do (so you can stop banging your head against the wall trying to get them to work!), and ten cool features that most people don't know about.

About Version Numbers

Outlook is part of a suite of applications called Microsoft Office. Microsoft offers a choice in how to buy Microsoft Office: as a subscription or as a one-time purchase.

The one-time-purchase version has a version number that represents the year it came out, like Office 2021. There are different editions of this product for different demographics, like Professional, Home and Student, or Enterprise. You get periodic automatic updates (if that option is enabled), but there are no major upgrade options. That means if you plan to upgrade to the next major release in the future, you will have to buy it at full price.

The subscription method is called Office 365, and it's the most popular one, both for business and personal uses. Office 365 is a general name for the subscription offering; 365 is not a version number. With the subscription method, you always have the most recent version at no extra charge, even if a major new version comes out. Microsoft silently rolls out new features and tweaks nearly every month via automatic download and installation. One day you'll open up Outlook and notice a new feature, or you'll see that the interface looks slightly different (and hopefully you'll think it's an improvement!). There are different Office 365 subscription plans for individuals, businesses, and schools that contain different combinations of the various applications. (They all include Outlook, though.)

Some business IT departments *really* don't like the fact that Microsoft frequently rolls out updates to Office without advance warning. They like to be able to control what updates are installed — and when. They like to get the updates well in advance and test them before they allow them to roll out to the users they support, to make sure there are no conflicts or bugs that will cause problems with other essential software that they use. For these companies, Microsoft offers an alternative: They will sell these companies a version of Office 2021 that does not automatically update. It stays exactly the same for months at a time, with changes rolled out every 6 months. This roll-out method is called the Long-Term Servicing Channel (LTSC).

So, generally speaking, what does all this mean to you?

>> You probably have Office 365. Most people do.

>> Which version you have really doesn't matter all that much. All versions get updated — just on different schedules.

>> You might see some minor differences in your Outlook interface compared to what's shown and described in this book. This is unavoidable.

Foolish Assumptions

As I wrote this book, I made certain assumptions about you, its reader. For one thing, I assume you know how to turn on your computer, use a mouse and keyboard, and navigate your way around Microsoft Windows 10. If Windows or Microsoft Office is strange to you, I recommend picking up Andy Rathbone's *Windows 10 For Dummies* or Wallace Wang's *Microsoft Office For Dummies*, respectively. Or, if you're of the senior set and more interested in home use than business, check out my book *Microsoft Office For Seniors For Dummies*. (All are published by Wiley.)

And speaking of Windows, I'm assuming you have the desktop version of Outlook running on Windows 11. (Yes, it also runs on laptops.) There are online and mobile versions of Outlook, and in fact I do cover them in Chapter 16, but most of this book is for users of the version that runs on Windows computers. There is also a Mac version of Outlook, and it works basically the same as the Windows version, but I don't cover it specifically.

I'm *not* making any assumptions about whether you're a home or business user; there's plenty of help in this book for both.

Interface Conventions Used in This Book

Outlook has many unique features, but it also has lots in common with other Windows programs: dialog boxes, drop-down menus, Ribbons, and so on. To be productive with Outlook, you need to understand how these features work and recognize the conventions I use for describing these features throughout this book.

Dialog boxes and windows

You deal with more dialog boxes in Outlook than you do in many other Microsoft Office programs. A dialog box is a box that pops up asking for information. Sometimes it's super simple, like a warning message asking you to click OK to continue. Other times there are dozens of options, like the dialog box that lets you set Outlook program options (covered in Chapter 14).

Here are the essential parts of a dialog box. You can see them in action in Figure I-1.

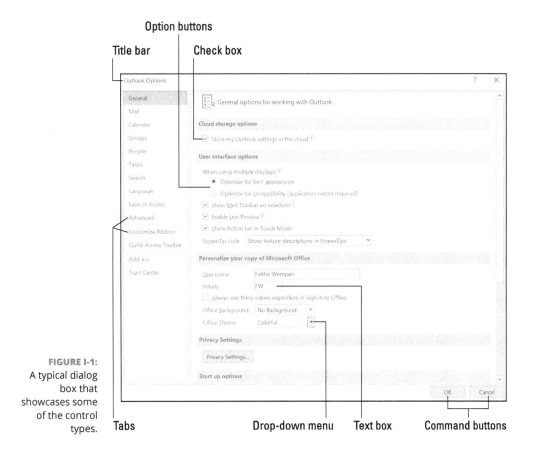

FIGURE I-1:
A typical dialog box that showcases some of the control types.

- >> **Title bar:** The title bar tells you the name of the dialog box or window.

- >> **Text boxes:** Text boxes are blank spaces into which you type information. When you click a text box, you see a blinking cursor, which means you can type text there.

- >> **Option buttons:** These are sets of round buttons where you can only select one of them at a time. When you click one, the others become unselected. They're used for situations where it's impossible to have more than one thing at a time, like Portrait vs. Landscape page orientation.

- >> **Check boxes:** These are square boxes for individual yes/no toggles. Even if there's a set of them, each one is separate.

- >> **Drop-down menus:** These look like rectangular buttons, but they have a down-pointing arrow at the right side. When you click them, a menu of options appears; click an option to make your selection.

- >> **Command buttons:** These rectangular buttons execute commands, like OK or Cancel. Sometimes they have an ellipsis on them (three dots, like this: . . .), which indicates that they open another dialog box.

- >> **Tabs:** Some dialog boxes have multiple pages, and each page has a tab you can click to display it. In Figure I-1 the tabs are just words in a bar along the left side, but in some dialog boxes the tabs run across the top of the dialog box window and look like actual file folder tabs.

Windows are closely related to dialog boxes; they're large boxes (typically resizable) designed to help you create or manage data. For example, when you schedule a new appointment on the calendar, a New Appointment window opens up, prompting you for the title, date, time, and any notes. The same is true for new email messages, new contacts, and so on.

Ribbons and tabs

Outlook features a strip of graphical buttons across the top called the Ribbon. See Figure I-2. You can find out what each button does by hovering the mouse pointer over it so a pop-up ScreenTip appears.

FIGURE I-2:
The Home tab of
the Ribbon in
Outlook.

The Ribbon is a multi-tabbed affair, and the tab names appear as a row of text above the Ribbon: Home, View, and so on. You start out on the Home tab, but you can click one of the other tabs to switch to it any time.

There's one special tab: File. This tab opens a whole different screen, called Backstage view. This screen lets you open and export data files, set program options, print, and perform maintenance-type functions like setting up rules, managing add-ins, and setting program options. See Figure I-3.

FIGURE I-3:
Backstage View
in Outlook.

Keyboard shortcuts

Normally, you can choose any Windows command in at least two different ways (and sometimes more):

» Click a button on the Ribbon or in the navigation pane.

» Press a keyboard combination. An example is Ctrl+B, which means holding down the Ctrl key and pressing the letter B. (You use this command to make text bold.)

» Press the F10 key to reveal the keyboard equivalents on the various Ribbon tabs and commands, and then press that key to make your selection. (This is way too much trouble for most people, but maybe you love a challenge).

Another fast way to get at your favorite Outlook features is the Quick Access Toolbar — a small strip of icons in the upper left corner of your screen. In Chapter 14, I describe how that works and how to make it do what you want.

Icons Used in This Book

Keep an eye out for the following icons sprinkled throughout the chapters — these little pictures draw your attention to specific types of useful information:

WARNING

The Warning icon points to something that can prevent or cause problems — good stuff to know!

REMEMBER

The Remember icon offers helpful information. (Everything in this book is helpful, but this stuff is even *more* helpful.)

TIP

The Tip icon points out a hint or trick for saving time and effort or something that makes Outlook easier to understand.

TECHNICAL STUFF

The Technical Stuff icon identifies background information that casual users can skip, although it may make for good conversation at a really dull party.

Beyond the Book

In addition to the material in the print or ebook you're reading right now, this product comes with some goodies on the web that you can access anywhere. No matter how well you understand the concepts of Outlook, you'll likely come across a few questions where you don't have a clue. To get this material, simply go to www.dummies.com and search for "Outlook For Dummies Office 2021 Edition Cheat Sheet" in the Search box.

1

Getting Started with Outlook

IN THIS PART . . .

Learn how to use Outlook to read and send email, send attachments, and create appointments and tasks as well as how to use the Calendar feature to help you meet important deadlines.

Explore the various parts of Outlook, including views, menus, and folders, as well as the search feature.

Discover how to create contacts and calendar appointments as well as how to use dragging, how to create and modify tasks, and how to further enhance your productivity.

IN THIS CHAPTER

» **Exploring what you can do with Outlook**

» **Switching to the Simplified Ribbon**

» **Reading and creating email**

» **Sending files by email**

» **Checking your calendar**

» **Entering appointments and contacts**

» **Managing tasks**

» **Keeping notes**

Chapter **1**

A First Look at Outlook

This book kicks off with Outlook's Greatest Hits — the things you'll want to do with Outlook every single day. The list sounds simple enough: sending email, making appointments, and so on. But there's more here than meets the eye; Outlook does ordinary things extraordinarily well.

Most people use only about 5 percent of Outlook's power. (Hey, that's kind of like how people only use a small percentage of their brains!) Even if you move up to using 10 percent of Outlook's features, you'll be amazed at how this application can streamline your life and spiff up your communications.

Why Outlook?

Millions of people use Outlook because millions of people use Outlook. That sounds redundant, but it's the truth. People choose Outlook not only because it has great features, but also because so many other people have already chosen it. Outlook is the standard tool for communicating, collaborating, and organizing for millions of people around the world.

Why does popularity matter? It's mainly a matter of standardization. When so many people use the same tool for organizing the things they do individually, it becomes vastly easier for everyone to organize the things they do together by using that tool. That's the case with Outlook. It's a powerful tool even if you work all alone, but that power gets magnified when you use it to collaborate with others.

Doing (Almost) Anything with a Few Clicks

Well, okay, maybe it takes more than a few clicks for the complicated stuff. (More on that complicated stuff in later chapters.) But a lot of what you will do every day in Outlook is super simple.

Here's the skinny on the basic things that you probably want to do first:

>> **Open an item and read it:** Double-click the item. It opens in a new window. If you single-click it, it displays in a preview pane (not in a new window).

>> **Create a new item:** Click the New button on the Ribbon at the top of the screen and fill out the form that appears. (The New button will have a more specific name depending on the module you're working with. For example, in the Mail module, the button is called New Email.) When you're done, click the Send button or the Save & Close button, depending on the type of item.

>> **Delete an item:** Click the item once to select it and then click the Delete button on the Ribbon at the top of the screen. You can also press the Delete key on your keyboard, or right-click the item and choose Delete.

>> **Move an item:** Use your mouse to drag the item to where you want it, such as to a different folder for storage.

Outlook can also do some sophisticated tricks, such as automatically sorting your email or creating form letters, but you'll need to understand a few details to take advantage of those tricks. The other 300-plus pages of this book cover the finer points of Outlook.

Switching to the Simplified Ribbon

REMEMBER

The figures you see in this book and the instructions you read assume you're using Outlook the way it comes directly from Microsoft — either out of a box or as a download — with all the standard options installed. If you don't like the way the program looks (or how things are named) when you install Outlook, you can change many of the things you see. If you change too much, however, some instructions and examples I give you won't make as much sense. I suggest leaving the interface alone until you're comfortable using Outlook. Chapter 14 covers a variety of customization options.

There is one important option you might need to adjust before you go any further, though. The Ribbon, which is the toolbar across the top of the screen, has two different ways it can appear. The Simplified Ribbon, which is the default for all new installs of Outlook, looks like Figure 1-1. The Classic Ribbon, which was the default in earlier versions of Outlook, looks like Figure 1-2.

FIGURE 1-1:
The Simplified Ribbon

FIGURE 1-2:
The Classic Ribbon

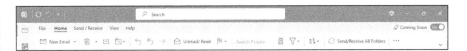

Ribbon Display Options arrow

This book's steps and figures show the Simplified Ribbon (Figure 1-1), so if your screen doesn't look like that, follow these steps to switch over to Simplified mode:

1. **Click the Ribbon Display Options arrow at the far right end of the Ribbon.**

   See Figure 1-2. A menu opens.

2. **Click Simplified Ribbon.**

   The Ribbon changes to Simplified mode.

I explain more about the two Ribbon modes in Chapter 2. Although I recommend that you use Simplified mode when following along with this book, I realize that some people who have been using Outlook for awhile with the Classic Ribbon just don't want to make the switch, so in this book I provide separate steps for each mode whenever there's a difference.

Using Email: Basic Delivery Techniques

Email is Outlook's most popular feature. I've run across people who didn't know Outlook could do anything *but* exchange email messages. It's a good thing that Outlook makes it so easy to read your email, although it's too bad so many people stop there.

Reading email

When you start Outlook, you normally see the Mail module, which is a screen with four columns. The leftmost column is the *navigation bar*. It contains buttons for each of Outlook's modules (sections), such as Mail, Calendar, People, and so on. You switch between modules by clicking one of those icons.

To its right is the Folder pane, which lets you switch between different locations, such as folders or data files. The third column contains your list of messages. The right column (called the Reading pane) contains the text of one of those messages. If the message is short enough, you may see its entire text in the Reading pane, as shown in Figure 1-3. If the message is longer, you'll have to open it, or scroll down in the Reading pane, to see the whole thing.

Mail

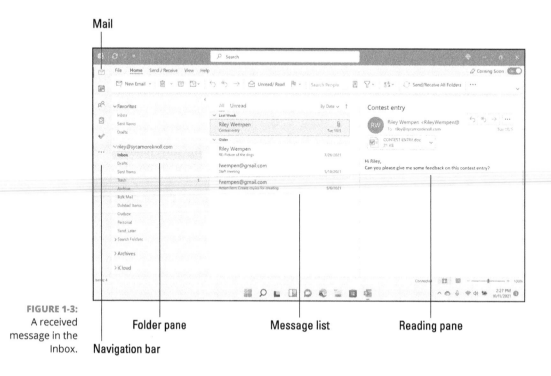

FIGURE 1-3:
A received
message in the
Inbox.

Folder pane   Message list   Reading pane

Navigation bar

To see an entire message, follow these steps:

1. **Click the Mail button in the navigation bar to make sure you are in the Mail module.**

   You don't need this step if you can already see your messages.

2. **Double-click the title of a message.**

   Now you can see the entire message on its own window.

3. **Press Esc to close the message.**

   The message window closes. (Note that closing a message does not delete it.)

TIP

A quick way to skim the messages in your Inbox is to click a message and then press the ↑ or ↓ key. You can move through your message list as you read the text of your messages in the Reading pane.

If you feel overwhelmed by the number of email messages you get each day, you're not alone. Billions of email messages fly around the Internet each day, and lots of people are feeling buried in messages. In Chapter 6, I show you the secrets of sorting and managing your messages, along with the Conversations feature, which makes it easy to deal with extended email discussions.

Answering email

Anytime you're reading an email message in Outlook, buttons labeled Reply and Reply All appear somewhere near the top of the screen. That's a hint.

To reply to a message you're reading, follow these steps:

1. **In the Mail module, select the message to which you want to reply.**

2. **Click the Reply button on the Home tab of the Ribbon.**

3. **Type your response.**

4. **Click the Send button.**

If you're reading a message sent to several people besides you, you have the option of sending a reply to everyone involved by clicking the Reply All button.

WARNING

Some people get carried away with the Reply All button and live to regret it. If you get a message addressed to lots of other people and click the Reply All button to fire back a snide response, you could instantly offend dozens of clients, bosses, or other bigwigs. Use Reply All when you need it, but make sure you really know who will be getting your message before you click the Send button.

When you reply to a message, by default, Outlook includes the text of the message that was sent to you. Some people like to include original text in their replies, but some don't. In Chapter 5, I show you how to change what Outlook automatically includes in replies.

Creating new email messages

The process of creating a new email message in Outlook is ridiculously simple. Even a child can do it. But if you can't get a child to create a new email message for you, you can do it yourself.

Follow these steps:

1. **To make sure you are in the Mail module, click Mail in the navigation bar.**

    Each of the modules has its own unique appearance, and you'll quickly learn to recognize at a glance which module you're working with at any point.

2. **Click the New Email button on the Home tab of the Ribbon.**

    An Untitled - Message window opens, containing a simple form you can fill out.

3. **Fill out the message form.**

    Put the recipient's address in the To box, type a subject in the Subject box, and type a message in the main message box. Figure 1-4 shows a completed example.

4. **Click the Send button.**

    Your message is on its way!

If you want to send a plain email message, these steps are all you have to do. If you prefer to send a fancier email, Outlook provides the bells and whistles — some of which are actually useful. For example, you might send a High Priority message to impress some big shots or send a Confidential message about a hush-hush topic. (Discover the mysteries of confidential email in Chapter 4.)

Sending a file

You can attach a file (or multiple files) to an outgoing email message. There are many different ways to do this, which I discuss in detail in Chapter 5. But for a teaser to that, here's one perfectly good method.

1. **Start a new email message in Outlook.**

   You just learned how to do this in the previous section.

2. **On the Message tab of the Ribbon, click Attach File.**

   A menu opens up with a bunch of recent data files on it. See Figure 1-5. If you see the file you want to attach, click it, and you're done; skip to Step 5. (If you are asked whether you want to Share Link or Attach as Copy; go with Attach as Copy.) If not, proceed to the next step.

3. **Click Browse This PC.**

   The Insert File dialog box opens.

4. **Locate and select the desired file and then click Insert.**

5. **Continue sending the message normally.**

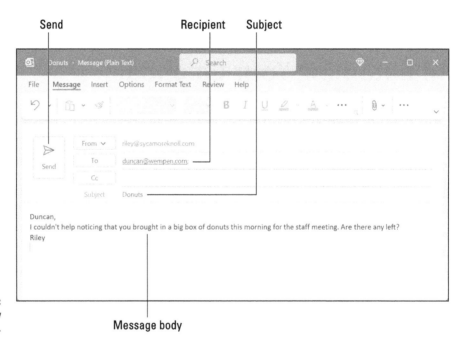

FIGURE 1-4:
Composing a new
email message.

You can also send links to files on your OneDrive; I get into that in Chapter 5, as well as how to send files directly from their home application. (For example, you can send a Word file to someone right from within Word.) So stay tuned for that!

Attach File

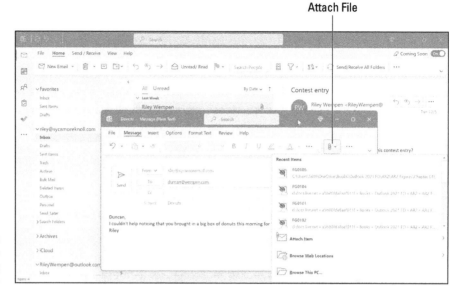

FIGURE 1-5:
Attaching a file to
an outgoing
message.

Maintaining Your Calendar

Time management is a myth. You can't get more than 24 hours in a day — no matter how well you manage your time. But you can get more done in a 24-hour day if you keep your calendar current. Outlook can help you with that.

Entering an appointment

If you've ever used an old-fashioned paper planner, the Outlook Calendar will look familiar to you. When you click the Calendar button in the navigation bar and then click the Day button on the Home tab, you see a grid in the middle of the screen with lines representing each segment of the day. You can adjust the length of the segments from as little as 5 minutes to as much as an hour, as shown in Figure 1-6.

To adjust the time intervals, right-click one of the times along the left edge and choose a different interval from the shortcut menu.

TIP

Calendar   This black line marks the current moment in time.

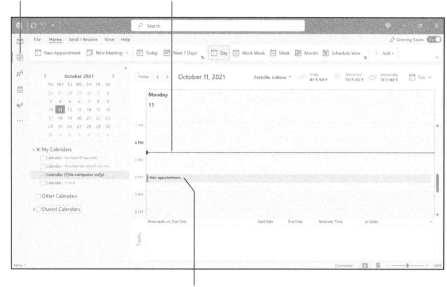

FIGURE 1-6:
Track your busy
schedule in the
Outlook
Calendar.

Click the line representing the desired time and then type the appointment name.

To enter an appointment at a certain time, follow these steps:

1. **Click Calendar in the navigation bar to switch to the Calendar module if needed.**

2. **On the Home tab, click Day.**

   You can create new appointments in other views, too, but let's stick to Day for now.

3. **Click the Today button.**

   Today's calendar appears if it did not already. A black line indicates the current time, as shown in Figure 1-6.

4. **Click the line next to the time you want your appointment to begin.**

   A colored bar appears there, ready for your typing.

5. **Type a name for your appointment.**

6. **Press Enter.**

If you want to enter more detailed information about your appointment — such as ending time, location, category, and so on — see Chapter 9 for the nitty-gritty on keeping track of all the details in your calendar.

Managing your schedule

Time management involves more than just entering appointments. If you're really busy, you want to manage your time by slicing and dicing your list of appointments to see when you're free to add even more appointments.

REMEMBER

You can choose from several different views of your calendar by clicking a button on the Home tab at the top of the Calendar screen:

>> Day

>> Work Week

>> Week

>> Month

>> Schedule View

If you need a more elaborate collection of Calendar views, click the View tab on the Ribbon and then choose one of the views listed under the Change View button. To really master time management, check out Chapter 9 to see the different ways you can view your Outlook Calendar.

Adding a Contact

When it's not *what* you know but *who* you know, you need a good tool for keeping track of who's who. Outlook is a great tool for managing your names and addresses, and it's just as easy to use as your "little black book."

To enter a new contact, follow these steps:

1. **Click People in the navigation bar to switch to the People module if needed.**

2. **Click the New Contact button on the Home tab of the Ribbon.**

    The New Contact entry form opens.

3. **Fill in the blanks on the form.**

    Figure 1-7 shows an example.

4. **Click the Save & Close button on the Ribbon.**

    Presto — you have a Contacts list!

People

FIGURE 1-7:
Fill in the form to
create the
contact.

Outlook's Contacts feature can be a lot more than a physical address book — if you know the ropes. Chapter 8 reveals the secrets of searching, sorting, and grouping the names in your list — and of using email to keep in touch with all the important people in your life.

Entering a Task

Knowing what you need to do isn't enough; you need to know what to do *next*. When you're juggling a thousand competing demands all at once, you need a tool that shows you at a glance what's up next so you can keep your work moving forward.

Outlook has several task management tools that help you organize your lengthy to-do list for peak performance. Those tools include the Tasks module, the To-Do module, and the To-Do bar. Chapter 10 describes all of them, but here's a quick way to get started.

To enter a new task, follow these steps:

1. **Click Tasks in the navigation bar to switch to the Tasks module if needed.**

The navigation bar might not show the Tasks icon, depending on your settings. If you don't see it, click More Apps (. . .) for a pop-up containing more icons, and then click Tasks.

2. **Click in the *Click here to add a new Task* text box and type the name of your task.**

3. **Press Enter.**

   Your new task moves down to the Task list with your other tasks, as shown in Figure 1-8. It also appears on your To-Do bar.

   If you do not see the To-Do bar, choose View ⇨ Layout ⇨ To-Do Bar ⇨ Tasks.

4. **Click the task you just created.**

   If the Reading Pane is visible, as it is in Figure 1-8, the task's details appear there. If you do not see the To-Do bar, choose View ⇨ Layout ⇨ Reading Pane ⇨ Right.

Outlook can help you manage anything from a simple shopping list to a complex business project. In Chapter 10, I show you how to deal with recurring tasks, how to regenerate tasks, and how to mark tasks as complete — and earn the right to brag about how much you've accomplished.

Tasks

Control the To-Do Bar and Reading Pane display here.

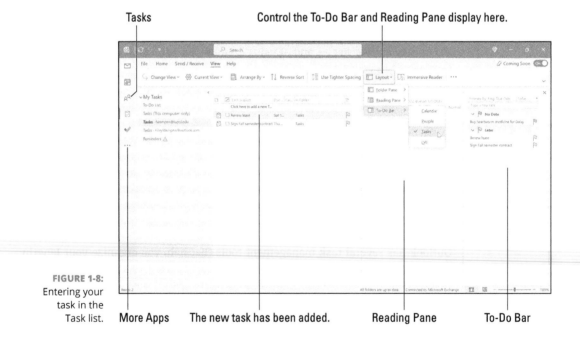

FIGURE 1-8: Entering your task in the Task list.

More Apps   The new task has been added.   Reading Pane   To-Do Bar

Taking Notes

I have hundreds of little scraps of information I need to keep somewhere, but until Outlook came along, I didn't have a place to put them. Now all the written flotsam and jetsam go into my Outlook Notes collection — where I can find them all again when I need them.

To create a new note, follow these steps:

1. Click Notes in the navigation bar to switch to the Notes module if needed.

If you don't see Notes in the navigation bar, click More Apps (. . .) and then click Notes.

2. Press Ctrl+Shift+N.

A blank note opens.

TIP

You could have also clicked New Note on the Ribbon in Step 2, but I wanted to show you an alternate method. A word about shortcuts: Ctrl+N starts a new item in whatever module you are working with; for example, in Mail it starts a new message and in Tasks it starts a new task. But Ctrl+Shift+N is special in that it always starts a new *note*, no matter which section of Outlook you are in.

3. Type the text you want to save.

The text you type appears in the note, as shown in Figure 1-9.

4. Press Esc.

The note you created appears in your list of notes. You can also click the Close (X) button in the upper right corner of the note to close it.

After you're in the habit of using Outlook to organize your life, I'm sure you'll want to move beyond the basics. That's what the rest of this book shows you. When you're ready to share your work with other people, send email like a pro, or just finish your workday by 5 p.m., you'll find ways to use Outlook to make your job — and your life — easier to manage.

FIGURE 1-9:
Preserve your prose for posterity in an Outlook note.

More Apps   **Notes**

IN THIS CHAPTER

» **Understanding Outlook's place in the Office universe**

» **Finding your way around in Outlook**

» **Using the Ribbon to issue commands**

» **Locating misplaced data with the Search feature**

» **Asking Outlook to help you**

Chapter **2**

Taking a Tour of the Outlook Interface

I recently heard that the average office worker spends 28 percent of each work week answering email. No wonder times are tough — everybody's too tied up with email to get anything done! When computers were invented, people thought they'd use them for something much more exciting than email. Oh, well. Welcome to the future — it's already here and it's already booked solid.

Fortunately, everyone gets more done now than in the past, partly because of tools like Microsoft Outlook. In fact, millions of people worldwide use Outlook to get more done every day. But most of those people use just a fraction of Outlook's power, so they work harder than necessary while getting less done. The people I've trained find that knowing a little bit more about what the app can do for them makes their lives easier. Let's hear it for making your life easier!

How Outlook Fits Into the Office Picture

Outlook is a part of Microsoft Office. It's called an Office *suite*, which means it's a collection of applications (apps for short) that work together, so you can easily create documents that contain multiple types of content. For example, you can copy a chart from a spreadsheet and paste it into a sales letter in a word processor.

Each of the Microsoft Office applications is designed to create a certain type of content, but they also work together as a team. It's kind of like the utensils you use for dining: You could eat your turkey dinner entirely with a fork, but it's much easier if you have a fork *and* a knife. And, of course, you want a spoon for the cranberry sauce. Each app in Microsoft Office specializes in something important: Microsoft Word for documents, Microsoft Excel charts for calculations, Microsoft PowerPoint for presentation graphics, and Microsoft Outlook for communications and organization. It's easy to use them separately and hugely productive to use them all together.

Until recently, Microsoft sold the Office suite as a packaged, store-bought product you could buy and use for years. They've changed their approach and now encourage everyone to rent Microsoft Office for a monthly or annual fee as part of a app called Office 365. Time will tell which approach is better. Microsoft clearly believes that software rental is the way of the future, so stay tuned.

As I mentioned in the Introduction, the product labeling is different depending on how you purchased the products. The one-time-purchase version is called Office 2021, and the subscription version is Office 365. This is mostly a matter of marketing, though, as the versions are nearly identical other than the names.

TECHNICAL STUFF

Outlook is also associated with several other Microsoft products. Microsoft Exchange Server is the backbone of the email system in many corporations, and Outlook is often the app that employees of those corporations use to read their company email. Microsoft SharePoint also connects to Outlook to help streamline the work of a group in much the same ways that Outlook speeds up the work of an individual. You don't need to worry about all this, though. You can start Outlook and use it the same way no matter which other apps it's bundled with.

Exploring Outlook's Main Screen

Outlook's interface is different from that of other Microsoft Office applications. Instead of offering to create a new document at startup, Outlook begins by displaying your email Inbox. From there you can navigate to one of the other modules or you can jump right into working with your mail.

Today, most people expect to find their way around a website or a computer app by clicking something on the left side of the screen and seeing something appear in the middle or on the right side of the screen. Outlook follows that pattern by putting the navigation controls on the left side of the screen — just the way you'd expect.

The Outlook main screen — which looks remarkably like Figure 2-1 — has all the usual parts of a Windows screen (see the Introduction if you're unfamiliar with how Windows looks), with a few important additions. At the left side of the screen, you see the navigation pane, and then the Folder pane. To the right of the Folder pane is the content that's specific to the module you're viewing; in the Mail module, there are two panes: a list of messages and a Reading pane. This area is different for each module. I also pointed these out back in Chapter 1.

Navigation bar

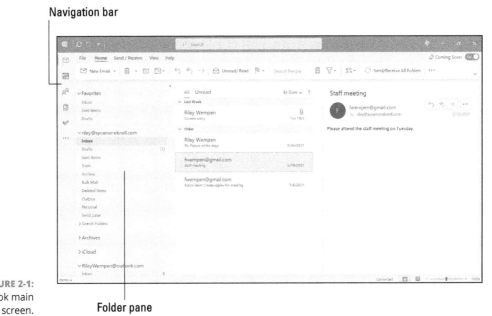

FIGURE 2-1:
The Outlook main screen.

Folder pane

Moving between modules

All the work you do in Outlook is organized into *modules*, or sections. Each module performs a specific job for you: The Calendar module stores appointments and manages your schedule, the Tasks module stores and manages your task list, and so on. Whenever you're running Outlook, you're always in one module or another.

Each module is represented by either a button or a text label in the navigation bar along the left edge of the screen, as pointed out in Figure 2-1. Clicking one takes you to the corresponding Outlook module:

>> **Mail** takes you to the Inbox, which collects your incoming email.

>> **Calendar** shows your schedule and all your appointments.

>> **People** calls up a module that stores names and addresses for you. Sometimes, Outlook calls this the Contacts module — but don't worry, they're the same thing.

>> **Tasks** displays your task list.

>> **To Do** provides a link to the data from Microsoft's To Do app, which is connected to the online version of Outlook (at Outlook.com).

>> **Notes** shows any notes you've created.

There are two additional modules, Folders and Shortcuts, but you will seldom use them. Folders shows a list of folders in which content is organized across modules; Shortcuts accesses any shortcuts you might have set up in Outlook.

By default, each module is represented by a small button, and only the first five buttons appear. To see the others, you have to click More Apps (...).

To change the number of icons that appear in the navigation bar, follow these steps:

1. **Click the File tab on the Ribbon and then click Options.**

   The Options dialog box opens.

TO DO VS. TASKS

Right before Outlook 2021 was released, Microsoft added a new icon to Outlook's navigation pane: To Do. It's the blue check mark right below the Tasks icon. It opens an in-Outlook version of Microsoft To Do, a new task management tool used in the online version of Outlook. If you use Microsoft To Do and also the desktop version of Outlook, having that icon there enables you to easily work with tasks from that app without leaving Outlook. There is also a Microsoft To Do app available for Android and iOS smartphones that connect to the same list (tied to your Microsoft account).

This addition is really confusing, to say the least, especially in its naming. What the heck, Microsoft? You have a Tasks module that contains both task lists and to-do lists, and now you're giving us a To Do module that has items called tasks? And the two modules are not connected to each other? And then there's a To-Do bar in Outlook on top of that? Sigh. But we'll bravely soldier through the confusion together in this book. I explain the To Do module in Chapter 10. You can ignore it for now.

2. **Click the Advanced tab in the navigation pane at the left.**

   At the top of the window you'll see the Outlook panes section.

3. **Click the Navigation button.**

   The Navigation Options dialog box opens. See Figure 2-2.

4. **Change the Maximum Number of Visible Items, if desired.**

   The default is 4.

5. **Use the Move Up and Move Down buttons to change the order of the modules (from left to right), if desired.**

   You might want to do this if you use Notes more frequently than Tasks, for example.

6. **Click OK.**

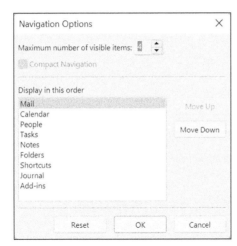

FIGURE 2-2:
Changing the navigation options.

Using the Folder pane

Outlook speeds your work by letting you deal with several kinds of information in one place. It does that by organizing those different types of information into folders. Most people only think about folders when they're dealing with email, which is why Outlook makes its folders completely visible only when you're dealing with email.

The Folder pane is on the left side of the screen, just to the right of the navigation bar. In the Mail module it shows a folder list. (It shows other stuff in some of the other modules.) By default it is expanded, so you can actually see it, as in Figure 2-1.

You can optionally collapse it by clicking the Minimize button, which is the little left-pointing arrow near the top of the Folder pane. When the Folder pane is collapsed, it resembles Figure 2-3. To re-expand it, click the Expand button (the same arrow but this time it points to the right). To keep it open, click the Pin button (which looks like a pushpin, and which isn't visible in Figure 2-3).

Expand button

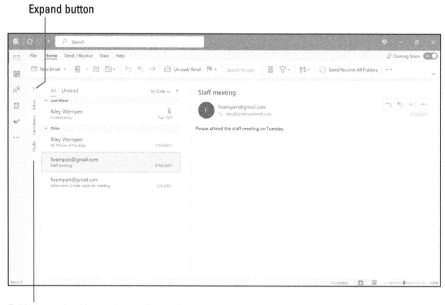

FIGURE 2-3:
The Outlook main
screen with the
Folder pane
collapsed.

Folder pane is skinny when collapsed.

Changing views in a module

The content you see on-screen in Outlook depends on which module you are using. Each module's screen is unique. When you're reading email, you see a list of your messages. If you're adding or searching for contacts, you see contact names. If you're viewing a calendar, you see . . . well, you see a calendar. You get the picture.

Outlook organizes what it shows you into units called *views*. There are different views available in each module, appropriate to the content you're working with. For example, in the Calendar module, there are views for Month, Week, Day, and so on. You can switch between views on the View tab of the Ribbon. Outlook comes with several preset views, and you can also create and save your own views. (I go into more details about views in Chapter 14.) Figure 2-4 shows the Work Week view in the Calendar module.

Click Today to return to today.

Click an arrow button to move to the next or previous week.

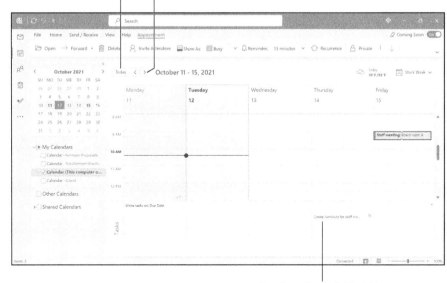

FIGURE 2-4:
A calendar in the
Work Week view.

A task on the Daily Task List

To check out your own calendar using the same view as in Figure 2-4, follow these steps:

1. **Click Calendar in the navigation bar (or press Ctrl+2).**

   Your calendar appears.

2. **Click the Work Week button on the Home tab of the Ribbon.**

   The Work Week view of your calendar appears. (A work week is 5 weekdays; a regular week shows all 7 days.)

3. **(Optional) Click the left and right arrow buttons above the left end of the calendar to change to a different week.**

4. **Click the Today button to return to today.**

Working with the To-Do bar

You can change the appearance of each module in a nearly infinite number of ways. For example, you may need to see the appointments for a single day or only the items you've assigned to a certain category. Views can help you get a quick look at exactly the information you need.

While viewing the Calendar, you can also view a To-Do bar along the right side of the screen, which lists any appointments and reminders coming up. To turn this on:

>> Using the Simplified Ribbon: Click the View tab on the Ribbon, click More Commands, point to Layout, point to To-Do Bar, and then click Calendar.

>> Using the Classic Ribbon: Click the View tab on the Ribbon, click To-Do Bar, and then click Calendar.

To turn it off again, repeat the process and choose Off from the menu, or click the Close (X) button in the upper right corner of the To-Do bar.

The bars listed on the To-Do Bar menu (Calendar, People and Tasks) can actually all be enabled/disabled separately, so you can potentially have all three showing at once. Try that and see how you like it; then turn off any of them that you don't find helpful.

Working with the Daily Task List

Another way to get extra info when using the calendar is to turn on the Daily Task List (View, Daily Task List, Normal). Doing so places a task list at the bottom of each day's column in Day, Week, or Work Week view, listing the tasks that are due each day. It's displayed in Figure 2-4, where it shows one task (on Thursday). Daily Task List doesn't appear in Month view.

There's one other viewing option to be aware of: Reading Pane. This one displays an extra pane on the right that shows details of whatever you've selected. For example, if you select an appointment on your calendar, the Reading Pane shows its information, just as if you had opened the appointment in a separate window. Figure 2-5 shows an example. You can turn the Reading Pane on or off, and decide where it displays (your choices are Right or Bottom). To do so:

>> Using the Simplified Ribbon: Click the View tab on the Ribbon, click More Commands, point to Layout, point to Reading Pane, and then click Right or click Bottom.

>> Using the Classic Ribbon: Click the View tab on the Ribbon, click Reading Pane, and then click Right or click Bottom.

By the way, each of the panes is resizable. Just position the mouse pointer on the divider between two panes and drag.

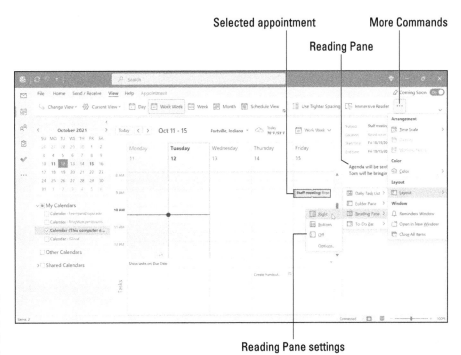

Selected appointment · More Commands · Reading Pane

Reading Pane settings

FIGURE 2-5:
Using the
Reading Pane to
see details of a
selected item.

Taking a peek

One nice feature in Outlook is a small pop-up window, called a Peek, which appears when you hover your mouse pointer over the Calendar, People, or Tasks button in the navigation bar. This handy feature helps you when you're replying to an email about an event that requires scheduling. You can take a quick peek at your calendar while continuing to work on that email, as shown in Figure 2-6.

REMEMBER

The Peek window is actually an undocked version of the To-Do bar. To prove this, open one of the Peek windows and then click the Dock the Peek icon in its upper right corner to dock the Peek window. Then hover the mouse pointer over the Close (X) button in the upper right corner of the docked peek window and check out the ScreenTip that appears: Remove the peek.

Navigating folders

The default set of folders that appears in your Folders pane in the Mail module depends on the kind of email account you have set up. You might not see the same folders as shown back in Figure 2-1; the Trash folder might be replaced by a Deleted Items folder, for example. Don't let such minor differences in the names throw you off. It's all good.

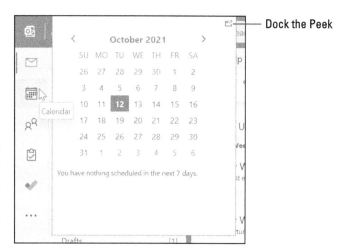
Dock the Peek

FIGURE 2-6:
The Peek feature
enables you to
take a quick look
at your calendar
while continuing
to read your
email.

Most people just stick with whatever default folders show up, and leave it at that. The names of the folders give you a pretty clear idea of what to expect from them. On the other hand, I know people who create elaborate filing systems by creating dozens of Outlook folders for their emails and even their tasks. It's personal: Some people are filers; some are pilers. Take your pick.

WARNING

The things that Outlook refers to as "folders" are not the same thing as what Windows calls "folders." You may be used to folders in Windows, which are what you use to organize files. You can copy and move files to and from folders on your hard drive as well as delete files from folders on your hard drive. Outlook doesn't deal with that kind of folder.

In Outlook, folders are organizing units within the app, where you can stash individual items like email messages. For example, you could create a Work folder and a Personal folder, and then sort your incoming email messages into one of the two as appropriate. These "folders" exist only within the Outlook data file; they aren't folders in the same sense as the ones in Windows.

To view a folder's content, click its name in the Folder pane. To move an item from one folder to another, select the item (such as an email message) and then drag and drop it onto the desired destination in the Folder pane.

I explain a lot more about folder management, including how to create new folders, in Chapter 6. Let me stress again, though, that you don't have to deal with Outlook folders at all if you don't want to. A lot of people don't. They just leave everything in their default locations.

Taking Control with the Ribbon

All Microsoft Office apps have a Ribbon, which is like a super toolbar across the top of the screen; you use the Ribbon to execute commands.

As I mentioned in Chapter 1, there are two modes the Ribbon can be in: Simplified and Classic. Simplified is the modern mode, and the default in new Outlook installations. Classic is the older style of Ribbon that you may be familiar with from other Office 365 apps — and from earlier versions of Outlook. Figure 2-7 compares the Simplified and Classic versions of the Mail module's Home tab.

The active tab's name is underlined.   More Commands button

Ribbon Display Options arrow

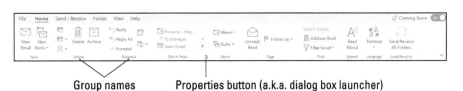

FIGURE 2-7:
The Simplified
Ribbon (top) and
the Classic
Ribbon (bottom).

Group names   Properties button (a.k.a. dialog box launcher)

Back in Chapter 1 I explained how to switch between the two modes. (In case you missed that and don't want to flip back there, here's how to do it: Click the Ribbon Display Options arrow on the right end of the Ribbon and choose either Simplified or Classic from the menu that appears.

The main difference is that Simplified mode has fewer buttons on it and the buttons aren't clustered into groups. Don't let Simplified mode fool you into thinking that all the Classic mode commands aren't there, though. Most of them still are. They're just tucked away. Many of the buttons in Simplified mode open menus containing more commands.

Personally, I like Simplified mode, and I use it on my personal PC. Not everyone warms up to it right away, though, so in this book whenever the steps are different depending on your chosen Ribbon mode, I provide separate steps for each, like I did earlier in this chapter when explaining how to control the To-Do bar and Daily Task List.

You can think of the Ribbon itself as a kind of notebook full of commands, and each tab as a different page in that notebook. In Classic mode, each tab contains a different set of groups, and each group has a different set of buttons. In Simplified mode, there aren't any groups on a tab.

In Outlook, each module (Mail, Calendar, People, Tasks, and so on) has its own version of the Ribbon, organized suitably for the purposes of the module. Most of the buttons are clearly labeled with the name of the thing they do, such as Reply, New Appointment, and so on.

In Classic Ribbon mode, the lower right corner of some groups has a small button called Properties; click it to see more detailed choices than you see on the Ribbon. See Figure 2-7. (Some sources call the Properties button a *dialog box launcher* since it typically opens some sort of dialog box related to its group.)

In Classic Ribbon mode, when the window is not wide enough to display everything on a tab, one or more groups collapses into a button. When you click the button, the individual commands from that group appear. Simplified Ribbon mode does things differently; it displays a More Commands button (. . .) at the right end of the Ribbon, and clicking that button opens a menu of additional commands. Some of the commands on this menu open their own submenus, as you saw back in Figure 2-5.

Viewing ScreenTips

TIP

Each button on the Ribbon displays a little pop-up tag called a ScreenTip when you hover the mouse pointer over it. The ScreenTip tells you the button's name and explains what will happen if you click it. Figure 2-8 shows an example.

ScreenTip

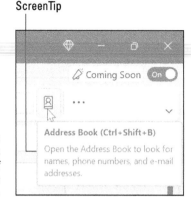

FIGURE 2-8:
A ScreenTip tells you the name of the tool you're using.

Some buttons have a little down-pointing arrow at the bottom or to the right of the button. Click the arrow to open a menu or list. One example that almost all Outlook modules have on the Home tab is a button called Move. Click the Move button to open its menu and see all the different places to which you can send an Outlook item. Another example is the New Items button, which I explain next.

Using the New Item(s) button

Every Outlook module has a New Item button, which enables you to create a new item in any module without leaving the module you're in.

In Simplified Ribbon mode, there's a button for this on the left end of the Home tab. Its official name is the New Item button, but its face shows *New* plus the type of item for the module you're working with. For example, in the People module, the button is New Contact. This button has an arrow on it that opens a menu, and from that menu you can choose a new item for any of the other modules. So, for example, while in the People module, you could create a new task or appointment. See Figure 2-9.

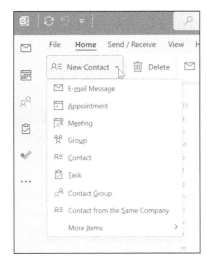

FIGURE 2-9:
In Simplified Ribbon mode, create a new item in any module.

In Classic Ribbon mode, you have the same capability, but the button situation is a bit different. In each module there is a button that creates a new item in that module, but there is also a separate New Items button (this time it's plural) that opens a menu from which you can choose a new item from any of the other modules. See Figure 2-10.

FIGURE 2-10:
In Classic Ribbon
mode, create a
new item in any
module.

Finding Things in a Flash with Search

Outlook makes it easy to accumulate bits and pieces of data. That can make it tough to find information. Outlook has a tool called Search that addresses that exact problem — and it's pretty slick.

Simple searching

TIP

At the top of the Outlook application window, near the center of the screen, you see the Search box. It's a box with a magnifying glass and the word *Search*. Click that box and a word or phrase you want to find within the current module. Then press Enter to execute the search.

The content changes to show only the items that contain the text you entered, as shown in Figure 2-11. For example, if you're in the Contacts module and you type *Sch*, you see only the records that contain those letters. In Figure 2-11, it has found two people named *Schmoe* and one named *Schneider*. Clear the search results by clicking the X on the right end of the Search box or by clicking the Close Search button on the Ribbon.

Type here to search.   Clear the search results.

FIGURE 2-11:
The Search box
helps you find
items in a jiffy.

Advanced searching

In some cases, searching for a certain group of letters isn't specific enough. For example, you may want Outlook to show just those people named Schmoe *and* who work for Schmoe Unlimited. You can create a more detailed search by doing the following.

1. Click in the Search box.

The Search box becomes active, and a menu of recently used actions appears. You can ignore this menu.

2. Click the Advanced Search icon (the down arrow).

A Search box appears, showing (at least) a Search In box and an Add More Options command. There may be other fields there, too, depending on the module. (Take a look at the Search box for the Mail module, for example, which has a lot more fields.) Figure 2-12 shows the People module's version, which is pretty simple.

3. Click Add More Options.

The Advanced Search Options dialog box opens.

4. Select the check box for the additional field(s) you want to search by.

For example, in Figure 2-13, I'm adding the Company field.

5. Click Apply.

The same menu appears as in Step 2. This time it not only has a Search In box, but it also has a text box for each of the fields you just added.

6. In the text box for each field, type the value you want to search for.

For example, I might type *Schmoe* for the Company field, as in Figure 2-14.

7. Click Search.

The search results appear for all items that meet your criteria. To clear the search, click the Close (X) button on the Search bar.

FIGURE 2-12:
Getting ready to add a field to your search criteria.

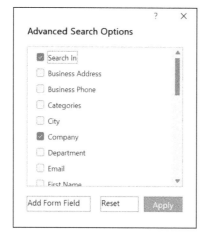

FIGURE 2-13:
Select the fields you want to search by.

FIGURE 2-14:
Enter the criteria for each of the fields you added.

TIP

By the way, once you add a field to the search criteria, that field stays there until you remove it. To remove a search criterion for future searches, click Add More Options to reopen the Advanced Search Options dialog box and then click Reset. Click Apply to apply your changes and close the dialog box.

The best way to understand the Search feature is to try it out. Just type some information into the box to see what you get and then click the X to create a new search. If you get a lot of results, try narrowing the list by adding more criteria.

Getting Help

The help system in Office applications (including Outlook) moves beyond helping you and actually tries to do things for you. That may sound creepy, but it's not. It's actually pretty useful.

Just do it for me!

The Help feature has changed somewhat in recent years in Office applications. There used to be a Tell Me What You Want to Do box featured prominently on the main screen, and you could type a question into it to get a list of actions that Outlook would perform for you upon request. It was separate from the Search box. In the current version of Outlook, the two boxes have been merged, so you can not only search for data with the Search box (as you just learned), but you can also search for actions to perform.

For example, suppose you want to reply to the selected email message but you don't remember how. In the Search box you could type *Reply* to see a list of actions, as in Figure 2-15. Each of those items on the Actions list is a live shortcut to that actual activity. So if you click Reply, a Reply window opens to help you start composing the reply.

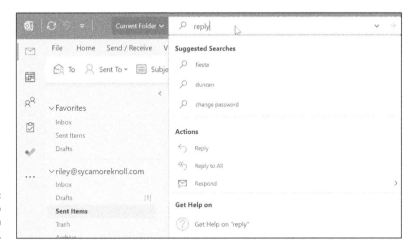

FIGURE 2-15:
Outlook offers to take an action on your behalf.

Just tell me what to do!

If you just want *information* about how to do something, and you don't want Outlook to do it for you, click Get Help On (whatever it was you typed) to open a Help pane and then read the step-by-step instructions that appear.

Want more options? Click the Help tab on the Ribbon for an assortment of help tools, such as Help (which opens that Help pane I just told you about), Contact Support, Troubleshoot, and Show Training.

IN THIS CHAPTER

» **Learning how to drag and drop**

» **Saving information from an email message to other formats**

» **Creating email messages from a contact or appointment**

» **Minimizing parts of the Outlook screen**

» **Getting to know the mouse buttons**

Chapter **3**

Getting on the Fast Track with Handy Shortcuts

T yping — ugh! Who needs it? It's amazing to think we still use a 19th-century device — the typewriter keyboard — to control our computers in the 21st century. We appear to be stuck with the QWERTY keyboard (the standard we all know and, uh, *love*) for a while longer, but we can give our carpal tunnels a rest now and then. By using the mouse, trackball, or touchpad, you can drag and drop rather than hunt and peck.

Most people recognize that a tool like Outlook can dramatically improve productivity, but many ignore Outlook's most powerful features and shortcuts. Some of those tools can be powerful weapons in your battle to make the most of your time, and I show you some of my favorites in this chapter.

Learning the Value of Dragging

If you want to work quickly in Outlook, a trick called *drag and drop* gives you the fastest and easiest way to get things done. When I say *drag*, I'm not referring to *RuPaul's Drag Race*. I mean the process of moving or copying items from one place to another with quick, easy mouse moves. This is by far the fastest way to complete many tasks in Outlook.

REMEMBER

Before you can drag an item, you have to *select* it, which simply means to click the item once. Then, the rest of the process is straightforward:

>> **Dragging** means clicking your mouse on something and moving the mouse to another location while holding the left mouse button down at the same time. The item you're dragging moves with the mouse pointer.

>> **Dropping** means letting go of the mouse button. The mouse pointer detaches from the object you dragged and leaves it in its new location.

TIP

If you change your mind mid-drag, you can press Esc to cancel a drag-and-drop operation.

When you drag an item, you see an icon hanging from the tail of the mouse pointer as you move the pointer across the screen. The icon makes the pointer look like it's carrying baggage, and to some degree, that's true. Dragging your mouse between Outlook modules "carries" information from one type of item to another.

If you hold down the Ctrl key while dragging, you get a bonus + sign on the mouse pointer, which means that you are making a copy rather than moving the item.

If the mouse pointer changes to a No sign (a red circle with a line through it), that means the location you are trying to drag to isn't valid for the item you are dragging. (For example, you can't drag anything onto the navigation bar.)

You can drag and drop items from any module to an item in any other module. That may seem like a simple concept, but it has enormous benefits, if you think about it. You can associate items from one module with items from another. You can attach a meeting attendee's contact information to an appointment in the Calendar, for example. Or you can email an action item from the Tasks module to a coworker.

You can also drag and drop items into folders in the Folder pane to organize them. For example, if you get a lot of email messages from clients at a particular company, you can create a folder in your Folder pane for that client and then drag and drop messages from your Inbox into that folder.

TIP

When you drag and drop items between different Outlook modules, you can sometimes create new types of items from the old information, depending on what you drag and where you drop it. For example, when you make an airline reservation and the airline emails you a summary of your itinerary, the most useful place for that information is in your calendar on the day of your flight. You could enter an appointment and type in all the information, but it's much faster to drag the airline's email message straight to your calendar. You not only save time, but all the information is absolutely accurate because it's the same information.

Everything you can do by using the drag-and-drop method can also be done through Ribbon choices or keyboard shortcuts, but you lose the advantage of having the information from one item flow into the new item, so you have to retype information. I don't have time for that, so I just drag and drop.

REMEMBER

After you've tried drag and drop, you'll see how much it helps you. And because I'm using this chapter to show you how to get everything done faster, I describe every action in terms of a drag-and-drop movement rather than through Ribbon choices or keyboard shortcuts. Throughout the rest of this book, I describe how to do things using the Ribbon, which is a more intuitive way to explain most Outlook features, but trust me, drag and drop is usually faster. So, when you read other parts of this book, don't think I'm discouraging you from trying drag and drop; I'm just trying to offer you the clearest explanation I can. (Whew! I'm glad that's off my chest.)

Creating Other Outlook Items from Email Messages

Nobody in business talks anymore — everybody sends email (or sometimes text messages). When your boss wants you to do something, you usually find out via email. But all those messages clutter your email Inbox so quickly that you can easily lose track of what you need to do.

Fortunately, it's easy to save the information from an email message in a variety of other module formats in Outlook. The following sections explain how to do it for tasks, appointments, and contacts.

Creating a task from an email message

TIP

Most productivity experts suggest that you convert emailed instructions into a To-Do list item right away to avoid losing track of important details. You can create a task from an email message by dragging the message to the Tasks icon on the navigation bar. You can add other information later, such as due date and category, but a single drag and drop is all you really need.

You can also take advantage the To-Do bar to give yourself a place where you can drag email messages for automatic conversion into tasks. I explained how to enable it in Chapter 2, in the section "Working with the To-Do Bar," but in those steps you enabled the Calendar part of it. So now let's enable the Tasks portion, as shown in Figure 3-1.

To-Do bar

FIGURE 3-1:
Drag tasks to the To-Do bar to help track when you have time to accomplish each item.

Start in the Mail module and do the following:

>> Using the Simplified Ribbon: Click the View tab on the Ribbon, click Layout, point to To-Do Bar, and then click Tasks.

>> Using the Classic Ribbon: Click the View tab on the Ribbon, click To-Do Bar, and then click Tasks.

Once the To-Do bar shows your Tasks list, you can simply drag and drop an email message onto it. A new line appears with the title of that email listed as a task. At the same time, a little red flag appears on your email message to show that you plan to get back to that item and take it on as a task.

TIP

Here's another tip for managing tasks. The Outlook Calendar features an optional strip at the bottom — called the Daily Task List — that lets you drag each task to a particular day, which helps you deal with the fact that many tasks take time. When your schedule is crowded and your email Inbox is cluttered, knowing what you need to do isn't enough; you also need to figure out when you'll have time to do it. I explained how to enable the Daily Task List in Chapter 2, in the section "Working with the Daily Task List."

The most productive thing about the Daily Task List is that you can drag unfinished tasks from one day to the next. That way, you don't lose track of tasks when your schedule gets interrupted.

YOUR ONE-PAGE PRODUCTIVITY SYSTEM

High-priced productivity gurus crank out overstuffed guidebooks like sausages. What's so productive about slogging through 400-page productivity books? Every productivity book says pretty much the same thing — and the stuff that matters fits on one page. So, I'll spare you 399 pages of jargon and gibberish — you're too busy for that.

Respond to every task *immediately* in one of four ways:

- **Do it** (if you can finish it in under 2 minutes).
- **Delete it** (after you've done it or determined that no action is required).
- **Defer it** (by dragging it immediately to your Outlook Daily Task List or calendar).
- **Delegate it** (if you have someone to whom you can delegate things — you lucky thing).

To reach peak productivity, you should constantly seek ways to do the following:

- **Centralize:** Store all your information in a single location. Outlook is a good place to do that.
- **Streamline:** Strive to touch any item no more than once.
- **Simplify:** A simple system you actually follow is better than a complex one you don't follow.

You should also strive to automate as many routine tasks as you can. Outlook offers powerful task-automation tools to help you zip through busy work. Some of my favorite tools are Rules and Quick Steps — both of which I discuss in Chapter 6. I'm also fond of Quick Parts, also covered in Chapter 6. Even if you only use a fraction of Outlook's power to streamline your work, you'll find that you get better results faster and with less effort.

Scheduling an appointment from an email message

Whether you're asking people to lunch, hosting a party, putting on a show, or organizing an exhibition, you probably already know how convenient email can be for organizing get-togethers.

When you receive a plain email announcement about an event and you want to plug its details into your calendar, you can do that in Outlook by following these steps:

1. **Click Mail in the navigation bar to switch to the Mail module.**

   A list of your received email messages appears.

2. **Select the message from which you want to make an appointment.**

3. **Drag the selected message to the Calendar icon in the navigation bar.**

   An Appointment form opens with the text from the message you dragged in the note section of the New Appointment form.

4. **Make any changes needed to the Start Time and End Time (see Figure 3-2).**

   The default Start Time is the next half-hour coming up, which is probably not what you want.

5. **If you want to include more information about the event, type that information in the appropriate box on the New Appointment form.**

   For example, you can change the Subject line text and the description in the body of the appointment.

6. **Click the Save & Close button.**

   You now have all the event information stored right in your calendar for future reference.

The great thing about creating an appointment from an email message is that all the details included in your message are right in your calendar. If you need driving directions, agenda details, or other information that was included in the message, just double-click the appointment in your calendar to get the lowdown. And if you use a smartphone with Outlook, all the information from your Outlook Calendar ends up on your mobile device. As a result, you'll have your appointment details handy wherever you go. I discuss mobile Outlook use in more detail in Chapter 13.

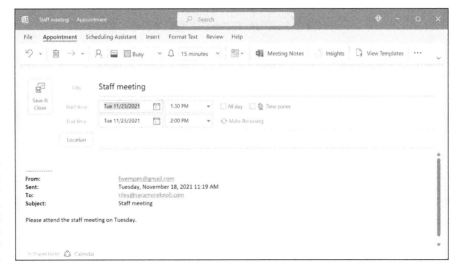

FIGURE 3-2:
When you drag
an email message
to your calendar,
the message text
is stored with
your new
appointment.

TIP

If you work in an office that uses Microsoft Exchange for email, you can take advantage of much more powerful features for organizing meetings. I cover those features in Chapter 15.

TABLET COMPUTING — HERE, BUT NOT ALL THERE

Everyone says that PCs are going the way of the dinosaur — to be replaced in a matter of months by sleek tablets with clever touchscreens. Bill Gates himself said exactly that . . . in November 2000. Okay, so Microsoft's plan to switch the whole world to tablets has fallen behind schedule by over two decades, but they've almost caught up. The latest versions of Microsoft Windows now make it possible for suitably equipped laptops and tablets to offer touchscreen operation — just like iPads and Android tablets and phones.

In some cases, it's possible to operate Outlook by swiping your finger across the screen rather than clicking and dragging your mouse. Unfortunately, some things that are possible aren't always practical. The version of Outlook you use on your desktop was built for use with a mouse, and many of the controls and menus that you might try to tap and swipe with your fingers are too small to use that way. You just end up making mistakes that are hard to correct.

In Chapter 13, I discuss the special version of Outlook that's made to use on phones and tablets. But that version omits many of the features that make the desktop version of Outlook so powerful, so you'll have to trust that there'll still be times when an old-fashioned mouse and keyboard will be a quicker way to get things done with Outlook.

Creating a new contact from an email message

You can drag an email message to the People button in the navigation bar to create a contact record that includes the email address. You not only save work by using this shortcut, but you also eliminate the risk of misspelling the email address.

To create a new contact record from an email message, follow these steps:

1. **In the Mail module, select the message for which you want to make a contact record.**

2. **Drag the selected message to the People button in the navigation bar.**

    The New Contact form opens with the name and email address of the person who sent the message filled in. Figure 3-3 shows a New Contact form created this way. Notice that the original message text appears in the Notes area.

3. **If you want to include more information, type it into the appropriate box on the New Contact form.**

    You can change existing information or add information: the company for whom the person works, the mailing address, other phone numbers, personal details (say, whether to send a complimentary gift of freeze-dried ants for the person's pet aardvark), and so on. If there isn't a specific field for the information you want to record, put it in the Notes box.

    TIP

    If the body of the email message contains information you want to use as contact information, select that information and drag it to the appropriate box of the New Contact form.

4. **Click the Save & Close button.**

    You now have the email address and any other information for the new contact stored for future reference.

TIP

Here's another quick way to capture an email address from an incoming message: Right-click on the name of the sender in the incoming message's From field (in the Reading pane; this won't work if you right-click on the From address in the message list). The From field is not a normal text box, so you may not think that right-clicking on it would do anything, but it does: A shortcut menu appears. Choose Add to Outlook Contacts to open the New Contact form and then follow the last two steps of the preceding list. If you don't see Add to Outlook Contacts on the menu, it means that address is already in your Contacts list. Instead, click Edit Contact to edit the contact that's already there.

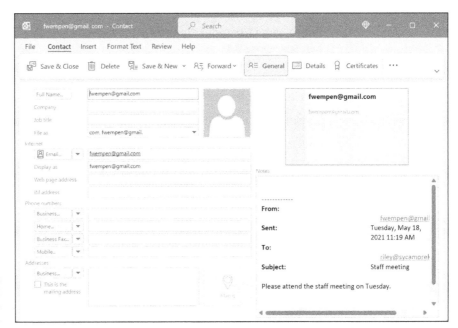

FIGURE 3-3:
A contact record
created from a
received email.

Creating Email Messages from Other Items

Just as you can make new items in other modules from an email, you can also reverse that and make new email messages from other modules' items. The following sections explain a couple of the most common scenarios around that.

Creating an email from a contact

Addressing messages is one of the most productive drag-and-drop techniques in Outlook. Email addresses can be cumbersome and difficult to remember, and if your spelling of an email address is off by even one letter, your message won't go through. It's best to just keep the email addresses in your Contacts list (a.k.a. the People module) and use those addresses to create new messages.

Create an email message from your Contacts list this way:

1. **Click People in the navigation bar to switch to the People module.**

   The Contacts list appears. You can use any view, but Business Cards view is easiest; you can click the first letter of the person's name to see that person's card. (For more about viewing your Contacts list, see Chapter 8.)

2. **Drag a name from your Contacts list to the Mail button in the navigation bar. See Figure 3-4.**

   The Message form appears with the address of the contact filled in.

3. **Type a subject for your message.**

   Keep it simple; a few words will do.

4. **Click in the text box and type your message.**

   You can also format text with bold type, italics, and other effects by clicking the appropriate buttons on the toolbar.

5. **Click the Send button.**

   The display returns to the Contacts list, and your message is sent.

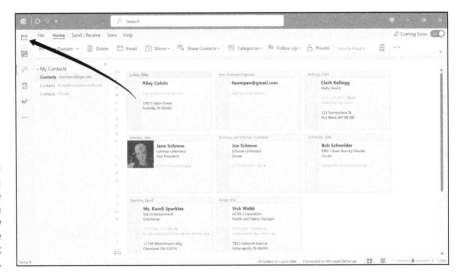

FIGURE 3-4:
Dragging a
contact to the
Mail button
creates a new
message
addressed to that
person.

Creating an email from an appointment

After you enter the particulars about an appointment, you may want to send that information to someone to tell that person what the appointment is about, where it occurs, and when it occurs.

To send an email message with information about an appointment, follow these steps:

1. **From the Calendar module, drag the appointment you're interested in from the Calendar to the Mail button in the navigation bar. See Figure 3-5.**

   The Message form appears. The subject of the message is already filled in.

2. **In the To text box, type the name of the person to whom you want to send a copy of the appointment.**

   Alternatively, you can click the To button and choose the person's name from the Address Book. If you use the Address Book, you have to click To again and then click the OK button.

3. **Click the Send button.**

   Your recipient gets an email message with details about the meeting. You can add additional comments in the text box.

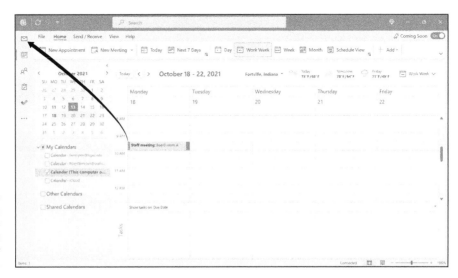

TIP

If you plan to invite other people in your organization to a meeting and you want to check their schedules to plan the meeting, you can also click the Schedule View button on the Home tab of the Ribbon. (You'll only see your own schedule unless you're connected to those other people's calendars, though, such as through a corporate Exchange server.)

Keeping the Interface Simple

The Outlook screen packs a lot of information into a small space. That seems efficient at first, but it's also distracting, and distraction is the enemy of productivity. You can minimize parts of the Outlook screen when you're not using them. By doing that, you'll be more focused on the tasks that require your concentration.

TIP

You can turn parts of the interface on and off, like the Folder pane, Reading pane, To-Do bar, and Daily Task List, as you learned in Chapter 2. Here's a quick review:

>> Using the Simplified Ribbon: Click the View tab on the Ribbon, click Layout (you might have to click More Commands (. . .) to find Layout), point to the element you want to turn off, and then click Off.

>> Using the Classic Ribbon: Click the View tab on the Ribbon, and in the Layout group, click the element you want to turn off and then click Off.

The To-Do bar also has a Close (X) button in its upper right corner; you can click it to quickly close the To-Do bar.

The Daily Task List and Folder pane both have Minimize buttons on them, which are tiny arrows in their upper right corner. When you click the Minimize button on one of these panes, the pane shrinks to a very thin bar, but is still available. To restore it to regular size, click the arrow again. Figure 3-6 shows the Daily Task List minimized and the Folder pane not minimized.

Minimize or restore the Folder pane.

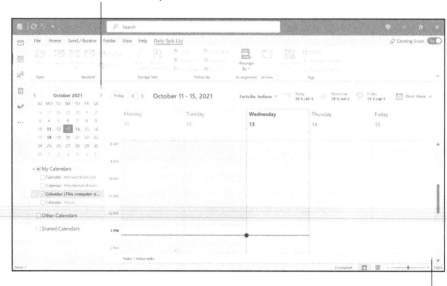

FIGURE 3-6:
You can view or hide various panes by making selections from the Layout group on the View tab.

Minimize or restore the Daily Task List.

Zen of the Right Button

So far, I've talked about holding down your mouse button as if your mouse has only one button. Many people use only the left button — and they get along just fine. But most PC mice have two buttons; some have even more.

TIP

When you *right-drag* an item (drag it by holding down the right mouse button instead of the left button), something different happens when you drop the item off: A menu asks what result you want. I don't always remember what's going to happen when I drag an item and drop it off, so I like to use the right-drag feature just to be sure.

For example, if you right-drag a contact to the Mail button, a menu with five choices appears:

>> Address New Message

>> Copy Here as Message with Text

>> Copy Here as Message with Shortcut

>> Copy Here as Message with Attachment

>> Move Here as Message with Attachment

>> Cancel

The next time you are going to drag something somewhere, try right-dragging instead and see what happens! There's no risk — the first item on the menu that appears is the one that you would have gotten automatically if you had left-dragged.

2
Taming the Email Beast

Learn how to write, send, and reply to emails as well as how to delete, forward, and save emails.

Explore how to use flags and reminders for messages, how to change your options for what happens when you reply to or forward a message, and how to attach files to messages as well as set up a signature for your emails.

Discover how to manage your messages, including filing messages, dealing with junk mail, and archiving messages, as well as how to use the Rules Wizard to help you filter your email.

Find out how to set up Outlook for multiple email accounts and data files, so you can manage messages from all your accounts in one place.

Chapter **4**

Email Essentials

When the first edition of *Outlook For Dummies* was published some 22 years ago, many readers had yet to celebrate the sending of their very first email. After this much time, email isn't something to celebrate anymore — not unless you celebrate washing the dishes or changing the litter box. (Woo-hoo!) Email has become every working person's biggest chore.

Many people put a lot more effort into email than is really necessary, especially if they have a tool as powerful as Outlook to speed things up. This chapter helps you crank up the speed at which you dispatch the various email messages that you must deal with, freeing up your time for more important things. Like playing Facebook games. (Your secret's safe with me.)

Front Ends and Back Ends

You need two things to send and receive email:

» A program that helps you create, save, and manage your messages

» A program that actually transports the messages to and from the other people with whom you exchange messages

Some technical people call these two parts the *front end* and the *back end*, respectively. Outlook is a front end for email. It helps you create, format, store, and manage your messages, but it has little to do with actually getting your messages to your destination. That work is done by a back-end service (such as Microsoft Exchange Server in your office), by your Internet service provider (ISP), or by an online email service (such as Outlook.com or Gmail).

REMEMBER

You can't send or receive email without an Internet connection. Your phone company and cable television provider probably offer Internet services that can be bundled with the services you already have. In many cases, they'll send someone to your home to get you up and running. Remember, though, that your easiest choice isn't always your best choice. Literally hundreds of companies are out there ready to give you Internet access, so it pays to shop around. (I tell you more about connecting Outlook to an email system in Chapter 7.)

Creating Messages

In many ways, electronic mail is better than regular paper mail (often referred to as *snail mail*). For one thing, email is delivered much faster than paper mail — almost instantaneously. I find that speedy delivery is really handy for last-minute birthday greetings. Email is also incredibly cheap; in fact, it's free most of the time.

As with just about anything in an Office application, there are several ways to create an email message in Outlook. Next I show you two of those ways: One of them easy but lacking in options, and the other is not-so-easy but a lot more customizable. Which is better? That depends on how much of a hurry you are in, and whether you love or loathe having lots of choices.

The quick-and-dirty way

Creating a new message is insanely easy. Follow these steps:

1. **Start Outlook.**

   The Mail module appears, showing your Inbox.

2. **Click the New Email button.**

3. **Enter an email address in the To box.**

4. **Enter a subject in the Subject box.**

5. **Enter your message in the Message box.**

6. **Click the Send button.**

    Nailed that one, didn't you? Was that easy or what? If I lost you at any point there and you feel like you need some more hand-holding, or if you're interested in exploring the available options, move on to the next section, where I satisfy both of those requests.

TIP

Outlook always starts up in the Inbox unless you configure it otherwise. If you want to start up in some other folder than your Inbox, click the File tab and select Options, click Advanced, and in the Outlook Start and Exit section, change the Start Outlook in This Folder setting. You can click its Browse button and browse all the folders in your Outlook data file. To start up in some other module, choose a folder that corresponds to that module (for example, Calendar, Tasks, or Notes).

The slow but complete way

You may prefer a more detailed approach to creating an email message. If you have a yen for fancy email — especially if you want to take advantage of every bell and whistle Outlook can add to your message — follow these steps. For some of the steps there are multiple ways of getting it done, and I'll tell you about some of the alternatives, so this may take awhile, but hang in there and you'll learn a lot!

1. **In the Mail module, click the New Email button on the Ribbon (or press Ctrl+N).**

    The New Message form opens, as shown in Figure 4-1. (Figure 4-1 shows the message as it will look at the *end* of these steps, but for now imagine it blank and pristine.)

TIP

    The Ctrl+N shortcut creates a new item in whatever module you are in. In Mail it's a new message, in Calendar it's a new appointment, and so on.

2. **If you see a From button above the To button, check to make sure the correct sending account appears next to the button.**

    You'll only see a From button (as in Figure 4-1) if you have multiple email accounts set up in Outlook. Chapter 7 explains how to set up multiple email accounts. If the correct email account isn't set as the sender, click From and choose a different account from the drop-down menu.

3. **Click the To text box and type the email address of the person to whom you're sending your message.**

    If you're sending messages to multiple people, separate their addresses using either commas or semicolons.

    If they are set up in your Outlook contact list, you can also type their name, and the email address will be pulled in automatically.

As you start typing a name, a list appears of people in your address book who match that text string in some way, and you can click a name from that list to instantly add it to the To box. That feature is called AutoName.

You can also click the To button itself, find the names of the people to whom you're sending the message in the Select Names dialog box (Figure 4-2), double-click their names to add them to the To text box, and then click the OK button.

4. **(Optional) Click the Cc text box and type the email addresses of the person to whom you want to send a copy of your message.**

You can also click the Cc button to add people from the Select Names dialog box. Once the dialog box is open, click a name and then click Cc to add it to the Cc box. (You can't just double-click the name like you did with To, because double-clicking always adds the name to the To line.)

5. **Type the subject of the message in the Subject text box.**

Keep your subject line brief. A snappy, relevant subject line makes someone want to read your message; a long or weird subject line doesn't.

If you forget to add a subject and try to send a message, Outlook opens a window that asks whether you really meant to send the message without a subject. Click the Don't Send button to go back to the message and add a subject. If you want to send your message without a subject, just click the Send Anyway button (but not before you've written your message).

6. **Type the text of your message in the Message box.**

The Message box is the big blank area under the Subject line.

7. **(Optional) Select the Review tab and click Spelling and Grammar (or press F7).**

Outlook runs a spell-check to make sure that your message makes you look as smart as you actually are. (Or even smarter.)

8. **Click the Send button (or press Ctrl+Enter or Alt+S).**

Outlook moves your mail to the Outbox. If your computer is online, Outlook immediately sends any messages from the Outbox.

9. **If Outlook does not immediately send your mail, click Send/Receive All Folders (or press F9) to force it to do a send/receive operation.**

When a message is sent, it automatically goes to the Sent Items folder. If the message stays in the Outbox folder, you may need to manually tell Outlook to go ahead and send it.

The Send/Receive All Folders command appears in several places. One is on the Home tab in the main Outlook window, another is on the Send/Receive tab. Yet another is as an icon on the Quick Access Toolbar in the upper left corner of the Outlook window. (It looks like two curved arrows chasing each other.) It works the same no matter where you select it.

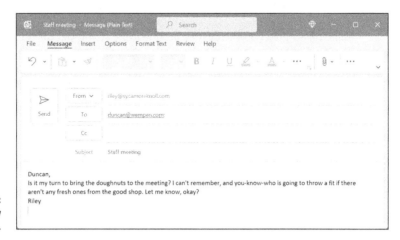

FIGURE 4-1:
The New
Message form.

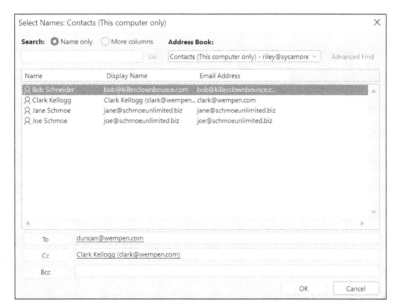

FIGURE 4-2:
Selecting
recipients from
the Select Names
dialog box.

Now that you have the basics down, let's look at some other options for sending email messages.

Blind copying for privacy

When you send a message to a large group, everyone who receives the message can see the email addresses in the To and Cc fields, which means you've just given out email addresses that some people might rather keep private. Everybody already gets way too many weird, unsolicited emails, and many people get peeved when you broadcast their address without permission.

Blind copies give you the best of both worlds. If you put all the email addresses in the Bcc field, nobody's privacy is compromised. Well, you can't put them *all* there, because there has to be at least one address in the To box. But you can do all the others that way. By using *Bcc* (an old abbreviation for *blind carbon copy* — a quaint reminder to those who'll admit they're old enough to remember carbon paper), you can keep secret addresses secret.

TIP

The Bcc field isn't always displayed when you create a message in Outlook. If you don't see a box labeled Bcc right below the Cc box when you're composing a new message, a reply, or a forward, select the Options tab on the Ribbon and click the Bcc button. (On the Simplified Ribbon you might need to click More Commands to find the Bcc button, depending on your window's width.) Alternatively, you can click the To or Cc button to open the Select Names dialog box and then enter at least one email address in the Bcc box; when you click OK to return to the message, you'll find a Bcc line.

Formatting a message

If you use Microsoft Word as your word processor, you're probably familiar with the formatting, graphics, tables, and all the tricks available in Word to make your email more attractive, like bullets, italics, and different colors and fonts. Those same tricks are available in Outlook by using the tools at the top of the message form on the Format Text tab. A subset of them are also on the Message tab.

If the controls on the Format Text tab and Message tab are unavailable, first make sure the insertion point is in the body of the message. Click there if needed.

If that doesn't work, Outlook is probably set up to default to a plain-text message format (that is, no formatting). To correct this:

» Using the Simplified Ribbon: Click the Format Text tab, click More Commands (if needed), click Format, and then click HTML or Rich Text.

» Using the Classic Ribbon: Click the Format Text tab, and in the Format group, click HTML or Rich Text.

HTML (Hyper Text Markup Language) format and RTF (Rich Text Format) are two different methods of allowing text formatting.

TIP

To change the default so that future new messages will be in a certain format, select File ⇨ Options ⇨ Mail and in the Compose Messages section, change the Compose Messages in This Format option to the desired format.

TIP

Microsoft recommends that you use RTF when you send messages inside an organization that uses Microsoft Exchange, and HTML format when you send to anyone else. The trouble is, how do you know who is using what kind of server? Outlook to the rescue! In the Outlook Options dialog box (File ⇨ Options), on the Mail tab, in the Message Format group, you'll find a handy setting called When Sending Messages in Rich Text Format to Internet Recipients. The default setting is Convert to HTML Format. There, problem solved! With this setting enabled, you can use RTF all the time without having to worry about compatibility.

Setting the message importance

Some messages are more important than others. The momentous report you're sending to your boss demands the kind of attention that wouldn't be appropriate for the wisecrack you send to your friend in the sales department. Setting the importance level to High tells the recipient that your message requires some serious attention. However, some spammers have caught on to this and send all their spam with high importance, so take it for what it's worth.

To set the importance for a message, follow these steps:

Simplified Ribbon:

1. **While typing a message in the Mail module, select the Message tab on the Ribbon.**

2. **Click More Commands.**

   If your window is wide enough that the High Importance and Low Importance buttons appear without having to click More Commands, skip this step.

3. **Click High Importance or Low Importance.**

Classic Ribbon:

1. **While typing a message in the Mail module, select the Message tab on the Ribbon.**

2. **In the Tags group, click High Importance or Low Importance.**

The High Importance button (with the red exclamation point) marks your message as High importance. The Low Importance button (with the blue arrow pointing downward) marks your message as Low importance. Notice, though, that there isn't a Normal Importance button in the Tags group. That's because Normal is the default. If you want to go back to Normal importance, repeat the above steps to toggle the High Importance or Low Importance indicator off again.

You might wonder why anyone would mark a message Low importance. After all, if it's so unimportant, why send the message in the first place? Apparently, some bosses like their employees to send in routine reports with a Low importance marking so the bosses know to read that stuff *after* all those exciting new email messages they get to read every day. You can also assign importance to messages received in your Inbox to tell yourself which messages can be dealt with later — if at all.

Setting sensitivity

You may want your message to be seen by only one person, or you may want to prevent your message from being changed by anyone after you send it. Sensitivity settings enable you to restrict what someone else can do to your message after you send it, and they let you set who that someone else can be.

To set the sensitivity of a message, follow these steps:

1. **As you are composing a message, click the File tab and click Properties.**

   The Properties dialog box opens.

2. **Click the list box arrow next to the word *Sensitivity* and select one of the levels shown: Low, Normal, or High.**

   See Figure 4-3. Most messages you send will have Normal sensitivity, so that's what Outlook uses unless you say otherwise.

3. **Click Close to close the dialog box.**

WARNING

Sensitivity means nothing, as a practical matter. Setting the sensitivity of a message to High doesn't make it any more private or confidential than any other message; it just notifies the recipient that the message contains particularly sensitive information. Many corporations are very careful about what kind of information can be sent by email outside the company. If you use Outlook at work, check with your system administrators before presuming that the information you send by email is secure.

Set the sensitivity.

| Properties | ✕ |

Settings

Importance Normal

Sensitivity Normal
- Normal
- **Normal**
- Personal
- Private
- Confidential

☐ Do not Au

Voting and Tracking o

☐ Use voting buttons

☐ Request a delivery receipt for this message

☐ Request a read receipt for this message

Security

Change security settings for this message.

Security Settings...

Delivery options

☐ Have replies sent to   Select Names...

☐ Do not deliver before   None   12:00 AM

☐ Expires after   None   12:00 AM

☑ Save copy of sent message

Contacts...

Categories ▼   None

Close

FIGURE 4-3:
The Properties
dialog box for a
message.

TIP

You might have noticed the Security Settings button in the Properties dialog box (refer to Figure 4-3). Select it to display a Security Properties dialog box. Unlike Sensitivity, Security Properties actually have the potential to protect your message in certain ways, such as by encrypting the message and its contents and/or using a digital signature to verify it came from you. However, you and your recipient must be set up on a compatible email system with something called an *Information Rights Management Service* to make that work. You can find out more about Information Rights Management at `https://support.office.com` and searching for information rights management.

Setting other message options

When you open the Properties dialog box as I describe in the previous section, you may notice a number of other options. These include Request a Read Receipt for This Message (which notifies you when your recipient reads your message) and Expires After (which marks a message as expired if your recipient doesn't open it before a time you designate). You can also access some of these options from the Options tab on the Ribbon, so you don't have to open the Properties dialog box. For example, you can choose Delay Delivery or Direct Replies To from there. (If using the Simplified Ribbon, you may have to click More Commands to see some of those options, depending on your window width.)

Those are all handy options, but if you want to use them, there's a catch: Your email system *and* your recipient's email system must support those features, or they probably won't work. If you and your recipient are on the same network using Microsoft Exchange Server, everything should work just fine. If you're not both using Outlook or on an Exchange network, it's a gamble. (See Chapter 15 for more about how to use the Outlook features that work only on Exchange Server.)

Adding an Internet link to an email message

All Microsoft Office programs automatically recognize the addresses of items on the Internet. If you type the name of a webpage, such as `www. dummies.com`, Outlook changes the text color to blue and underlines the address, making it look just like the hypertext link you click to jump among different pages on the Internet. That makes it easy to send someone information about an exciting website; just type or copy the address into your message.

If the webpage address doesn't start with `www`, Outlook might not recognize it as a web address; if that happens, just put `http://` or `https://` in front of it. Depending on what the recipient uses to read email, they should be able to just click the text to make a web browser pop up and open the page you mention in your message.

Still not working? You can select Link from the Message tab and create a hyperlink using the Insert Hyperlink dialog box. (This only works if the message format is set to HTML or RTF; if it's Plain Text, that dialog box won't open for you.)

Dictating a message

If you don't type very well (or quickly), for whatever reason, here's a great time-saver: You can use Office's voice recognition software to dictate the message right into a new message window. Here's how that works:

1. **Start composing the message as you normally would.**

   Enter the recipients and a subject and set any message options desired.

2. **Click in the message body and position the insertion point where you want the dictated text to start.**

   If it's a blank message, just click anywhere in the message body.

3. **On the Message tab of the Ribbon, click Dictate.**

   Depending on your window width, you might need to click More Commands to see the Dictate command if you're using the Simplified Ribbon.

   A Listening prompt appears in a status window to let you know your microphone is active. See Figure 4-4.

4. **Talk! Just start dictating the words you want to appear in the message.**

   If you need to pause dictating, click the microphone icon to pause the recording. Then click it again to resume.

TIP

You can dictate certain formatting and punctuation using special commands, like *bold*, *question mark*, and *backspace*. While dictating, say *What can I say* into the microphone to open a help pane that shows you the sported punctuation, commands, and symbols. You can also find this same help information by searching the Help system in Outlook.

5. **When you're finished dictating, click the Close (X) button in the upper right corner of the status window.**

6. **Read the dictated text closely and make any corrections needed.**

7. **Continue sending the message as you normally would.**

Click More Commands if needed to access the Dictate command.

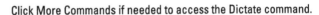

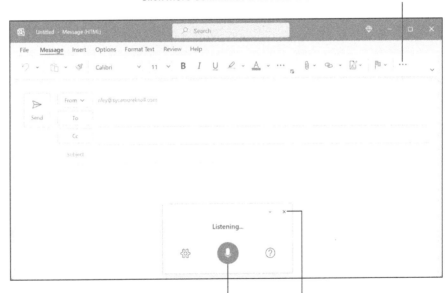

FIGURE 4-4:
The microphone is waiting for your dictation.

Click the microphone to pause or continue.   Close this window when done dictating.

Reading and Replying to Email Messages

Outlook has a couple of ways to tell you when you receive an email message. The status bar in the lower left corner of the Outlook screen tells you how many email messages you have overall in your Inbox and how many of those are unread. The word *Inbox* in the Folder pane also changes to boldface type when you have an unread email (see Figure 4-5). When you look in the Inbox, you also see titles of unread messages in boldface.

This folder name is bold because it's the active folder.

Number of unread messages in the folder

Unread messages appear in bold.

FIGURE 4-5:
Numbers next to
your Inbox icon
tell you how
many unread
messages you
have.

Number of messages in the active folder, both total and unread

To open and read an email message, follow these steps:

1. **In the Mail module, double-click the title of the message you want to read.**

   The message opens in its own window.

2. **Click the Close button (X) or press Esc to close the message when you're done.**

   Opening the message by double-clicking it is optional because you can read it perfectly well in the Reading pane, so an alternative would be to simply click the desired message to select it in the Inbox message list.

TIP

Viewing previews of message text

When you start getting lots of email, some of it will be important, but some of it will be relatively unimportant — if not downright useless. When you first see the mail in your Inbox, it's helpful to know which messages are important and which are not so you can focus on the important stuff. You can't count on the people who send you email to say "Don't read this; it's unimportant" (although a Low importance rating is a good clue). Outlook tries to help by letting you peek at the first few lines of a message.

By default, Message Preview is turned on and set to 1 line, as you've seen in the figures that show the Mail module so far in this book. You can change that to 2 lines, 3 lines, or Off. Message Preview is redundant if you have the Reading pane turned on, but if you don't, you might find the preview helpful.

To control the previews of your unread messages, follow these steps:

1. **In the Mail module, select the View tab on the Ribbon.**

2. (Simplified Ribbon only) Click the Current View button to open a menu of viewing options.

   This step isn't needed if you're using the Classic Ribbon.

3. **Click Message Preview.**

   A menu appears. See Figure 4-6.

4. **Click the desired setting (1 line, 2 lines, 3 lines, or Off).**

5. **If prompted to change the settings in All Mailboxes or This Folder, choose whichever is your preference.**

   Figure 4-6 shows the Inbox with the Reading pane turned off and Message Preview set to 3 lines.

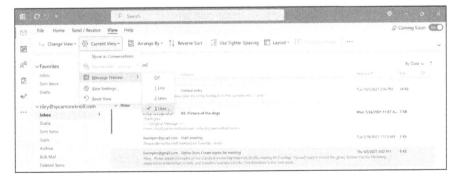

FIGURE 4-6:
You can see a preview of your unread messages after enabling Message Preview.

Every module in Outlook has a collection of views you can use to make your information easier to use. The Message Preview is a good way to browse your incoming email if you don't use the Reading pane. In Chapter 14, I show you some other views that can make your collection of email messages more useful.

TIP

As I've mentioned, a great way to zoom through your Inbox is to use the Reading pane — an area of the Outlook screen that displays the contents of any message you select. It's on by default, and positioned to the right of the message list. You can turn it off, or you can position it below the message list. To set up your Reading pane, follow these steps:

1. **In the Mail module, select the View tab on the Ribbon.**

2. **Click the Reading pane button.**

3. **Choose Right, Bottom, or Off.**

   You can't go wrong with any of the three choices; if you don't like one, change to another. When you turn on the Reading pane, you can skim through your messages by pressing either the ↑ or ↓ key.

Sending a reply

The thing I love about email is that sending a reply is so easy. You don't even need to know the person's address when you're sending a reply; just click the Reply button and Outlook takes care of it for you.

To reply to a message, follow these steps:

1. **In the Mail module, click the title of the message to which you want to reply.**

   The message you clicked appears in the Reading pane, and you can see the contents of the message. I'm assuming here that the Reading pane is enabled; if it's not, enable it as described in the preceding section.

2. **Choose one of these options:**

   - To reply to the person in the From field, click the Reply button.

   - To reply to the people in the Cc field *and* the person in the From field, click the Reply All button.

   A Reply screen opens in the Reading pane area, where the original message was just seconds ago.

TIP

   If you want to compose the reply in its own window, click Pop Out. That gives you a little more room to see what you are doing in the Message box.

   You may receive (or send) email that's addressed to a whole bunch of people all at one time. At least one person should be named in the To field; more than one person can also be in the Cc field, which is for people to whom you're sending only a copy. It doesn't make much functional difference whether a recipient is a To or a Cc; all recipients can reply to, forward, or ignore the message. So why even make the distinction? It's mainly a matter of who you want to take action on the message versus who is just observing. If I were to receive a message from my boss and I were in the To line, I'd expect my boss to want a response from me. If I'm only on the Cc line, I assume that I can just file it away for reference.

You don't always need to reply to the people in the Cc field or you may want to reply to only some of them. To include only some additional recipients from the original, click the Reply button and add the desired people again to the Cc field. Alternatively, click the Reply All button and then delete the users from the Cc field you don't want to include.

3. **Type your reply in the Message box.**

   Don't be alarmed when you discover some text already in the Message box — it's part of the message to which you're replying. Your blinking cursor is at the top of the screen, so anything you type precedes the other person's message. (This arrangement means the person who gets your message can review the original message as a memory-jogger when they receive your reply.) Figure 4-7 shows a reply ready to send.

Pop Out opens the reply in a separate tab.

Send the message.

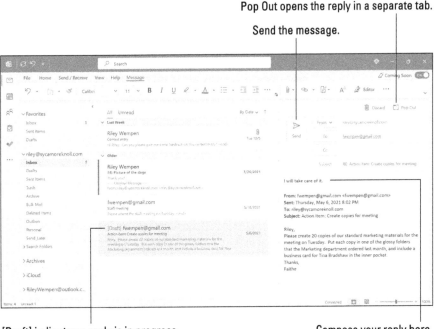

FIGURE 4-7:
The Reply screen.

[Draft] indicates a reply is in progress.

Compose your reply here.

4. **Click the Send button.**

Your message is sent, the Message form disappears, and the message you replied to reappears.

5. **Press Esc to close the Message screen.**

The message you replied to disappears and your Inbox reappears.

Resending messages

Another great thing about email is the way it makes it so easy to ask people to do what you want. Unfortunately, people often overlook things because they get so much email. When you find yourself making repeated requests, it's time to take advantage of Outlook's Resend feature. That way, you don't have to completely retype your original request; you can simply find the original message and resend it, along with a cheerful reminder about how long ago you sent the original request.

WARNING

This method of resending works only with certain types of email accounts. It doesn't work with Exchange, SharePoint, or Outlook.com accounts, for example. If you try these steps and you don't see the options described, your account type probably doesn't support it. You can still resend a message by forwarding it.

To resend a message, follow these steps:

1. **In the Mail module, click the Sent Items folder in the Folder pane.**

2. **Find the message in which you made the original request and double-click it.**

That opens the original message in its own window. This is required; unfortunately, resending a message isn't something you can do from the Reading pane.

3. **Do one of the following:**

   - Simplified Ribbon: On the Message tab, click More Commands, point to Actions, and then click Resend This Message.

   - Classic Ribbon: On the Message tab, in the Move group, click More Move Actions and then click Resend This Message.

That automatically opens a new copy of your previous message, exactly as it looked when you originally sent it.

4. **Type a quick reminder, or change the message if appropriate.**

5. **Click the Send button.**

If you do this enough times, it becomes impossible for people to ignore you.

WARNING

DON'T GET CAUGHT BY PHISHING

Sneaky people are always looking for new ways to trick you, especially on the Internet. In recent years, a common scam called *phishing* has cost people time, money, and grief after they responded to an email by an impostor who claimed to represent a bank or another financial institution.

If you get an email that purports to be from a bank or another business and it asks you to click a link to log on to verify personal information, especially passwords, don't fall for it. The link will probably direct you to a website that might *look* legitimate — but the personal information you're asked to enter can then be used for fraud or identity theft. Contact the business directly — preferably by phone — to make sure the email isn't a fake. One way to confirm that an email is phony is to hover your mouse over a link in the message until the URL or Internet address pops up. If the address it links to isn't the same as the address of the institution that claims to be sending the message, it's a phishing scam. Just delete it.

If you really want to check in with the purported sender of the email in question, go to your browser and log in to the organization's website — if it's an organization with which you're familiar. If it's an odd-looking message that comes from a strange place, stay away from it.

Read it to me!

The Read Aloud feature is sort of the opposite of the Dictation feature you learned about earlier in this chapter, but rather than you speaking aloud to Outlook, Outlook speaks aloud to *you*. You can use this feature whenever reading is not your first choice of activity — like when you can't find your reading glasses.

Here's how it works:

1. **Open a received message and position the insertion point at the spot where you want Outlook to start reading.**

   You can either open it in its own window or display it in the Reading pane.

2. **Click Read Aloud.**

   If you opened the message in its own window, Read Aloud is on the Message tab; if you are reading it in the Reading pane, Read Aloud is on the Home tab.

   If you are using the Simplified Ribbon, you might need to click More Commands to access Read Aloud.

   Outlook immediately starts reading the message out loud. If you don't hear it, check your speakers and your computer's volume level.

A Reading toolbar appears on the right side of the message body, with tools for controlling the reading. You can click the Pause button there to pause it, for example, as shown in Figure 4-8.

3. **When you're done being read to, click Read Aloud again to turn the feature off.**

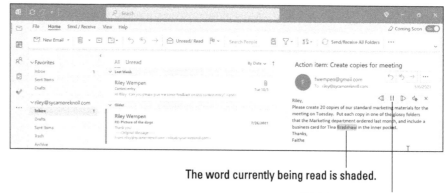

The word currently being read is shaded.

Click here to pause or resume.

That's Not My Department: Forwarding Email

You may not always have the answer to every email message you get. You may need to send a message to somebody else to answer, so pass it on.

To forward a message, follow these steps:

1. **In the Mail module, in the list of messages, click the title of the message you want to forward.**

   The message you selected appears in the Reading pane. You can forward the message as soon as you read it.

2. **Click the Forward button.**

   The Forward screen opens, replacing the Reading pane. The subject of the original message is now the subject of the new message, except the letters FW: (for Forward) are inserted at the beginning.

3. **Click the To text box and type the email address of the person to whom you're forwarding the message.**

If the person to whom you're forwarding the message is already in your Address Book, just start typing the person's name, and Outlook figures out the email address for you.

4. **Click the Cc text box and type the email addresses of the people to whom you also want to forward a copy of your message.**

   Many people forward trivia (such as jokes of the day) to their friends by email. Most recipients are included as Cc addresses.

WARNING

   Remember, business email etiquette is different from home email etiquette. Many employers have strict policies about appropriate use of their corporate email systems. If you work for such a company, be aware of your company's policies.

   If you want to pester your friends by sending silly trivia from your home computer to their home computers (as I do), that's your own business.

5. **In the text box, type any comments you want to add to the message.**

   The text of the original message appears in the text box. You can preface the message that you're forwarding if you want to give that person a bit of explanation; for example: "This is the 99th message I've had from this person. Somebody needs to get a life." Figure 4-9 shows the message ready to send.

6. **Click the Send button.**

   Your message is on its way.

FIGURE 4-9:
The Forward screen is nearly identical to the Reply screen, except the recipient isn't filled in automatically. (It's been manually entered in this figure.)

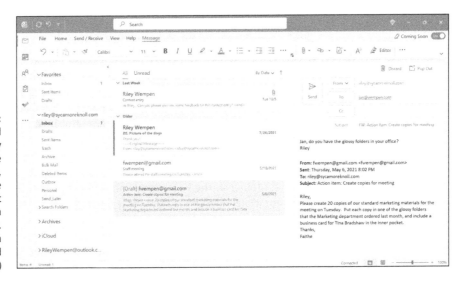

Deleting Messages

You can zap an email message without a second thought; you don't even have to read the thing. As soon as you see the Inbox list, you know who's sending the message and what it's about, so you don't have to waste time reading Burt's Bad Joke of the Day. Just zap it.

TIP

If you accidentally delete a message you didn't want to lose, undo your last action by pressing Ctrl+Z immediately. If you've done some other actions since the accidental deletion, click the Deleted Items folder in the Folder pane. You'll find all the messages you've deleted in the last few months (unless you've emptied the Deleted Items folder). To recover a deleted message, just drag it from the Deleted Items list to the icon for whichever folder you want to put it in.

To delete a message, follow these steps:

1. **In the Mail module, in the message list, select the title of the message that you want to delete.**

   You don't have to read the message; you can just delete it from the list.

2. **Delete the message by doing any of the following:**

   - Press the Delete key on your keyboard.
   - Press Ctrl+D.
   - Right-click the message and choose Delete from the menu.
   - Click the Delete tab on the Home tab of the Ribbon.

When you delete messages, Outlook doesn't actually eliminate deleted items; it moves them to the Deleted Items folder. (With some mail accounts and mail systems it's called Trash rather than Deleted Items. Same thing.) If you have unread items in your Deleted Items folder, the folder name is followed by the number of unread items — the same way Outlook annotates the Inbox with the number of unread items.

You can get rid of the deleted message permanently by right-clicking the Deleted Items (or Trash) folder in the Folder pane and then choosing Empty Folder. After you empty your Deleted Items folder, the messages that were in it disappear forever.

TIP

If you get tired of emptying the Deleted Items or Trash folder, you can tell Outlook to do it for you automatically each time you exit the application. Choose File ➪ Options ➪ Advanced. In the Outlook Start and Exit section, select the Empty Deleted Items Folders When Exiting Outlook check box.

Saving a Draft of a Message

If you get interrupted while writing an email message, all is not lost. You can return to it later. When you start composing a message and then navigate away from it without sending it, Outlook automatically saves your work in the Drafts folder. (You can make sure it does by pressing Ctrl+S for Save, but it saves automatically, so that's a bit of overkill.) When you are ready to continue working on it, navigate to the Drafts folder, click the message, finish it up, and click Send. Or, if you decide you want to delete the draft, click the Discard button above the message composition pane.

Saving a Message as a File

You may create or receive an email message that's so wonderful (or terrible) that you just have to save it. You may need to print it to show to someone, save it to disk, or export it to a desktop publishing application, for example.

Why would you want to save a message as a file rather than just keeping it around inside Outlook? Two reasons. The first is that every message you keep in Outlook increases the size of your Outlook data file, making Outlook start and exit more slowly. The second is that if you keep messages in Outlook and then your Outlook data file becomes corrupted, you may lose that message. By saving it outside of Outlook, you keep it safe(r).

To save a message as a file, follow these steps:

1. **In the Mail module, with the message open, select the File tab on the Ribbon and then choose Save As (or press F12).**

   The message can either be displayed in the Reading pane or open in its own window.

   The Save As dialog box opens.

2. **Use the navigation pane on the left side of the Save As dialog box to choose the drive and folder in which you want to save the file.**

   By default, Outlook initially chooses your Documents folder, but you can save the message on any drive and in any folder you want.

3. **Click the File Name text box and type the name you want to give the file.**

   Type any name you want; if you type a filename that Outlook can't use, it opens a window telling you that the filename is not valid.

4. **Click the Save as Type box, as shown in Figure 4-10, and choose Text Only as your file type.**

   You have several file types to choose from, but the Text Only file format is most easily read by other applications. The different file type options are:

   - **Text Only (*.txt):** A very simple file format that removes all of the message's formatting. As the name implies, it saves only the text of the message.

   - **Outlook Template (*.oft):** This format is for saving a message that you want to use repeatedly in Outlook. It saves the message's formatting as well as any attachments.

   - **Outlook Message Format (*.msg):** This format keeps all the message's formatting and attachments, but it can only be read by Outlook.

   - **Outlook Message Format - Unicode (*.msg):** This is the same as the previous file format, but it uses international characters that can be read by versions of Outlook that use different languages. This is Outlook's default setting.

   - **HTML:** This is webpage format. It can be read using any browser.

   - **MHT files:** This is also a type of webpage format, but it saves graphics embedded in the file. It's also sometimes called single-file webpage. Any browser can read it.

5. **Click the Save button (or press Enter).**

   In Figure 4-10, the Save button is under the open menu, so it's not visible.

   The message is saved to the folder you specified in Step 2.

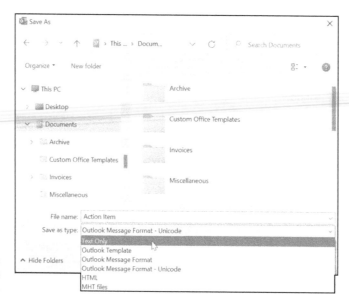

FIGURE 4-10: The Save As dialog box.

IN THIS CHAPTER

» Using flags and reminders with messages

» Saving copies of sent messages

» Setting options for replies and forwarding

» Including your name with your comments in replies

» Attaching files to messages

» Setting up a signature

» Translating a foreign-language message

Chapter **5**

Taking Email to the Next Level

O utlook can do all sorts of tricks with the mail you send out as well as with the messages you receive. You can flag messages with reminders, customize your messages with a signature, or add special formatting to the messages you send as replies.

WARNING

One of Outlook's strengths is its ability to support lots of different kinds of email accounts — everything from a simple web-based account like Gmail to a business account running through a Microsoft Exchange server. This wide variety of account support sometimes makes for a bit of chaos when talking about Outlook's features, though, because not all features are available for all types of accounts. If at any point what you see on your screen doesn't match what you read in this book, that's probably the reason. To reduce confusion, I will tag some of these instances when they pop up. There are also some email features that work only if both the sender and the recipient are using Microsoft Outlook. I'll point these out as we go along, too.

Nagging by Flagging

Flagging a message makes it stand out in your Inbox, so you can see it at a glance. Over time, flags have become one of my favorite Outlook features. I get thousands of messages each week, and I need help remembering to get back to important messages that otherwise might get lost in the shuffle. If I can't respond to an important message right away, I like to flag that message as soon as I read it, so I'm sure to get back to it.

You can also plant a flag in a message you send to others to remind them about a task they have to do if both you and the other person use Microsoft Outlook.

One-click flagging

When you hover your mouse over a message in your Inbox, at the right end of the subject line, you'll see a little gray outline of a flag — sort of a shadow flag. When you click that little shadow, it changes from gray to red to show you've flagged the message. Whenever you look at your list of messages now, you know which messages need further attention. The messages you've flagged also appear in the Task list so you can keep track of flagged messages even after they've slipped to the bottom of the screen. Figure 5-1 shows a flagged message with the To-Do bar displaying tasks so you can see the corresponding entry there.

Corresponding entry in To-Do bar

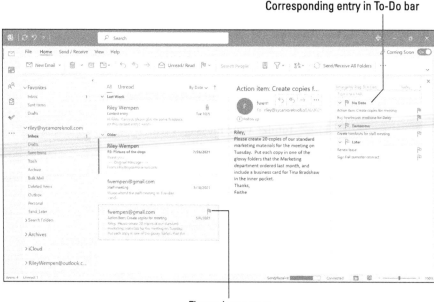

FIGURE 5-1:
The Inbox with a message flagged.

Flagged message

After you've attended to your flagged message, click the flag again. Depending on the type of flagging available for your email account (see the next section), the flag will either disappear entirely or will be replaced by a check mark.

TIP

If you click a message's flag and nothing happens, try restarting Outlook to see if that clears up the problem.

What kind of flagging have you got?

Before we go any further, you need to know what kind of flagging your email account type supports, so do this experiment:

 Select an email message in your Inbox.

It doesn't matter which one; this step is just to make tagging available.

2. **On the Home tab, click the Follow Up button.**

It's the button that looks like a red flag.

Alternately, you can right-click the message's flag. A menu appears that resembles one of the two menus shown in Figure 5-2.

FIGURE 5-2:
The Follow Up menu for an account that doesn't support flagging (left) and for one that does (right).

If you see a super-simple menu like the one on the left in Figure 5-2, your email account doesn't support full-featured flagging. You'll be able to toggle a flag on/off for a message, but that's all. If you see the full-featured menu like the one on the right, your email account *does* support flagging, and you're good to go with the following sections.

TECHNICAL STUFF

If flags are important to you and you have one of those accounts that doesn't allow much flag flexibility, check to see if the account is configured as an IMAP/SMTP account (File ⇨ Account Settings ⇨ Account Settings). If it is, you could delete the account from Outlook and set it up again, this time using Advanced settings, as a POP account. Chapter 7 covers setting up mail accounts. There's a gotcha, though: Doing so will delete all your previously received messages from that account from the current computer. There are also some functional differences between IMAP and POP accounts, some of which aren't obvious from the outset. See Chapter 7 for more on that.

Setting a flag's status

After you set a flag, you can click that flag again to turn it off. What "off" looks like depends on what level of flagging your email account supports, though.

If your account supports only basic flagging, clicking the flag again makes the flag disappear, like it never happened. Basic flags are strictly an on/off affair.

If your account supports full-featured flagging, clicking the flag again replaces it with a check mark to indicate that it has been dealt with. If you click it yet again, the flag reappears. If you want to clear the flag entirely, right-click the flag and choose Clear Flag.

Setting flags for different days

When you click to add a flag to a message, a copy of the message appears in the To-Do bar, along with the list of things you're scheduled to do today, as you saw in Figure 5-1. If tomorrow rolls around and you haven't either cleared the flag or marked it as completed, that email message will appear in red in your Inbox to help remind you to deal with it. It will also show up in red on your Task list.

In real life, though, not everything is due the same day it is tagged. You might prefer to put off a task until tomorrow or next week. If you right-click the flag icon (provided your account supports flagging), you see a list of possible due dates for a flag, including Today, Tomorrow, This Week, Next Week, No Date, and Custom. That list appears on the right side of Figure 5-2.

You can also assign a custom date to the flag. In fact, you can assign *two* dates: a Start date and a Due date. Follow these steps:

1. **Right-click the flag on the message you want to work with and choose Custom.**

   The Custom dialog box opens. You could have also gotten here by clicking the Follow Up button on the Home tab and then clicking Custom.

2. **(Optional) Enter a date in the Start Date box.**

If you don't specify a Start date, it'll be today's date. You can click the down arrow to the right of the text box to choose from a date picker if you like, as in Figure 5-3.

3. **Enter the desired end date in the Due Date box.**

Again, you can use a date picker if you like.

4. **Click OK.**

FIGURE 5-3:
Choose an exact
Start date and/or
End date.

After you've picked a due date, you can change it by dragging the item from one due date to another on the To-Do bar. For example, you can drag an item from the Today group to the Next Week group (if both groups are visible). You can also right-click the flag and choose a different due date.

Changing the default flag date

For unusually busy people and compulsive procrastinators, you can change the default due dates of your flags by following these steps:

1. **Click the Follow Up button on the Ribbon.**

The flag shortcut menu appears (like the one shown on the right side of Figure 5-2).

2. **Choose Set Quick Click.**

A dialog box opens, and the list box in that dialog box offers several choices for a due date, as shown in Figure 5-4.

If there's no Set Quick Click command on the menu, you probably don't have the type of email account that allows this, so move along.

3. **Pick the date that suits you.**

   The date you choose becomes the default flag due date.

If you have trouble committing to a date, you can choose No Date and just wait until someone complains. Or if you're ruthlessly optimistic, you can set the default to Complete, where simply clicking on a flag magically completes the task.

Adding a reminder to a flag

Outlook flags can pop up and remind you to do something at any time you choose. To add a reminder to a flag, you use the same Custom dialog box that you saw back in Figure 5-3. Follow these steps:

1. **Right-click the flag on the message you want to flag and choose Add Reminder.**

   You could also go through the Follow Up command on the Home tab to do this.

   The Custom dialog box opens, with the Reminder check box selected. See Figure 5-5. The default reminder date/time is 4:00 p.m. today.

2. **Click the list box arrow at the right end of the Flag To text box and choose one of the menu items (or type your own choice).**

   Follow Up is the default, but there are several other choices, like Review and Forward.

3. **Enter a date and time for the reminder.**

   You can type the date and time or click the down arrows on their boxes to select without typing.

See the little speaker icon to the right of the reminder time? You can click it to open a Reminder Sound dialog box, where you can choose what sound will play with the reminder pop-up. Fun!

4. **Click OK.**

When the reminder date you entered in the Custom dialog box arrives, a reminder dialog box helps give you a gentle nudge.

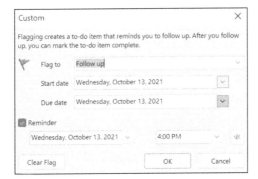

FIGURE 5-5:
The Custom dialog box with a reminder flag being set.

Attaching a flag to an outgoing message

When you send someone a message, wouldn't it be nice if you could (gently) let them know that you expect them to act on it on a certain date? You can do that! Provided the recipient's email program supports the feature, a reminder can pop up and pester them. (Who could resist that?)

As you are composing the email message, do the following to add a flag to it:

1. **Start composing a new email message as you normally would.**

2. **On the Message tab, click Follow Up, and then click Add Reminder.**

   A special version of the Custom dialog box appears. The top part is basically the same as the one you saw back in Figure 5-5, but there's also a separate section at the bottom for a recipient flag. See Figure 5-6.

3. **Mark the Flag for Recipients check box.**

   This enables separate flagging for recipients.

4. **Select the Reminder check box at the bottom of the dialog box.**

   This enables setting a reminder for recipients.

5. **Set the desired date and time for the recipient reminder.**

6. Click **OK.**

7. Finish composing and sending your message as you normally would.

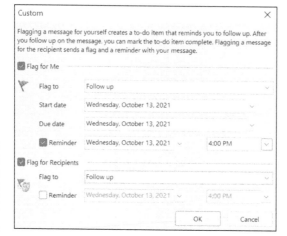

FIGURE 5-6:
For an outgoing message you can have separate flags for yourself and for your recipients.

Here's the deal with adding a reminder to a message, though — it may not come through the way you expect. It all depends on the email application the person is using to read your message and the level of support for flagging that their account has. So you can't count on them seeing your flag and/or your reminder.

If the recipient's account and mail program *do* fully support flags, the message they receive will look like the one in Figure 5-7. Notice that there's a flag, but not the same kind of plain flag you've seen before; it's a little flag with an outline of a person on it. That indicates it's an incoming flag that you haven't accepted yet. If you click it, it changes to a regular flag.

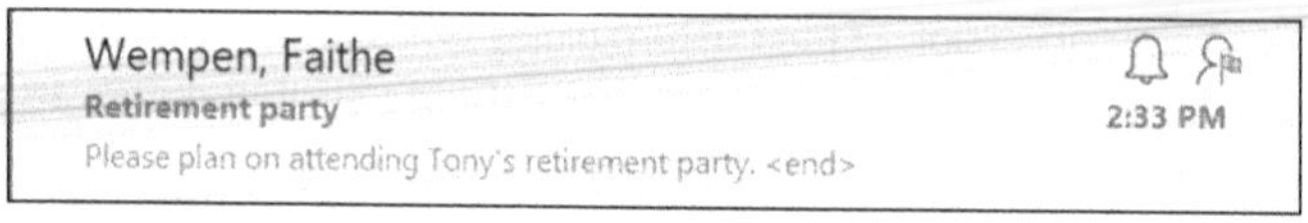

FIGURE 5-7:
Incoming messages with flags and reminders show a different flag icon.

> Wempen, Faithe
> **Retirement party**   2:33 PM
> Please plan on attending Tony's retirement party. <end>

Changing the date on a reminder

Procrastination used to be an art; Outlook makes it a science. Here's how to change the reminder date for a reminder flag that someone sent you:

1. **Right-click the flag on the incoming message you want to change and choose Add Reminder.**

   The Custom dialog box opens, like the one you saw earlier in Figure 5-3.

2. **Change the date and/or time as desired.**

3. **Click OK.**

Saving Copies of Your Messages — or Not

By default, Outlook saves copies of all your sent messages in your Sent Items folder. (Some mail systems call it Sent Mail or Sent Messages, but it's the same thing.) That's super handy when you need to refer to what you sent, but if other people use your computer and you're concerned about privacy, you might want to disable that feature at some point.

To save copies of your messages, follow these steps:

1. **Select the File tab and click the Options button.**

   The Outlook Options dialog box opens.

2. **Click the Mail button in the navigation window on the left.**

   The Mail settings appear.

3. **Scroll down to the Save Messages section (see Figure 5-8) and select or deselect the Save Copies of Messages in the Sent Items Folder check box.**

   It should already be selected by default; clear it at your own risk for extra privacy if you want.

4. **Click OK.**

Select or deselect this check box to save copies of your sent messages (or not).

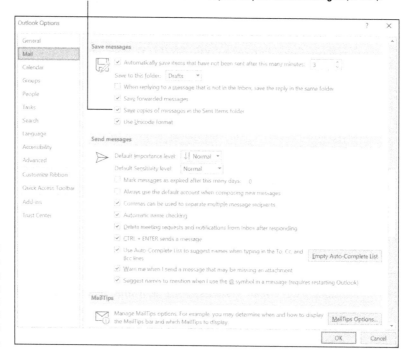

FIGURE 5-8:
You can decide
whether to save
copies of the
messages you
send by using the
Outlook Options
dialog box.

Setting Your Reply and Forward Options

When you forward or reply to messages, Outlook has certain rules it follows as to how the original text gets quoted and formatted. For example, should the original message be included as part of the email, or attached as a separate file? Should its text be indented? Should it be prefixed with something, like an arrow symbol or your name? Many options are available.

To set your options, follow these steps:

1. **Select the File tab on the Ribbon and click the Options button.**

   The Outlook Options dialog box opens.

2. **Click the Mail button in the navigation window on the left.**

   The Mail settings window opens.

3. **Scroll down to the Replies and Forwards section.**

4. **Open the When Replying to a Message List and choose your preferred style.**

   When Outlook is first installed, Include Original Message Text is the default option. The diagram on the left side of the menu shows how the message will be laid out when you choose each option, as shown in Figure 5-9.

5. **Open the When Forwarding a Message list and choose your preferred style.**

6. **Click OK.**

   The Outlook Options dialog box closes.

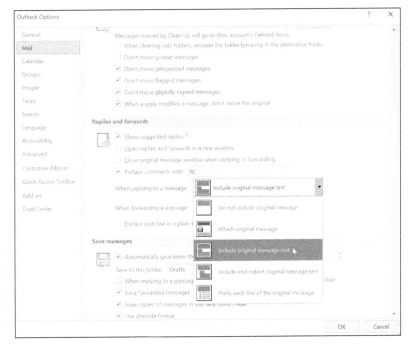

FIGURE 5-9:
Change the appearance of your replies and forwards in the Mail settings window.

You can select and delete the text of the original message when you create a forward or reply, but including at least a part of the original message makes your response easier to understand. You also have the option of selecting and deleting the parts of the original text that aren't relevant to your reply.

Adding Comments to a Reply or a Forward

When you forward or reply to a message, you can type your reply above the quoted original — and that's fine, if the original is short and simple. But if the original message is convoluted and asks multiple questions, it might help to type your reply within the original message, responding to each question where it appears.

The only problem with typing replies within the original quoted message is that it isn't always clear what's your new typing and what's from the original. To fix that, Outlook enables you to preface any inline replies you make with your name (or whatever other text you want). It also makes your reply text bold, so it stands out more.

REMEMBER

This feature tags only those replies that occur in line with the original quoted message, not replies you type above the quoted text.

To tag your inline replies with your name, follow these steps:

1. **Select the File tab on the Ribbon and click the Options button.**

   The Outlook Options dialog box opens.

2. **Click the Mail button in the navigation window on the left.**

   The Mail settings window opens.

3. **Scroll down to the Replies and Forwards section.**

   You may remember this part of the dialog box from Figure 5-8 earlier in the chapter.

4. **Select the Preface Comments With check box if it is not already selected.**

5. **In the Preface Comments With text box, type the text you want to accompany your annotations.**

   Whatever you enter will be used as the prefix to all the text you type when you reply to messages. Your initials might be a good choice here, or your name.

6. **Click OK.**

   The next time you are composing a reply, you'll see the results of this setting if you type in the body of the original quoted message, as shown in Figure 5-10.

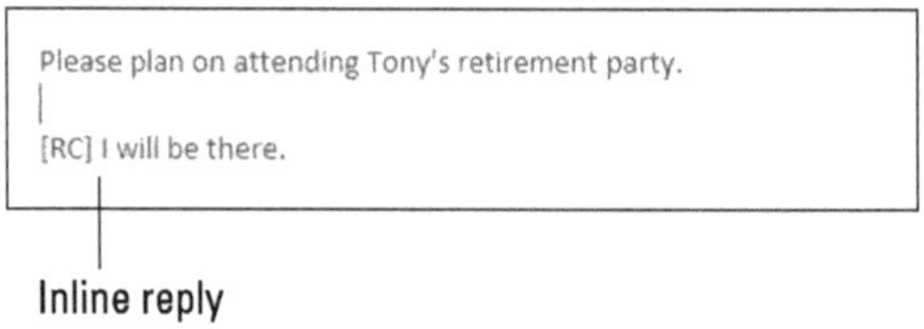

FIGURE 5-10:
Your initials shows up to indicate your reply.

> Please plan on attending Tony's retirement party.
>
> [RC] I will be there.

Inline reply

Sending Attachments

Almost any type of file can be sent as an attachment to an email. For example, you can send word processing documents, spreadsheets, pictures, and videos.

WARNING

There are a few types of files that Outlook won't usually allow you to send or receive because they are commonly used to spread viruses. Most executable files (that is, files that run programs) with extensions like .com, .exe, .bat, and .vbs are blocked. Some mail servers also look inside .zip files and reject them if there are any of the disallowed file types inside.

If you need to send those kinds of files, it's better to save them to a cloud storage drive like OneDrive and then provide a link to them via email. Another workaround is to compress the executable file in a .zip file, a format that Outlook does allow. On an Exchange system, the email server administrator can unblock certain file types that would normally be blocked. Keep in mind that just because your mail server will allow you to send it doesn't mean the recipient's mail server will allow it to be received. Further, you won't usually receive any kind of warning; the mail server just ignores it. So if you sent someone a large attachment, you might follow up with another email (no attachment this time) checking to see if they received it.

WARNING

Mail servers also have their own rules about the maximum attachment size for both sending and receiving. So again, if you send a large attachment and you don't hear anything from the recipient, follow up.

There are two ways of sending an attachment. One is to attach the file directly from within Outlook, as you learned in Chapter 1. I'll review that process next. Then I'll explain the second way, which is to send a file from the application in which you created it.

Sending a file from Outlook

If you're already in Outlook, the easiest way to send a file to someone as an attachment is usually to just start a new message and attach the file to it. This method works great with a wide variety of file formats — basically any file type that Outlook does not disallow can be sent this way. You don't even have to have an application capable of opening/editing it.

Follow these steps to attach a file to a new outgoing email message in Outlook:

1. **Start composing a new message as you normally would.**

   Fill in the recipient(s), the subject, and the message body.

2. **Click the Attach File button on the new message window's Ribbon.**

   A list drops down to show the names of the files you've worked on most recently. There's a pretty good chance the file you want to attach is in that list.

3. **If you see the name of the file you want to send, click that name in the list and skip to Step 7.**

4. **Click Browse This PC.**

   The Insert File dialog box opens, as shown in Figure 5-11. It looks like the dialog box you use for opening files in most Windows programs, and it works like opening a file, too.

5. **Click the name of the file you want to send.**

   The selected file's name appears in the File Name box at the bottom of the dialog box.

TIP

   To attach multiple files at once, hold down Ctrl as you click each file you want to attach. This only works if the multiple files you want to attach are in the same location.

6. **Click the Insert button.**

   The name(s) of the file(s) appear in the Attached box in the Message form's message header.

7. **Finish composing your message as you normally would and then click Send to send it.**

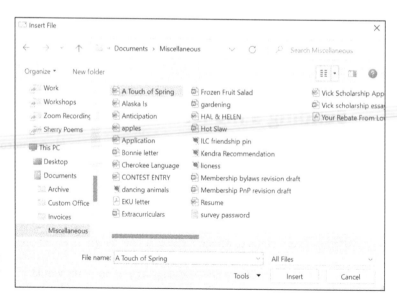

FIGURE 5-11:
The Insert File
dialog box.

Another approach for sending an attachment is to find the file on your computer using File Explorer, right-click on that file, choose Send To from the shortcut menu, and then click Mail Recipient. You can also drag and drop attachments directly into Outlook's New Message form.

Sending a file from another application

You probably do most of your daily work in programs other than Outlook. You might create documents in Microsoft Word or build elaborate spreadsheets with Excel. When you want to send a file by email, Outlook gets involved.

You can email a file either as a copy or as a link. If you send a copy, each recipient gets their own separate copy of the file. If you send a link, each recipient gets the same hyperlink that points to your original copy stored on your OneDrive.

OneDrive is a cloud-based file storage system that's available for free to anyone with a Microsoft account who has an Internet connection — and that's pretty much anyone who uses Windows and/or Office. You don't *have* to use OneDrive for storing your Office application files, but there are many advantages to doing so, like always having access to them no matter where you are, and no matter what disaster might have befallen your home, office, or computer. (Not to get morbid, but these things do happen.) You don't even have to be connected to the Internet all the time, because OneDrive files are cached on your local hard drive. When you are Internet-connected, the Internet version is synched automatically.

Sending a file as a link from Microsoft Word

To email a file as a link from Microsoft Word, follow these steps. (It's the same steps for Excel and PowerPoint, too.)

1. **Open the file in Microsoft Word (or Excel, or PowerPoint).**

    The file opens on-screen.

2. **Save it to OneDrive if it's not already saved there.**

    Click File and then look in the navigation bar on the left. If you see Save As, the file isn't saved to OneDrive yet. Click OneDrive as the location and save the file. If you see Save a Copy, it is already saved to OneDrive and you're good to go; press Esc to get out of there.

3. **Click Share in the upper right corner of the application window.**

    A Send Link dialog box opens.

4. **In the To: box, enter the email address of the person you want to send the file to.**

   To enter multiple addresses, separate them with semicolons.

5. **Type a message to the recipient if desired in the Include a Message (Optional) box.**

   This message will appear as the email message body. Figure 5-12 shows an example.

6. **Click Share.**

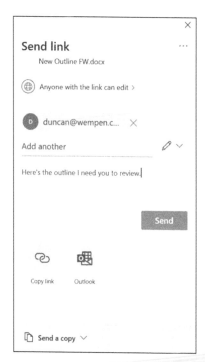

FIGURE 5-12:
You can email a
link to a
document right
from Microsoft
Word.

Sending a file as a copy from Microsoft Word

You can also send a copy of a document as an email attachment. This method sends a separate copy to each recipient, and doesn't require the file to be stored on OneDrive. To email a file as a copy from Microsoft Word, follow these steps:

1. **Open the document in Microsoft Word.**

   The document opens on-screen.

2. **Click Share in the upper right corner of the Word window.**

   A Send Link dialog box opens (like the one you saw earlier in Figure 5-12).

3. **At the bottom of the dialog box, click Send a Copy.**

4. **In the pop-up menu that appears, click the format in which you want to send the file: Word document or PDF.**

   PDF is a good choice if you don't want the recipient to be able to make changes; Word document is a good choice if you do. Either way, a New Message window opens in Outlook. (If Outlook wasn't already open, it opens at this point.) The new message has the document already attached.

5. **In the To box, enter the email address of the person you want to send the file to.**

   To enter multiple addresses, separate them with semicolons.

6. **Change the subject line text if desired.**

   By default it's the filename.

7. **Type a message below the attachment if desired.**

   Figure 5-13 shows a completed message ready to send.

8. **Click Send.**

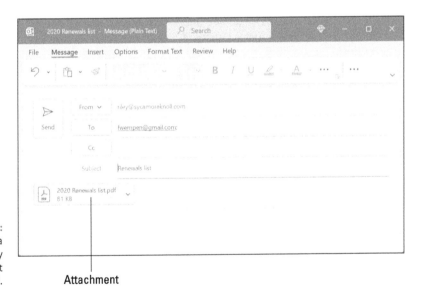

FIGURE 5-13:
You can email a
file as a copy
from Microsoft
Word.

Attachment

Whew! When you're just sending one Word file, these steps seem like a long way to go, but they'll always get your document on its way.

Emailing Screenshots

They say a picture is worth a thousand words. Many of those words can become four-letter words when your computer is acting up, making it tough to describe the nature of your problem accurately. Outlook can help when other computer programs give you grief.

A *screenshot* is a picture of your computer screen that you capture to show what's going on. This book contains dozens of screenshots of Microsoft Outlook, which I include to make it easier for you to understand what I mean. You can do exactly that same thing with the screenshot feature in Microsoft Outlook. You can send a screenshot to help someone solve a problem with their computer, but you can also send a screenshot of nearly anything that appears on your screen, including cat photos, selfies, or inspiring, made-up quotes. The possibilities are endless.

TIP

One way to capture a screenshot is to press the PrintScreen key, which copies a screenshot to the Clipboard. You can then paste it into the body of an email (press Ctrl+V) or into a graphics program such as Paint.

To include a screenshot in an email message, follow these steps:

1. **While composing an email message or reply, make sure the message format is either HTML or Rich Text.**

   Plain text messages don't accept inline graphics. You learned how to set the message format in Chapter 4.

2. **Click in the message body to move the insertion point where you want to place the screenshot.**

3. **Click the Insert tab on the Ribbon.**

4. **Do one of the following:**

   - Using the Simplified Ribbon: Click More Commands and point to Screenshot.

   - Using the Classic Ribbon: Click the Take a Screenshot button in the Illustrations group.

   Either way, a gallery of thumbnail images opens. See Figure 5-14. Those are the other windows that are open on your computer (except minimized ones).

5. **Click one of the screens from the gallery.**

   The screenshot you selected appears in the body of your email message.

6. **Finish your email message and send it to your recipient.**

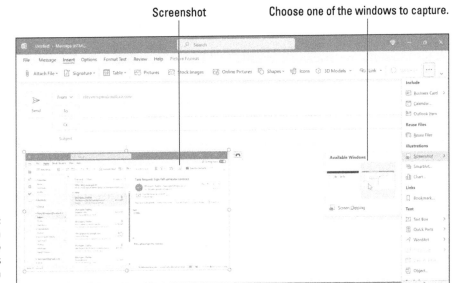

Screenshot   Choose one of the windows to capture.

FIGURE 5-14:
You can email a
screenshot to
show what's
going on with
your computer.

Creating Signatures for Your Messages

Many people like to add a signature to the end of every message they send. A *signature* is usually a few lines of text that identifies you to everyone who reads your message and tells something you want everyone to know. Many people include their name, the name of their business, their business's web address, their motto, a little sales slogan, or some squib of personal information.

You can tell Outlook to add a signature automatically to all your outgoing messages, but you must first create a signature file.

To create your signature file, follow these steps:

1. **Select the File tab on the Ribbon and click the Options button.**

    The Outlook Options dialog box opens.

2. **Click the Mail button in the navigation pane on the left.**

    The Mail settings window opens.

3. **In the Compose Messages section, click the Signatures button.**

    The Signatures and Stationery dialog box opens to the E-Mail Signature tab.

4. **Click the New button.**

    The New Signature dialog box opens.

5. **Type a name for your new signature.**

   The name you type appears in the New Signature box. You can name a signature anything you want.

6. **Click OK.**

   The New Signature dialog box closes.

7. **Type the text of the signature you want in the Edit Signature box and add any formatting you want.**

   To change the font, size, color, or other text characteristics, use the buttons just above the text box. If you're more comfortable creating highly formatted text in Microsoft Word, you can create your signature in Word and then copy and paste it in the Edit Signature box. Figure 5-15 shows a completed signature example.

REMEMBER

   Many people receive email on their cell phones and other kinds of devices that don't know what to do with fancy formatting, so you may be best off with a fairly plain signature. Also, try to be brief. You don't want your signature to be longer than the message to which it's attached.

TIP

   If you work in a company in which everyone uses similar company-approved signatures, you can copy a signature from an email you get from someone else and change the specific details about phone number, address, and so on, from their information to yours. Just open an incoming message from a colleague, run your mouse over the signature to select it, press Ctrl+C to copy it, then click in the New Signature box (or Edit Signature box) and press Ctrl+V to paste it in. At that point, you can edit the signature as you wish.

8. **Click OK.**

   Your new signature is now saved, and the Signatures and Stationery dialog box closes.

9. **Click the OK button in the Outlook Options dialog box.**

   The Outlook Options dialog box closes.

   Your new signature will now appear on every new message you send. If you create more than one signature, you can switch to a different default signature by following Steps 1–3 and then choosing the signature you want from the New Messages menu in the Choose Default Signature section. If you want to include a signature in your replies and forwards, choose the signature you want from the Replies/Forwards menu in the Choose Default Signature section.

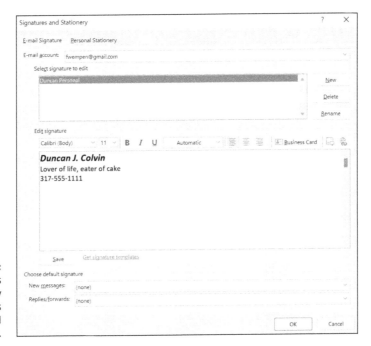

FIGURE 5-15:
The Signatures
and Stationery
dialog box's
E-mail
Signature tab.

TIP

If you use more than one email address, you can choose your signatures in a couple ways:

>> **Set up Outlook to use different signatures on different email addresses:** For example, assume that one address is for business and another is for personal messages. You can create a businesslike signature for the first and a more casual signature for the latter. To designate which signature goes with which address, select the address from the E-mail Account drop-down menu in the Choose Default Signature section and then pick the signature you want to use for that email address. Repeat this for each additional email address for which you want to include a signature.

>> **Choose signatures one at a time:** When you finish writing the body of an email message, click the Insert tab on the New Message form's Ribbon and then click the Signature button to see the list of signatures you've created. Click the name of the signature you want to use to make it appear in your message.

Translating a Foreign-Language Message

Have you ever received an email message in a language you don't speak? One way to translate it is to paste the text from the message into one of the many web-based translation websites, but with Outlook you don't have to go to that trouble. You can translate some messages (in some languages) without leaving Outlook!

Outlook's translation is only for incoming messages, not outgoing ones.

To translate a message you've received, follow these steps:

1. **Select the message you want to translate.**

   You can either open it in its own window or display it in the Reading pane.

2. **Click the Translate button on the Ribbon.**

   If you opened the message in its own window, the Translate button is on the Message tab; if you're viewing the message in the Reading pane, the Translate button is on the Home tab.

3. **Click Translate Message.**

The text in the message changes to English (or your preferred language, if your system is set to some other default language).

You can set your translation preferences from the Outlook Options dialog box's Language tab. A shortcut for getting there is Translate ⇨ Translation Preferences.

Chapter **6**

Conquering Your Mountain of Messages

So, you say you spend too much time on email? Everybody does. Some experts estimate that the average business employee spends up to 2 hours each day on email, and it's getting worse every year.

Fortunately, Outlook has some handy tools for coping with the flood of electronic flotsam and jetsam that finds its way into your Inbox. You can create separate folders for filing your mail, and you can use Outlook's View feature to help sort your incoming messages into manageable groups. You can even archive old messages to keep your Inbox from getting too bloated.

This chapter also introduces the Rules Wizard, which works its magic on your Inbox, automatically responding to incoming messages according to your wishes. You can move all messages from certain senders to the folder of your choice — for example, send everything from Spam-O-Rama.com to oblivion — send automatic replies to messages about certain subjects, or delete messages containing words that offend you.

Speaking of spam, an even more effective way to deal with offensive or aggres-sively useless messages is to use the junk email filters built into Outlook. The filters should already be turned on, but you can crank up the settings to have even less junk mail cluttering up your Inbox.

Organizing Folders

You're probably familiar with organizing items into folders. Windows organizes all your other documents into folders, so why should Outlook be any different? Well, Outlook *is* a little different from Windows regarding folders. But the idea is the same: Create a folder and drag stuff to it.

Creating a new mail folder

The simplest way to manage incoming mail is to just file it. Before you file a mes-sage, you need to create at least one folder in which to file your messages. You only need to create a folder once; it's there for good after you create it (unless, of course, you later decide to delete it). You can create as many folders as you want; you may have dozens or just one or two.

For example, I have folders for filing mail from specific clients. All the email I've received in connection with this book is in a folder called Outlook For Dummies. (Clever title, eh?) A folder called Personal has messages that aren't business related.

To create a folder that's a subfolder of your Inbox, follow these steps:

1. **In the Mail module, select Inbox in the Folder pane (or press Ctrl+Shift+I) to make sure the Inbox is selected.**

   The Inbox is selected by default when you open Outlook, but it might not be if you've been doing other things since you started up.

2. **Right-click the Inbox folder in the Folder pane and choose New Folder.**

   A blank text box appears beneath the Inbox folder in the Folder pane.

3. **Type a name for your new folder, such as** *Personal*, **as shown in Figure 6-1, and press Enter.**

   You can name the folder anything you like. You can also create many folders for saving and sorting your incoming email. Leaving all your mail in your Inbox gets confusing. On the other hand, if you create too many folders, you may be just as confused as if you had only one.

FIGURE 6-1:
Creating a
new folder.

There's another way to create a new folder that involves a dialog box, but you have to use the Classic Ribbon to get to it, or use a keyboard shortcut. Here's how that works.

1. **In the Mail module, select the Inbox in the Folder pane.**

2. **Do one of the following:**

   - Switch to Classic Ribbon mode, and then on the Folder tab, click New Folder.

   - Press Ctrl+Shift+E.

3. The Create New Folder dialog box opens. See Figure 6-2.

4. **Make sure that your Inbox is selected in the Select Where to Place the Folder list.**

   The new folder will be a subfolder of whatever folder you select here.

5. **Type the desired name for the folder in the Name box.**

6. **Click OK.**

FIGURE 6-2:
The Create New
Folder dialog box.

WARNING

If you have an IMAP mail account, you might not be able to create a subfolder of your Inbox. If you get an error message to that effect at Step 6, try again (starting at Step 4), but this time, in the Select Where to Place the Folder list, click your email account name (top level of the folder hierarchy, one level up from the Inbox). The result is that your new folder is at the same level of hierarchy as the Inbox, rather than being subordinate to it. It works just fine either way.

Moving messages to another folder

Filing your messages is as easy as dragging them from the folder they're in to the folder where you want them. Just click the Inbox to look at your messages when they arrive and then drag each message to the folder where you want your messages to stay.

For a different way to move messages to another folder, follow these steps:

1. **In the Mail module, click the title of the message you want to move.**

   The message is highlighted.

2. **Select the Home tab on the Ribbon and click the Move button.**

   A drop-down menu opens, showing shortcuts to frequently or recently used folders associated with your email account.

3a. **If the destination you want appears on the list, select it.**

   The message is moved to the folder you chose. You're done; skip the rest of these steps.

   OR

3b. **If the folder you want doesn't appear on the list, click Other Folder.**

   The Move Items dialog box opens, showing all the available folders. See Figure 6-3.

4. **Click the desired location from the list of folders.**

5. **Click OK to complete the move.**

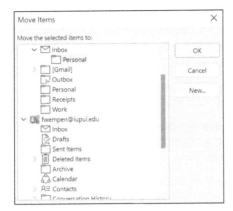

FIGURE 6-3:
The Move Items
dialog box.

Organizing Your Email with Search Folders

The Search Folders feature in Outlook is designed to help you organize the messages in your Inbox and other folders. Search Folders provides a single place where you can always look to find a certain kind of message. A search folder doesn't actually move your messages; it's really a kind of imaginary location for your messages so you only have to look at one type of message at a time.

When you first start Outlook, there aren't any search folders in the Folder pane. If you want to use Search Folders, you'll need to add one of the default Outlook search folders or create your own custom search folder.

Setting up a search folder

To set up a search folder, follow these steps:

1. **In the Mail module, click the Inbox to select that folder in the Folder pane.**

   If you have more than one email address, you might have multiple Inbox folders in the Folder pane. Click the Inbox associated with the email address you want to use with this new folder.

REMEMBER

2. **If you are using the Simplified Ribbon, switch to the Classic Ribbon.**

3. **Select the Folder tab on the Ribbon and then click the New Search Folder button (or press Ctrl+Shift+P).**

   The New Search Folder dialog box opens, as shown in Figure 6-4.

   The Ctrl+Shift+P shortcut works only if you are using the Classic Ribbon.

4. **Select the type of search folder you'd like to add from the list in the New Search Folder dialog box.**

More than a dozen different kinds of folders are available. You can either use a predefined folder or create your own type of search folder (by choosing Create a Custom Search Folder at the bottom of the list).

5. **If a Choose button appears at the bottom of the New Search Folder dialog box when you select a certain search folder, click the button and fill in the requested information.**

When you click some of the search folder types to select them, the bottom of the New Search Folder dialog box changes, offering you a choice suitable to the type of folder you're creating. The controls that appear when you click Choose depend on the criteria for inclusion in the folder. For example, if you're setting up a search based on certain names, the Select Names dialog box appears. Just work with whatever pops up.

You might not see a Choose button at all, depending on what you selected.

6. **Click the OK button.**

The New Search Folder dialog box closes and your new search folder appears in the navigation pane. You can re-run this search at any time by clicking the search folder's name there.

7. (Optional) Switch back to the Simplified Ribbon.

FIGURE 6-4:
The New Search
Folder dialog box.

Some useful predefined search folders in the New Search Folder dialog box are:

>> **Mail Flagged for Follow Up:** This search folder shows only the messages you've flagged. When you remove the flag from a message, you'll no longer see it in this search folder, but you can still find it in the Inbox or folder where it actually resides.

>> **Large Mail:** This search folder organizes your messages by how much storage space they require. Normally, you're probably not too concerned with the size of the messages you receive — but don't be surprised if the system administrators where you work ask you not to store too much mail in your Inbox. If you have lots of messages with attachments (or messages in which friends include their photographs), you may find your Inbox filling up quickly.

You can use the Large Mail search folder to figure out which messages are taking up the most space — and eliminate the largest ones. The messages you'll see in this folder are categorized by size, starting with Large and moving up to Huge and Enormous.

>> **Unread Mail:** This search folder shows you only the messages you haven't read yet. When you read a message in this folder, it disappears from the folder, but you'll still be able to find it in your Inbox.

You need not limit yourself to the search folders that Outlook provides. You can also create your own custom folders. For example, if you receive regular messages about sales in a certain region, you can set up a custom search folder that automatically shows you all the messages you've received with that information.

Using a search folder

You don't need to do anything special to use a search folder. Just click the name of the search folder you want to look at in the Folder pane and then a list of those messages appears. When you're ready to go back to your Inbox, just click the Inbox button in the Folder pane to see your whole collection of messages again.

Deleting a search folder

Some searches need to be frequently repeated — and some don't. If you won't need to run a particular search in the future, you can easily delete it.

Search folders don't contain the original messages, but only pointers to them. Therefore, deleting a search folder doesn't delete the messages it contains. They're still safe and sound in their original locations.

To delete a search folder, follow these steps:

1. **In the Mail module, in the Folder pane, right-click on the search folder you want to delete.**

2. **Choose Delete Folder.**

3. **Click Yes.**

   Your search folder disappears from the Folder pane.

Playing by the Rules

Rules are another of my favorite features in Outlook. The Rules feature lets you make Outlook act on certain kinds of email messages automatically. For example, I get tons of email messages, and I can easily waste the whole day sorting through them. I have much more entertaining ways to waste my time, such as pasting sticky notes to my forehead and having imaginary conversations with celebrities. That's why I set up Rules in Outlook to automatically sort my incoming mail into different folders; it lets me spend a little less time wading through all those messages and more time on my overactive fantasy life.

I show you several rule-creation methods in the upcoming sections. I start you out with the complete method so you can see the breadth of what's available, and then I show you some ways to shortcut that rather long process.

Creating a rule: the complete method

You usually discover the need to create a rule right after getting a message that ticks you off. By creating a rule, you'll never have to read another message from that so-and-so again — unless that so-and-so is your boss. In which case you may have to make another kind of rule.

Rules can do much more than just sort incoming messages. You can create rules that automatically reply to certain messages, flag messages with a particular word in the subject, delete messages from specific people — the sky's the limit.

The Rules Wizard is called a *wizard* because of the way the program leads you step-by-step to create each rule. Don't let all the steps worry you — the process is actually pretty simple. To create a simple rule to move an incoming message from a certain person to a certain folder, follow these steps:

1. **In the Mail module, select the Inbox in the Folder pane.**

2. **On the Home tab of the Ribbon, click the Rules button (or click More Commands and then click Rules), and then click Manage Rules & Alerts.**

   Don't click Create Rule on the Rules button's menu; that gives you a limited number of options based on whichever message is currently selected. Selecting Manage Rules & Alerts opens the Rules and Alerts dialog box, but you're still one click away from the Rules Wizard.

3. **If you have more than one email address set up in Outlook, make sure the correct one is selected from the Apply Changes to This Folder drop-down menu at the top of the Rules and Alerts dialog box.**

4. **Click the New Rule button.**

   The Rules Wizard dialog box opens. The dialog box contains a list of the types of rules you can create, as shown in Figure 6-5.

   The Rules Wizard offers several common types of rules you may want to create, such as:

   - Move messages from someone to a folder.

   - Move messages with specific words in the subject to a folder.

   - Move messages sent to a public group to a folder.

5. **Choose the type of rule you want to create. For this example, choose Move Messages from Someone to a Folder.**

6. **Click Next.**

   The Rules Wizard dialog box changes to ask about the conditions you want to set. See Figure 6-6. For this example, the condition will be a particular sender.

7. **Make sure that the From People or Public Group check box is selected in the Step 1 section.**

   It should be selected by default.

8. **In the Step 2 box, Click the People or Public Group hyperlink.**

   The Rule Address dialog box opens.

9. **Do one of the following to specify the address(es) to include in the rule:**

   a. Type each email address in the From box at the bottom of the Rule Address dialog box, separating them with semicolons.

   b. Double-click the name of each person whose messages you want to move to a new folder. Doing this adds the names to the From box without you having to type them.

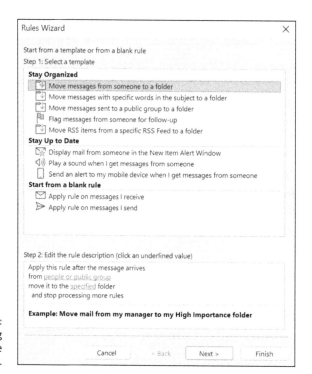

FIGURE 6-5:
Start by choosing
the kind of rule
you want.

FIGURE 6-6:
Set up the
conditions for the
rule.

10. **Click OK to close the Rule Address dialog box.**

The name(s) you've selected replace the words People or Public Group in the Step 2 box.

11. **Click Next to move to the next screen of the Rules Wizard.**

Here you can specify what happens to the messages that meet the criteria. In the Step 1 section, notice that Stop Processing More Rules is selected, as well as Move It to the Specified Folder. Those are the defaults.

12. **In the Step 2 box, click *specified* (the underlined word there).**

A Rules and Alerts dialog box opens, offering you a choice of folders to which you can move the message, as shown in Figure 6-7.

13. **Double-click the name of the folder to which you want to move messages.**

The dialog box closes and the name of the folder you chose appears in the sentence in the Step 2 box.

TIP

14. **Click Next to move to the next screen in the Rules Wizard.**

On this screen you can set up any exceptions to the rule. For this example you won't have any exceptions, because we're keeping things simple, but keep this in mind for later use.

15. **Click Next to move to the next screen in the Rules Wizard.**

Here you can specify a name for the rule and set a few options for it.

16. **Type the name in the Step 1 box, replacing the default name.**

17. **Click the Finish button.**

The Rules and Alerts dialog box opens again, providing a list of all your rules. Each rule has a check box next to it. You can turn rules on and off by selecting or deselecting the check boxes. If a check mark appears next to a rule, it's turned on; otherwise, the rule is turned off.

18. **Click the OK button to close the Rules and Alerts dialog box.**

TIP

You don't have to click through every single step of the Rules Wizard, as you did in the preceding steps. After Step 10 above, in the Step 2 box you can click *specified*, choose the folder location, and then jump right to Step 17.

FIGURE 6-7:
Choose the folder
to which your
messages will go.

Creating a rule: the quick method

If you have received an email that has some property that you want to create a rule on (such as its sender or subject), follow these steps to see how easy it is to make that rule:

1. **In the Inbox, select the email to use as an example for the rule creation.**

2. **On the Home tab of the Ribbon, click Rules (or click More Commands and then click Rules), and then click Create Rule.**

   The Create Rule dialog box opens.

3. **Select the check boxes for each of the properties of that email message that you want to include in the rule.**

   For example, in Figure 6-8 I am making a rule about the sender's email address; I'm not including the Subject Contains or Sent To properties.

4. **Select the check box for the action you want to happen.**

   For example, in Figure 6-8 I am choosing to move the item to a folder. If you choose this, click Select Folder and select which folder it should be.

5. **Click OK.**

   The rule is created and a confirmation message appears. From this box you can optionally select the Run This Rule Now on Messages Already in the Current Folder check box.

6. **Click OK to clear the confirmation message.**

TIP

If you start using this abbreviated method and realize you need the full version, click Advanced Options in the Create Rule dialog box to switch over to the Rules Wizard.

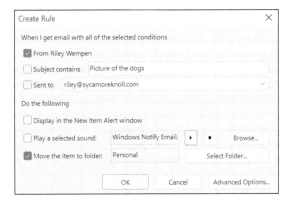

Running a rule

Normally, rules go into action when messages arrive in your Inbox. When you create a rule to move messages from a certain person to a certain folder, the messages that arrive after you create the rule get moved, but the messages sitting in your Inbox keep sitting there.

If you want to apply a rule to the messages already sitting in your Inbox, follow these steps:

1. **From the Home tab, click Rules (or click More Commands and then click Rules), and then click Manage Rules & Alerts.**

   The Rules and Alerts dialog box opens.

2. **Select the rule(s) you want to run.**

   All the rules are selected by default; deselect the check box for each rule you *don't* want to run.

3. **Click the Run Rules Now button at the top of the dialog box.**

   The Run Rules Now dialog box opens.

4. **Click the name of the rule you want to run, placing a check mark next to it.**

5. **Click the Run Now button.**

   At this point, you can't see the result of your rule because the Rules and Alerts dialog box is covering the screen.

6. **Click Close to close the Run Rules Now dialog box.**

7. **Click OK or Cancel to close the Rules and Alerts dialog box.**

Filtering Junk Email

If you feel overwhelmed by junk email, you're not alone; more junk email messages are now sent over the Internet than legitimate ones. It's safe to assume that if you get email, you get junk email — also known as *spam.*

Outlook has a filtering system that looks over all your incoming mail and automatically moves anything that looks like junk email to a special folder. You can delete everything that gets moved to your Junk Email folder now and again — after checking to make sure Outlook didn't mistakenly move real email to your Junk Email folder.

No machine is perfect, and no program that runs on a machine is perfect. I don't entirely know how Outlook figures out which messages are junk and which are real. I find that some junk email still gets through, but Outlook catches more than half the junk messages I get. Once or twice, I've seen it dump items from real people into the Junk Email folder. (Outlook once sent a message from my father to the Junk Email folder; I've been checking the Junk Email folder regularly ever since.) Some folks prefer to use software that works with Outlook to filter out junk mail.

REMEMBER

If you don't think Outlook is up to the job, you'll want to invest in what is commonly referred to as *antispam software*, which is often part of a larger *security suite* of applications that protects your entire computer. McAfee and Symantec are two popular brands.

Fine-tuning the filter's sensitivity

Depending on your Outlook settings, automatic filtering might already be on (and perhaps set to Low), or it might be off. The Low setting is rather conservative, finding the most obvious spam but not preventing most email from getting through that is at least somewhat plausible as legitimate mail. The High setting is more aggressive, but it sometimes filters out messages you want to see.

To adjust Outlook's junk email settings, follow these steps:

1. **In the Mail module, select the Home tab, click the Junk button (or click More Commands and then click Junk), and then click Junk Email Options.**

   The Junk Email Options dialog box opens, as shown in Figure 6-9, with the Options tab on top.

2. **Click the option you prefer.**

The options Outlook offers you include the following:

- **No Automatic Filtering:** At this setting, every sleazy message goes right to your Inbox — unchallenged. If that's your cup of tea, fine. Most people want a little more filtering. If you choose this option, some of the check boxes at the bottom of the dialog box won't be available to you.

- **Low:** The junkiest of the junk gets moved, but a lot of nasty stuff still gets through.

- **High:** This setting is aggressive enough that you can expect to see a certain amount of legitimate email end up in the Junk Email folder. If you choose this setting, check your Junk Email folder from time to time to be sure that important messages don't get trashed by mistake.

- **Safe Lists Only:** This setting moves all messages out of your Inbox except for the ones from people or companies that you've designated in your Safe Senders lists.

Also, the check boxes at the bottom of the Options tab offer you a range of other choices:

- **Permanently Delete Suspected Junk Email Instead of Moving It to the Junk Email Folder:** I think this might be a bit too aggressive, but it's your choice. I haven't seen a perfect Junk Email filter yet, so it's probably better to push junk messages over to the Junk Email folder and manually empty the folder occasionally. On the other hand, you may work in a company that limits the amount of email you're allowed to store, and the messages in your Junk Email folder count against your limit. Thus, zapping junk email may be the best option.

WARNING

- **Disable Links and Other Functionality in Phishing Messages:** *Phishing* isn't just an incorrectly spelled pastime; it's a way of doing something very wrong to lots of unsuspecting recipients. *Phishing* is the term used for an email message that tries to impersonate a bank or a financial institution in an effort to steal your personal information or infect your computer with a virus. It's often the first step in an identity theft operation, so Outlook tries to detect false emails and disable the web links they contain. Even so, you should never give personal financial information or passwords to anyone in response to an email message. Go straight to your financial institution by phone or log on to its website directly (not by clicking the links in an email). You could be the victim of all kinds of bad stuff if you're not careful. Let Outlook provide you with some added protection — turn on this option if it's available. (This option is not available for some email account types, such as accounts that use an Exchange server.)

- **Warn Me About Suspicious Domain Names in Email Addresses:** Some places have a bad reputation — on the Internet and off. If you receive an email from a suspicious location, Outlook will warn you so you don't get yourself into trouble. Mama said there'd be websites like this. She also told you to eat your vegetables. Did you? I didn't think so. Well, I'm telling you to turn this option on, too.

TIP

If those last two options are grayed out (unavailable), choose a setting other than No Automatic Filtering in the options above the check boxes and they will spring to life.

3. If those last two options are grayed out (unavailable), choose a setting other than No Automatic Filtering in the options above the check boxes and they will spring to life.

TIP

4. **Click the OK button.**

    The Junk Email Options dialog box closes.

There you are! With any luck, you'll no longer need to wade through messages about get-rich-quick schemes or pills that enlarge body parts you don't even have.

Filtering your email with sender and recipient lists

Outlook's junk email feature lets you decide if you want to set up your own *safe* and *blocked* lists. You can make a list of people whose messages should *always* be moved to the Junk Email folder (or people whose messages should *never* be moved there). Check out the other tabs of the Junk Email Options dialog box (Figure 6-9) for descriptions of the types of senders you can enter:

>> **Safe Senders:** When you get a message from an email address or domain that you specify here, Outlook makes sure not to treat the message as junk email — no matter what else the message says.

>> **Safe Recipients:** If you receive messages from an online mailing list, the messages often appear to come from many different people, but they're always addressed to the list. (For example, if you belong to any of the groups on Yahoo! Groups, you'll see this.) In this case, you'd put the name of the list in your Safe Recipients list.

>> **Blocked Senders:** This is the opposite of the two preceding choices: Messages from the addresses or domains on this list are always treated as junk email.

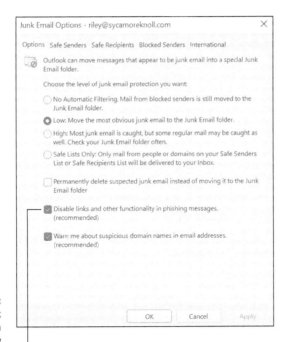

FIGURE 6-9:
Set your junk
email protection
as high or as low
as you like.

This option may not be available, depending on your account type.

>> **International:** Quite a lot of spam comes from overseas. You might see a seemingly endless stream of spam from senders whose email addresses end in strange letters, such as spamsender@spam.ru. Those odd letters at the end of the address are called *top-level domains*, and they indicate the country of origin of the sender. For example, .ru is the top-level domain for Russia — a common source of spam these days.

TIP

If you receive frequent spam from some of these top-level domains, you can have Outlook automatically send all incoming messages from them directly to the Junk Email folder. On the International tab of the Junk Email Options dialog box, click the Blocked Top-Level Domain List button and select top-level domains, as shown in Figure 6-10. Similarly, if you get lots of spam in foreign languages, you can also have Outlook ban those messages. Also on the International tab, click the Blocked Encoding List button and select the respective languages.

If you regularly get legitimate mail from senders whose messages use a particular top-level domain, you don't want to block that domain, even if you get lots of spam from it. The same goes for messages that are encoded with foreign language sets — don't block languages that are used by legitimate senders.

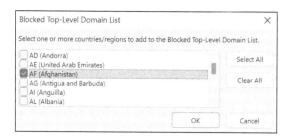

To add an individual to your Blocked Senders list, follow these steps:

1. **When you get a message from someone you don't want to hear from anymore, select the message.**

2. **Click the Junk button (or click More Commands and then click Junk) on the Home tab on the Ribbon.**

3. **Choose Block Sender.**

   This same method works for adding people, domains, or groups to the Safe Senders and Safe Recipients lists. Just select the message, click the Junk button on the Home tab on the Ribbon, and choose the list to which you want the sender added. Of course, if you want to be more precise, you can go directly to the appropriate tab in the Junk Email Options dialog box and type in the addresses or domains you want to filter.

These other junk email options on the Safe Senders tab could save you time:

>> **Contacts:** A check box at the bottom of the Safe Senders tab is labeled Also Trust Email from My Contacts. If you select that box, messages from anyone in your Address Book automatically get treated as safe messages.

>> **Recipients:** If you select the check box labeled Automatically Add People I Email to the Safe Senders list, Outlook will automatically accept messages from the people to whom you've sent messages.

>> **Import and Export:** If you have a particularly long list of people to add to your Safe Senders list or Blocked Senders list, you can create a list in Notepad and then import that list to Outlook with the Import from File option. Companies with lengthy client lists might make this feature available to all their employees.

Filtering domains

Outlook gives you one rather powerful option among your junk email choices that you need to be careful about. That option involves filtering domains. If you do business with people at a certain company, you can enter that entire company in your Safe Senders list by following these steps:

1. **In the Mail module, select the message.**

2. **Click the Junk button (or click More Commands and then click Junk) on the Home tab on the Ribbon.**

3. **Choose Never Block Sender's Domain @example.com.**

WARNING

Use the domain-filtering feature with care. If you add the domain of a friend who sends you email via a spam-prone provider to your Safe Senders list, you partly defeat the purpose of your junk email filters.

Archiving for Posterity

It doesn't take long to accumulate more messages than you can deal with. Some people just delete messages as they read them. Others hold on to old messages for reference purposes. I hold on to all the messages I've ever sent or received in Outlook because I never know when I'll need to check back to see what someone said to me (or, for that matter, what I said).

WARNING

Some companies are required by law to retain all messages for a certain period of time. This is a serious issue if you work in a highly regulated industry, such as banking, finance, or health care. Failure to save messages for the right amount of time can land you or your company in deep doo-doo, so it pays to be aware of your company's retention policy.

The problem with storing lots of messages is that Outlook slows down when you store too many of them. A huge collection of messages is not only cumbersome to manage, but system administrators at a large company may not let you store more than a certain amount of email because it clogs up the system.

Archive is a feature that's built right into Outlook to help you store messages and other Outlook items you don't need to look at right now but that you still might want to refer to in the future. If you use Outlook on an Exchange network at work, archiving makes it easy to get along with your system administrators by slimming down the number of messages you're storing in the email system.

Even if you don't want to use the Archive feature right now, you may want to understand how it works. Outlook can be set up to archive items automatically using the AutoArchive feature, which may look to you as if your Outlook items are disappearing. In the following sections, I show you how to find the items that Outlook has archived for safekeeping.

If the Archive feature seems scary and complicated to you, try not to worry. I agree that Microsoft hasn't done a good job of making the Archive feature understandable. When you get the hang of it, however, archiving could become valuable to you.

Although email messages are what people archive most often, nearly all Outlook items can be sent to the archive — calendars and tasks, for example — except for contacts.

Setting up AutoArchive

Unless you change Outlook's AutoArchive settings, Outlook does *not* archive your items automatically. Some businesses, however, might have it enabled for their users. Other companies might instead use an autodelete service to purge old messages, but check your company's email retention policy before you make any changes to the AutoArchive settings.

If you want to turn on AutoArchive, see how Outlook is set up to archive your old items, or change the way Outlook does the job, follow these steps:

1. **Select the File tab and click Options.**

   The Outlook Options dialog box opens.

2. **Click the Advanced button in the navigation pane on the left.**

3. **In the AutoArchive section, click the AutoArchive Settings button.**

   The AutoArchive dialog box opens, as shown in Figure 6-11. (Figure 6-11 shows AutoArchive enabled, which may or may not be the case for you initially.)

FIGURE 6-11:
The AutoArchive
dialog box.

Don't go barging through the AutoArchive dialog box changing things willy-nilly — at least not until you look to see what's already set up. Four important tidbits that the AutoArchive dialog box normally tells you are:

>> Whether the AutoArchive feature is turned on

>> How often Outlook archives items

>> How old items have to be for Outlook to send them to the archive

>> The name and location of the archive file

If you turn on AutoArchive without changing any of the other AutoArchive settings, Outlook automatically archives items every 14 days, sending items that are more than 6 months old to the archive file listed in the AutoArchive dialog box. For most people, those settings are just fine. Some people prefer to turn off the AutoArchive feature and run the archive process manually, as I describe shortly. You can turn on or off the AutoArchive process by selecting or deselecting the Run AutoArchive Every check box at the top of the AutoArchive dialog box. You can also change how often AutoArchive runs by replacing the 14 in the text box with any number between 1 and 60.

TIP

If all you do is turn on AutoArchive and make no other changes here, you might be surprised to find out that your Inbox — as well as some other folders — will *not* be autoarchived. Each folder has its own AutoArchive settings, which can be different from other folders' AutoArchive settings. If you want to autoarchive all your folders with identical settings, make sure to also click the Apply These Settings to All Folders Now button in the AutoArchive dialog box — that is, all folders except for the Contacts folder, which can't be archived. Autoarchiving *all* your folders might not be a great idea if you never clean out your Deleted Items or Junk Email folders, because you'd wind up archiving lots of spam and deleted messages.

Setting AutoArchive for individual folders

It might be a better idea to set up the AutoArchive settings for each of your folders individually so you can have more control over what gets autoarchived and what doesn't. For this example, I use the Inbox folder and set it to autoarchive every 6 months:

1. **In the Mail module, select Inbox in the Folder list.**

   The Inbox is highlighted.

2. **On the Ribbon, select the Folder tab and click the AutoArchive Settings button in the Properties group.**

   The Inbox Properties dialog box opens, displaying the AutoArchive tab.

3. **Select Archive This Folder Using These Settings.**

4. **Confirm that the drop-down menu is set to Months.**

If you'd rather autoarchive messages from your Inbox that are much more recent, you can choose Weeks or Days. But hang with me for this example for the moment.

5. **In the Clean Out Items Older Than text box, type the number *6* if it doesn't already appear there.**

The Inbox Properties dialog box should now indicate that items older than 6 months will be cleaned out, as shown in Figure 6-12. You can put any number between 1 and 999 in the text box — which means you can autoarchive messages from the Inbox that are anywhere from a day old to 999 months old.

6. **Select Move Old Items to Default Archive Folder.**

WARNING

This setting will probably already be selected, but make sure that the Permanently Delete Old Items option is *not* selected. If you selected that option, all old Inbox messages would be deleted instead of archived.

TIP

If your mail account is hosted on an Exchange server, you will have two other tabs in this dialog box: Permissions (where you can control who can archive items) and Synchronization (where you can set up synchronization between the server and the offline copy of the archive folder). Neither are commonly adjusted; feel free to leave these at their defaults.

7. **Click the OK button.**

Even though you're only setting the AutoArchive settings for a single folder, you must turn on Outlook's AutoArchive setting. If AutoArchive is already turned on (as I describe in the previous section), the Inbox Properties dialog box will close and you're all set.

TIP

After you click OK, if a window pops up stating There Are No Global AutoArchive Options Set, this means that Outlook's AutoArchive setting isn't turned on. Luckily, this window gives you the option of turning it on just by clicking the OK button. Click OK to turn on autoarchiving for Outlook and for the Inbox.

Repeat these steps for each folder you want to use AutoArchive. Even if you have a folder that you don't want to autoarchive, at least check what its current AutoArchive settings are.

WARNING

When you enabled Outlook's AutoArchive feature, you also probably inadvertently activated AutoArchive for some other folders that you might not want to have archived; there's no way to autoarchive a folder without also turning on Outlook's AutoArchive setting. When Outlook is first installed, the Calendar, Tasks, Journal, Sent Items, and Deleted Items folders are all set to autoarchive if Outlook's Auto-Archive setting is turned on. I did say this was scary and complicated, didn't I?

FIGURE 6-12:
Setting the Inbox
folder to
autoarchive
messages that
are older than
6 months.

If this all seems confusing, this should help: If you followed the previous examples exactly (and why wouldn't you?), every 14 days, Outlook will run AutoArchive. When Outlook runs AutoArchive, it will move all messages from the Inbox (as well as any subfolders in the Inbox folder) that are *older than* 6 months old into the archive. Any messages that are newer than 6 months stay in the Inbox. Now it doesn't seem so scary or complicated, does it?

TIP

Whenever you create a new folder, it's automatically set *not* to autoarchive, even if you previously applied your autoarchiving settings for all folders. If you want your new folder to autoarchive, go through the previous steps for that folder. Also, when you turn on AutoArchive for Outlook, the Deleted Items folder is set to autoarchive using the default settings. If you don't clean out your Deleted Items folder, all the emails you thought you'd never see again will instead be archived for posterity. You should consider setting the Deleted Items folder to not autoarchive.

Starting the archive process manually

You can archive messages any time you want by following these steps:

1. **Choose the File tab.**

2. **Click Info in the navigation pane on the left.**

   It is probably already selected.

3. **Click the Tools button.**

4. **Click the Clean Up Old Items button.**

   The Archive dialog box appears, as shown in Figure 6-13.

5. **Choose the settings you want and then click OK.**

If you start the archive manually, you get slightly better control of the process. You can:

» Give a cutoff date for archiving items (say, the first of the year).

» Determine which folders to archive and where to send the archived items.

» Archive different Outlook folders to different archive files.

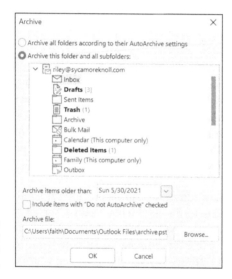

FIGURE 6-13:
Manually
archiving the
Inbox folder.

WARNING

The disadvantage to all this control is that it's possible to make an innocent mistake and send archived items to a place you can't find again easily. Try not to change the name or location of the files to which your archived items are sent. Outlook doesn't provide much help with keeping track of archived files.

Finding and viewing archived items

Sometimes, AutoArchive seems like magic. Older items are mysteriously filed away without any action on your part. Isn't that easy? Sure — until you suddenly need to *find* one of those items that magically moved to your archive. Then, you have to figure out where it went and how to get at it again.

I usually like to talk up the good points of Outlook, but honestly, this is one place where the Outlook developers fell down on the job. Although it's easy to move items into your archive, it's pretty confusing to get them back. What's the point of archiving items if you can't find them again?

Anyway, when you want to take another look at the items you've archived, open the Archive folder, which Outlook also refers to as a *data file*.

To open a data file that contains your archived items, follow these steps:

1. **Click the File tab, click the Open & Export button, and click the Open Outlook Data File button.**

    The Open Outlook Data File dialog box opens.

2. **Select the file you want to open.**

    The file you selected appears in the File Name text box. For example, to open the default archive file, choose Archive.

3. **Click the OK button.**

    The name of the data file you opened appears in the navigation pane, below your normal set of folders.

Simple enough, right? Yes, but there's a virtual fly in the virtual ointment. You probably don't know the name of the archive file you want to open, and it might not show up in the list of files in the Open Outlook Data File dialog box.

TIP

To find out the name of the archive data file to open, follow these steps:

1. **Click the File tab.**

2. **Click the Info button.**

3. **Click the Tools button.**

4. **Click the Clean Up Old Items button.**

5. **Look in the Archive File text box.**

    This is the archive file's location.

    Don't change anything about the information; otherwise, Outlook may start sending your archived items someplace else.

TIP

My favorite trick for capturing a long name in a dialog box is to copy the information. Here's what it looks like in fast-forward:

1. **Click the name once.**

2. **Press Tab.**

3. **Press Shift+Tab.**

4. **Press Ctrl+C.**

5. **Click the Cancel button.**

   Congratulations, you just sneakily copied that archive file path to the Clipboard. Now you can follow the steps given earlier in this section, and paste the name you want into the Open Outlook Data File dialog box's File Name text box by pressing Ctrl+V. Then rejoice that you don't have to remember that long, crazy filename.

Closing the archive data file

You can keep your archive data file open in the Folder pane as long as you want, but most people prefer to close it after they find what they need. Outlook runs a little faster when you close any unnecessary data files.

To close an archive data file, follow these steps:

1. **In the Folder pane, right-click on the name of the archive data file.**

   Click the top-level heading (which will be *archive* if you used the default name), not one of the subfolders. A shortcut menu appears.

2. **Choose Close "archive."**

   The archive data file might be called something other than *archive* — and if so, the name of your particular archive data file will appear instead of the term *archive*. Your archive folder disappears from the Folder pane.

Arranging Your Messages

Nobody gets a *little* bit of email anymore. If you get one message, you get a ton of 'em, and they can quickly clog your Inbox. In no time, you find yourself scrolling through an endless stream of new messages, trying to find that one proverbial needle in the haystack that you needed a week from last Tuesday. Fortunately, Outlook offers you a whole bunch of different ways to arrange that mess of messages so you have a fighting chance of figuring out what's important, what can wait, and what can be ignored or deleted.

Filtering your messages

There are three labels at the top of the list of messages. The two leftmost labels are called All and Unread. Clicking All displays all of your messages. If you click Unread, you only see the messages you haven't viewed yet; once you read a message, it disappears from this view, although you can see it again if you click All. The third label tells you what sort order is applied; I explain it in the next section, "Sorting Your Messages."

Sorting your messages

The label on the right above the list of messages in your Inbox describes the system Outlook is using to sort the message list. If By Date appears, your messages are displayed in the order in which you received them. That's how you want to view your messages almost all the time. The arrow button to the right of By Date switches between ascending and descending order (that is, oldest or newest first).

TIP

To change the way Outlook arranges your messages, click By Date to reveal a menu of all the arrangements you can use, as in Figure 6-14. The down- or up-pointing arrow to the right of the arrangement choice specifies ascending or descending order. Click the arrow to reverse the order.

USING THE FOCUSED INBOX

If your mail comes from an Exchange, Microsoft 365, or Outlook.com email account, you have an extra mail management option called Focused Inbox. When this option is enabled, instead of seeing All and Unread options, you'll see Focused and Other. Focused shows only important messages; Other shows messages that don't seem important, like spam and ads.

You can enable the Focused Inbox feature from the View tab by clicking the Focused Inbox button to toggle it on or off. If your email account doesn't support the feature, you won't see that button on the Ribbon at all.

Outlook does a decent job of guessing which messages are important, but you can fine-tune it to be better. When a message appears under Focused but it's not important, right-click it and choose Move to Other (or Always Move to Other if you want all future messages from this sender to be moved also). If the opposite happens and it's actually important but it has ended up in Other, right-click it and choose Move to Focused (or Always Move to Focused).

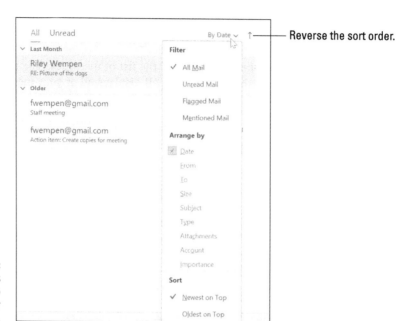

Reverse the sort order.

FIGURE 6-14:
Outlook offers
plenty of ways to
arrange your
folders.

>> **Date:** When you first set up Outlook, this is how your Inbox is arranged. Your messages appear in the order in which you received them — just as you'd expect.

>> **From:** As you might guess, this arrangement organizes your message collection according to the person who sent the message. Choosing the From arrangement is a little bit faster than setting up a search folder, but sometimes, a search folder is still the best way to track messages from *specific* important people.

>> **To:** Most messages you receive are addressed to you — but not always. Sometimes, you receive messages addressed to a list of people, so your name doesn't appear in the To field of the message. This arrangement separates your messages according to whether your name is in the To field of each message.

>> **Categories:** You might not use categories, but if you do, you can sort messages according to them. See Chapter 14 for information about assigning categories. This option might not appear for an IMAP account.

>> **Flag Status:** You can sort messages according to whether or not they have a flag set and what that flag's status is. Flagged items appear last if you're sorting in ascending order, and first if you're sorting in descending order. Like Categories, this option might not appear for an IMAP account.

>> **Flag Start Date or Flag Due Date:** You can sort either by Start Date or Due Date, which is helpful if you have assigned dates to flagged items. (See Chapter 5 for details on using flags.)

» **Size:** Everyone knows that size doesn't matter; it's the sentiment that counts. Well, okay, not always. Size is important to certain system administrators — and it isn't *always* a personal problem. Some email messages include photographs, music, and all sorts of heavyweight files that can really clog your company's email servers. Thus, when your system administrator asks you to thin out your Inbox, make some use of this feature: Identify and delete or archive the messages that are the most overweight. You can do this by sorting by size from largest to smallest and then taking a critical look at the items at the top of the list.

» **Subject:** This arrangement sorts alphabetically by whatever is in the Subject line of the message.

» **Type:** Not every item that arrives in your Inbox is a simple message; you may also receive Meeting Requests, Task Requests, and all sorts of other items. When you want to separate the messages from the Meeting Requests and so on, switch to the Type arrangement so the most interesting messages rise to the top of the list.

» **Attachments:** When you go to your Inbox, you may not be looking for a message; you may be hunting for an attachment. Arranging your messages by attachment lets you examine the likely suspects first.

» **Account:** You can set up Outlook to collect email from several different email addresses at the same time, and each of your email addresses gets its own Inbox. But if you move messages from your different email addresses into the same folder — as you might do when you periodically clean up your Inboxes — there may come a point down the road when you want to see which of those messages in the folder came from which of those addresses or just to look at the messages sent to one of those addresses. If you want to see only the messages sent to a single address, choose the Account arrangement and then click the arrow next to the names of accounts you don't want to see. With this arrangement, Outlook shows you only the messages from the accounts that interest you. Unless you mush all your incoming mail from your different mailboxes into a single Inbox, the Account arrangement won't help you much when you're viewing the Inbox.

» **Importance:** First things first — you know the saying. When you need to see the messages marked with High Importance first, this is the arrangement you want to use.

If you want to arrange your messages when the Reading pane is off, click the View tab and choose the arrangement you want to use from the choices in the Arrangement group, and change the sort order by clicking Reverse Sort from there.

Viewing conversations

Whether you just trade a few emails back and forth with one other person or engage in large group discussions that continue for weeks, Outlook's Conversations arrangement groups together all related messages that have the same subject. With a single glance, you can see the latest entry in a conversation thread as well as older messages from the conversation. A conversation starts as soon as someone replies to a message, clicking either the Reply or Reply All button. No matter who else responds or contributes, all new messages become part of the conversation.

To enable conversation viewing, follow these steps:

1. **In the Mail module, click the View tab.**

2. **Do one of the following:**

   - Using the Simplified Ribbon: Click Current View and then click Show as Conversations.

   - Using the Classic Ribbon: In the Messages group, click Show as Conversations.

   A dialog box appears asking if you want to see conversations only for this folder or for all mailboxes.

3. **Click This Folder.**

When conversation display is enabled, you can tell whether a message in your Inbox is part of a conversation when you see a small triangle positioned just to the left of the sender's name, indicating that more messages are inside.

When you click a message that's part of a conversation, the most recent message received in the conversation is displayed in the Reading pane. Click the triangle to the left of the message's Mail icon to expand the complete list of messages you have sent or received that are part of the conversation, as shown in Figure 6-15. Even if some of these messages are located in the Sent folder or were moved to another folder, they still appear in the conversation list. If a message is moved to the Deleted Items folder, however, it won't appear in the conversation list.

You can reply to any message in the conversation list. If you reply to a message that isn't the most recent, you see a warning and get the chance to open the latest message in the conversation.

WARNING

When you reply to a message that's part of a conversation, don't change the subject of the message. If you do, Outlook doesn't consider it part of the conversation anymore; Outlook identifies a conversation partially by a message's Subject field. Don't worry if messages come in with the same Subject field that aren't part of a conversation; Outlook is smart enough to know the difference and doesn't add them to the conversation.

Mail icon

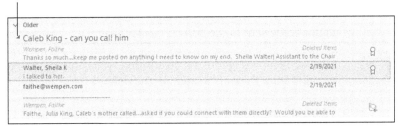

FIGURE 6-15:
All the messages
from a
conversation
are grouped
together.

TIP

To fine-tune the way conversations are displayed, do one of the following to open a menu of conversation options and make your selections:

>> Using the Simplified Ribbon: On the View tab, click Current View and then point to Conversation Settings.

>> Using the Classic Ribbon: On the View tab, click the Conversation Settings button.

You can choose whether or not to show message from other folders, for example.

Ignoring conversations

There often comes a point in a conversation where the discussion is no longer of interest or relevance to you. It's not uncommon for a conversation to completely spiral off-topic — what started out as a conversation about when to have the next team meeting becomes a seemingly endless string of back-and-forth jokes about how hot the conference room gets in the winter.

If you no longer want to follow a conversation, you have an easy way to ignore it. Select any message from the conversation and then do one of the following:

>> Using the Simplified Ribbon: On the Home tab, click the Delete button's down arrow and choose Ignore.

>> Using the Classic Ribbon: On the Home tab, in the Delete group, click Ignore.

You can also ignore a conversation by right-clicking on any of the messages in the conversation and selecting Ignore from the drop-down menu — or with any message selected from the conversation, you can press Ctrl+Delete.

When you ignore a conversation, all messages from the conversation that are in the Inbox — and in any other folder you moved messages from the conversation to — are dumped into the Deleted Items folder (or Trash folder, depending on the mail server's name for it). All traces of the conversation are gone from your Inbox and other folders, but messages from the conversation that are in your Sent folder aren't moved. If any new messages from the conversation arrive, they're also automatically sent to the Deleted Items folder.

TIP

If you accidentally ignore a conversation, you can unignore it. Simply move the messages from the conversation in the Deleted Items folder back into the Inbox.

Cleaning up conversations

When someone replies to a message, most email programs — by default — include the text of the original message in the reply. When Outlook is first installed, it's set to do this. To see this setting, click the File tab, click the Options button in the navigation pane on the left, click the Mail tab, and scroll down to the Replies and Forwards section in the Outlook Options dialog box.

If everyone who sends a reply in a conversation includes the text of previous messages from the conversation, each subsequent message becomes a snapshot of the entire conversation thread up to that point. This creates a lot of redundancy because a lot of the same information is repeated in each message. (Do I need to repeat that?)

Outlook can detect this redundancy and remove messages from a conversation that contain information that's already included elsewhere in the conversation. Outlook calls this *cleaning up*.

TIP

The quick-and-dirty way to clean up a conversation is to select a message in the conversation you want to clean up and press Alt+Delete.

The longer way to clean up is as follows:

1. **In the Mail module, select the conversation you want to clean up.**

   The most recently received message of the conversation is selected. You can do this in any folder that contains a message from the conversation.

2. **Do one of the following:**

   - Using the Simplified Ribbon: On the Home tab, click the Delete button's down arrow and choose Clean Up Conversation (see Figure 6-16).

   - Using the Classic Ribbon: On the Home tab, in the Delete group, click the Clean Up button and choose Clean Up Conversation.

   A Clean Up Conversation dialog box opens.

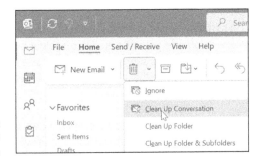

FIGURE 6-16:
Cleaning up a
conversation.

3. **Click Clean Up.**

All messages from the conversation that Outlook detects as redundant are removed from all the folders they're in and moved to the Deleted Items folder. Messages in the Sent folder stay put.

From the menu in Step 2, you can also select Clean Up Folder to clean up all the conversations within the selected folder. Clean Up Folder & Subfolders goes one step further and cleans up all conversations that are in the selected folders and all subfolders. For example, if you created a Personal folder that lives inside your Inbox folder, selecting the Inbox folder and then choosing Clean Up Folder & Subfolders automatically cleans up all conversations in both folders.

Don't be surprised if Outlook doesn't remove many messages. Outlook takes a rather conservative view on what it considers redundant, and it also doesn't move replies that have modified a previous message or messages that have Follow Up flags.

If you want to give Outlook more latitude with what it can move when it cleans up a conversation, you need to change a few settings:

1. **Select the File tab and click the Options button.**

The Outlook Options dialog box opens.

2. **Click Mail in the navigation pane.**

The Mail settings open.

3. **Scroll down to the Conversation Clean Up section.**

A number of options are listed that affect when Outlook will and won't move messages from a conversation, as shown in Figure 6-17. Make adjustments to the settings that best fit your needs.

Pay close attention to the Cleaned-Up Items Will Go to This Folder text box. Outlook sends cleaned-up items to the Deleted Items folder by default. But if you want to send cleaned-up items someplace else, such as a folder in an archive file, this is where you make that change. Click the Browse button and select where your cleaned-up items should go.

TIP

If you find that Outlook doesn't move any messages when you click Clean Up, someone probably made changes somewhere within the previous message text in their message reply before clicking the Send button. To get Outlook to clean up a conversation where this happens, make another change to the Conversation Clean Up settings: Deselect the When a Reply Modifies a Message, Don't Move the Original check box. The danger in doing this is that the text from previous messages may have been changed for good reason — such as someone answering someone else's questions within the text of the original message.

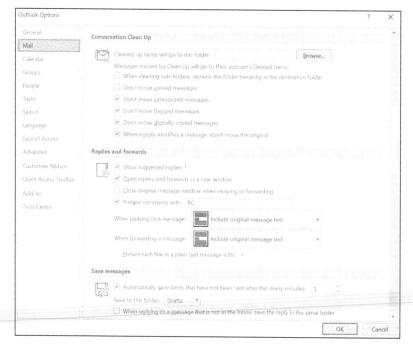

FIGURE 6-17: Conversation Clean Up options.

Simplifying Tasks Using Quick Steps

By now, you've no doubt noticed that some Outlook actions take multiple clicks of the mouse to complete, such as the process of replying to a message and then deleting it. That's not a big deal if you only perform a particular action every once in a while, but if it's something you do regularly in Outlook, it can quickly become a pain. If you do certain tasks on a regular basis, Outlook's Quick Steps feature can come to your rescue.

Quick Steps lets you reduce multistep tasks to a single click of the mouse.

Quick Steps will be available in one of two places, depending on the Ribbon mode you are using and the type of email account.

>> If you're using the Simplified Ribbon, Quick Steps might be a drop-down menu near the middle of the Home tab. Click its down arrow to see its commands. Or, it might be accessible from the More Commands button's menu as a submenu, as in Figure 6-18.

>> If you're using the Classic Ribbon, Quick Steps is a group on the Home tab. Click the More button to see the available commands.

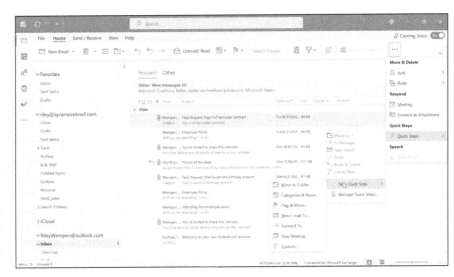

FIGURE 6-18:
If Quick Steps does not appear on the Home tab, you'll find it here on the More Commands button's menu from the Home tab.

Even though the Quick Steps controls are visible only when using the Mail module, you can use Quick Steps to speed up actions with most of Outlook's modules, such as Calendar or Tasks.

When you first install Outlook, five (or six) Quick Steps are already created and ready for you to use. You can see these on the submenu in Figure 6-18.

>> **Move To:** Use this Quick Step if you frequently move messages to a specific folder. If you've yet to move a message to a folder in Outlook, the Quick Step shows Move To: ?. If you've already moved messages to folders, this Quick Step replaces the ? with the name of the last folder you moved a message to, such as Move To: Personal.

>> **To Manager:** This Quick Step automatically opens a Message form for forwarding the selected message to a particular recipient, but it doesn't delete the selected message. If you use Outlook in a corporate setting, this is usually set up to forward the message you're currently reading to your manager.

>> **Team Email:** Use this Quick Step to open the New Message form and populate the To field with a particular set of recipients. If you use Outlook in a corporate setting, this is usually set up — by your administrators — to open a message that's already addressed to all members of your team to include your manager and everyone who reports directly to your manager. You can create Groups that include the people you choose, not just your boss and your colleagues, and send emails to all of them. You create Groups in the People module.

>> **Done:** Available only for certain types of email accounts (such as Exchange server accounts), Done marks a task as complete, or an item as read, and then moves it to a specified folder.

>> **Reply & Delete:** The name pretty much says it all: When you select this Quick Step, Outlook automatically opens a Message form for replying to the sender of the selected message and moves the selected message to the Deleted Items folder.

>> **Create New:** Strictly speaking, this isn't really a Quick Step; it opens the Edit Quick Step Wizard, which allows you to create your own custom Quick Steps.

Except for the Reply & Delete Quick Step, each of these Quick Steps requires you to make some decisions the first time you use them. This is because Outlook doesn't know yet where you want your messages moved to or who your manager is. If it did, that might be a little scary. Thus, you're going to have to tell Outlook what it needs to do when you select a particular Quick Step. After you do this, you never have to do it again — Outlook will remember what you want it to do whenever you select the Quick Step.

Each of the Quick Steps is a bit different, but I use the Move To Quick Step as an example here:

1. **In the Mail module, select a message in the Inbox.**

   It can be any message. Don't worry about it actually being moved. As long as this is the first time you're using the Move To Quick Step, the message you select won't be moved; Outlook just needs to know which type of Outlook element you're creating the Quick Step for.

2. **From the Home tab, open the Quick Steps menu and choose Move To: ?.**

I explained how to open the Quick Steps menu at the beginning of this section.

The icon may or may not say Move To: ?.

The First Time Setup dialog box opens, as shown Figure 6-19. Your system may not say Move To: ? but might instead have just a folder name, such as Personal. If the dialog box already has a folder name in it, Outlook is just trying to be helpful by suggesting the last folder to which you moved a message; the First Time Setup dialog box will still open.

3. **Select the folder to which the Quick Step will move messages.**

Select a folder in the Move to Folder box by clicking the arrow at the end of the box. If you don't see the folder you want, choose the Other Folder selection, which opens the Select Folder window so you can see a detailed list of all available folders. You can also create a new folder using the Select Folder window.

4. **Make sure the Move to Folder check box is selected.**

If you want each message marked as read when the Quick Step moves it, make sure the Mark as Read check box is also selected.

If you want to change the Quick Step's icon, add actions to it, or create a keyboard shortcut for the Quick Step, click the Options button to access those settings.

5. **Type a name for the Quick Step in the Name text box.**

You probably noticed that as soon as you selected a folder in the Move to Folder box, Outlook also placed that folder name in the Name text box. If you're happy with the name that Outlook chose for the Quick Step, skip ahead to the next step. If you want to give the Quick Step a different name, just type it into the Name text box. You should give the Quick Step a name that will help you remember what the Quick Step does; *Move to Personal folder* would be a pretty good name for a Quick Step that moves a message to a folder called Personal, don't you think? For those who prefer brevity, *Personal* works, too.

6. **Click the Save button.**

The First Time Setup dialog box closes.

Whenever you want to move a message to the specific folder, just select the message and click the Quick Step you created. The message will automatically move to the folder and be marked as read.

Once you get the hang of using Quick Steps, you should be able to create Quick Steps that perform many functions with a single click of the mouse; creating a Quick Step that does your job for you might be beyond the reach of Outlook.

FIGURE 6-19:
The Quick Step
First Time Setup
dialog box.

Creating and managing Quick Steps

In addition to the Quick Steps that appear in the Quick Step box when Outlook is first installed, you have even more Quick Step templates you can choose from. To use these additional Quick Step templates, follow these steps:

1. **In the Mail module, from the Home tab, open the Quick Steps menu.**

   I explained how to open the Quick Steps menu at the beginning of this section.

2. **Point to New Quick Step.**

   A menu of additional Quick Step templates appears, which you saw back in Figure 6-18. Selecting any of these templates opens the First Time Setup dialog box, offering choices that apply to the particular type of task you selected. For example, if you select Move to Folder, the First Time Setup dialog box asks you to pick which folder it will move the messages to, and it also gives you the option of marking the messages as read.

   These additional Quick Step templates are as follows:

   - **Move to Folder:** This is essentially the same as Move To.

   - **Categorize & Move:** This moves the selected message to a specific folder, marks the message as read, and assigns a category color and name to the message. This one might not appear if you're working with an IMAP account.

   - **Flag & Move:** This moves the selected message to a specific folder, marks the message as read, and assigns a flag to the message.

   - **New Email To:** This opens a New Message form with the To field already filled out with a particular recipient.

   - **Forward To:** This is essentially the same as To Manager.

   - **New Meeting:** If you often send meeting invites to the same group of people, use this Quick Step to open a New Meeting form with the To field already filled in with the invitees.

- **Custom:** This opens the Edit Quick Step dialog box so you can create your own custom Quick Step.

3. **Select a Quick Step template.**

   As you saw with the Move To Quick Step, a First Time Setup dialog box opens.

4. **Make your choices and name your template.**

   Depending on the task, you'll need to tell Outlook where to move a message, how to categorize a message, what flag to set, to whom to send or forward a message, or to whom to send a meeting invitation. After you input this information into the First Time Setup dialog box, be sure to also give this Quick Step a name that will help you remember what it does.

5. **Click the Finish button.**

   The First Time Setup dialog box closes.

TIP

Instead of selecting New Quick Step from the menu, you could choose Manage Quick Steps, which opens the Manage Quick Steps dialog box, as shown in Figure 6-20. Here, you can do a bunch of different things to your Quick Steps, such as change the order in which they appear in the Quick Step box on the Ribbon, change what they do, duplicate them, delete them, and create new ones. If your Quick Steps are becoming an unruly mess and you want to start over from square one, click the Reset to Defaults button and all the Quick Steps will revert to what they looked like when you first installed Outlook.

FIGURE 6-20:
The Manage
Quick Steps
dialog box.

Creating Quick Parts to save keystrokes

When you find yourself typing the same text into email messages over and over, you can reduce your effort by saving frequently used text as a Quick Part. Quick Parts sounds like Quick Steps; they're different things, but they're ridiculously simple.

To create a Quick Part, follow these steps:

1. **While replying to an email message, if the message is being composed in the Reading pane, click Pop Out to open it in its own window.**

   That's necessary because you need access to the Insert tab, and you don't get that when composing or replying in the Reading pane.

2. **Drag your mouse over some text in the message to select it.**

   The text you select is highlighted.

3. **Click the Insert tab and choose Quick Parts.**

   If you're using the Simplified Ribbon, you might need to click More Commands for access to Quick Parts.

   If you're using the Classic Ribbon, Quick Parts is in the Text group.

   A menu appears.

4. **Choose Save Selection to Quick Part Gallery.**

   The Create New Building Block dialog box opens.

5. **Type a new name for your Quick Part if you don't like the one you see.**

   The suggested name might be fine, but you may prefer something else. You can also assign a category and description to your Quick Part, but that makes very little difference in how you use it, so you can leave those options alone.

6. **Click OK.**

TIP

After creating a Quick Part, you can make it appear in the body of a new email or a reply in a flash: Click the Insert tab on the Ribbon, click Quick Parts in the Text group, and then click the Quick Part you want. It's so easy, you'll never want to send an original email again.

IN THIS CHAPTER

» Choosing your email provider

» Buying a domain name

» Setting up email accounts in Outlook

» Sending messages from different accounts

» Modifying mail account settings

» Managing Outlook data files

Chapter **7**

Managing Multiple Email Accounts and Data Files

A lot of people just have one email address. They set it up in Outlook when they first start using the program, or someone else sets it up for them, and that's that. But you, my friend, are not a lot of people, or you wouldn't be reading this chapter. You long for more — more flexibility, more privacy, more side hustles, or maybe even the ability to have an alter-ego that you can use on the down-low, like `Freaky4U@FantasiesComeTrue.biz`. (No, that's not a real email address. Yes, I checked.) In this chapter, I show you how to set up additional email accounts in Outlook, and provide some advice as to how to acquire those email addresses from various services.

Choosing an Email Provider

If you use a computer at home, you probably already have an *Internet service provider (ISP)*. That's the company you pay a monthly fee to for your Internet connectivity. Depending on where you live, your ISP options might include your cable TV provider, telephone company, or satellite service provider. I'm not going to try to sell you on one type of service or another, because the performance and the deals vary a lot based on location, and you probably already have a provider anyway.

A lot of people, when they first get Internet service, get an email address supplied by their ISP. It's easy, and free, and they don't know any better. Pity them.

Nearly every ISP offers free email accounts along with their ISP services. They often make their email amazingly easy to set up and start using. Everyone in your family can have their own email address. They *really* want to be your email provider as well as your ISP — no extra charge! Sounds too good to be true, doesn't it?

And that's because there's a fishhook in that worm that can prevent you from shopping around later for a better ISP deal. After you set up an address with an ISP, and send email from that address for a year or more, it gets more and more difficult to change to a different ISP, because you have to notify everyone you know of your new email address. And "everyone" can be a daunting list to come up with, because you've probably forgotten all the services and shopping sites that you created accounts with using that email address. So you're stuck with that ISP forever, no matter how high they jack up their prices, because it's such a pain to have to change email addresses.

As an alternative, you can get your own email address from lots of different services; many of them are free. Google offers Gmail, for example, and Microsoft would be happy to give you a free Outlook.com account. (Outlook.com email accounts also work with a lot of Outlook's fancier features that many accounts from ISPs don't.) If you want to upgrade to more sophisticated services, you can also check out Microsoft 365 plans, which range from simple personal accounts to sophisticated offerings for huge multinational corporations. That's nice to know if you're the kind of person who thinks big.

WARNING

Some web-based email services don't work very well (or at all) with Outlook. That's because web-based email, by its very nature, uses a web-based email client — that is, a program you can use to read and manage your messages. The email address and the web-based client application are a matched pair. So if you want to use a third-party client like Outlook to read and manage the mail, it might require some special setup, or it might not be possible at all, depending on the service. When you're shopping for the perfect email provider, look for services that advertise POP3 and/or IMAP access as an option. (I explain what those are later in this chapter.) This should ensure that the service will work with Outlook at least at a basic level. However, if the web-based client provides other Outlook-like services such as a Contacts list or a calendar, you still might not be able to access those via Outlook.

Buying Your Own Domain Name

If you want to spend about $100 a year (maybe a little less), you can have your own domain name, and have as many email addresses as you want under it. For example, if your name is Mordecai Roblevsky, you could buy the domain `roblevsky.com` and set up the address `Mordecai@Roblevsky.com`. If you have a more common name, such as John Smith, it might be too late to grab your name as an email address. You could either choose a variation on your name or change your name to Roblevsky.

TIP

If you're interested in buying a domain name and setting up your own custom email account, check out GoDaddy (`www.godaddy.com`). GoDaddy provides good service overall — despite how racy its TV commercials get. It can register your domain name and host its email services for a reasonable yearly fee. No, it's not free, but isn't it cool to have your very own email domain? Not to mention it gives a much more professional impression if you're a business owner, and it's an email account that nobody will ever take away from you — unless you fail to pay the yearly fee for it, of course.

There are three steps involved in this buy-your-own-domain process:

1. **Register the domain name.**

   It has to be a name not taken already, of course. You can pay for just one year at a time, or pay several years in advance. This part costs anywhere from $5 to $20 a year. To do this you deal with a domain registrar company. GoDaddy.com is one, but there are many others. Your registrar keeps track of your contact information and the fact that you own the domain. Well, actually, you are renting it, for as long as you keep paying its fee. But you have the right to do what you want with it.

2. **Sign up for hosting.**

   Your hosting company is the company that runs the web and email servers for your domain. If you have a website associated with your domain, the hosting company will store that website on its servers and direct web traffic to it when people enter your domain name in their browsers. More to the point of this book, the hosting company will also let your domain use its email servers to send and receive mail. The hosting company can be the same as the registrar company (and in fact, it's administratively a lot easier that way), or it can be a separate company.

3. **Create the email accounts.**

   Use your hosting company's web-based control panel to set up the email accounts you want to have and assign their passwords. You can create whatever accounts you wish. Anything before the @ sign is totally up to you. Everything after the @ sign is your domain name. So, for example, Mordecai could set up accounts for everyone in the Roblevsky family: levi@roblevsky.com, toby@roblevsky.com, and so on. Or Freaky4U@Roblevsky.com. It's all about choices.

Setting Up Email Accounts in Outlook

After you've signed up for an email account, you can set up Outlook to send and receive email from that account. You might already have an email account set up in Outlook (and I'm willing to bet you do if you've made it this far in the book), but the new accounts you set up will co-exist with it peacefully.

REMEMBER

If you're a corporate user, your system administrators may not want you to mess around with account settings, and the bosses may have special arrangements and settings they want you to use when you work from home. Either way, it's best to ask first.

Understanding POP3 vs. IMAP

Most email accounts, including the ones you create for your own domain and the accounts you get from your ISP, support one of two types of access: *Post Office Protocol 3* (POP3, or just POP for short) and *Internet Mail Access Protocol* (IMAP, pronounced "eye-map"). For a web-based email account to work with Outlook, it must support either POP3 or IMAP access. Some accounts support both, so you can choose which one to use.

The main difference between the two is that with IMAP, all your messages remain on the server, and whenever you connect to the server, your local email client updates your mail folders from the server information. When you delete messages from your Inbox in Outlook, they are also deleted from the server copy of your Inbox. The advantage to this system is that if you access your email from multiple devices, each device will show the latest up-to-date version. Your Inbox is device-independent. This is the type of account you want if you regularly check your email from multiple places, like a desktop, tablet, and smartphone.

With POP, on the other hand, the focal point is your local PC and your local email client (for example, Outlook). When you connect to the POP3 mail server by sending/receiving messages, any new messages are transferred to the local PC and the server has no further involvement with them. You can set up Outlook to remove transferred messages from the server immediately or to save them for a certain amount of time as a backup there, but the server doesn't concern itself with, for example, whether the message has been read or replied to.

POP3 is an older technology, designed for the time when hardly anyone had more than one computing device and it was probably a desktop PC. However, POP3 still has some advantages. For example, you can access the full archive of your old messages any time you are on your computer — whether the Internet is working or not. And because your old mail is stored on your local PC, not on the server, you'll never have to worry about your email server storage allotment maxing out. With POP you can also choose to aggregate the incoming email from multiple POP3 accounts into a single Outlook data file, making data file backup and transfer a little easier. POP3 accounts also support more Outlook features than IMAP accounts do. Flagging is one example; you don't get its full features with an IMAP account.

Most email systems that support one of these also support the other, so when you set up the account in Outlook (or whatever email client you are using, such as the mail app on your smartphone), you can specify which you want. Choose based on your situation.

WARNING

Once you have set up an email account in Outlook as either IMAP or POP3, you can't switch to the other. You have to delete the account from Outlook and recreate it. Doing so will delete any messages that have been stored on the local copy of Outlook (which is more significant for POP3 than for IMAP).

Collecting the needed information for setup

To set up an email account in Outlook using default settings, you don't need a lot of technical information — usually just your email address and its password. Outlook can usually figure out the rest. Today's Outlook rocks compared to earlier versions in that regard, so if you haven't set up an email account in Outlook for several versions, you're in for a pleasant surprise. So if you're the non-techie type, try that first. (Skip ahead to the next section.)

But if you think you might need some non-default settings for your email account, or if you just want to be prepared, gather some information from your email server provider beforehand:

>> Email address and password. That one's a no-brainer. Of course you need that.

>> Incoming mail server address. The format for this address is *text.text.text*. It might look something like imap.secureserver.com or pop.secureserver.com. The last two parts of that might be the same as your domain name (if you have your own mail server, for example) or it might be some more generic name.

>> Outgoing mail server address. The format for this address is also *text.text.text*. It might look like smtp-out.secureserver.com. It will probably include the letters *smtp* in the first slot.

TECHNICAL STUFF

SMTP stands for Simple Mail Transfer Protocol. It's the protocol for sending mail. (POP3 and IMAP are both protocols for *receiving* mail.)

>> Port numbers for incoming and/or outgoing mail.

>> Whether or not the server requires an encrypted connection, and if so, what encryption method.

>> Whether or not the server requires logon using Secure Password Authentication, either for sending or receiving or both.

You can get this information from your provider's support section of its website in most cases. If you're on your own, call the tech support line for your online service or ISP to get all the proper spellings of the server names and passwords. (Don't forget to ask whether they're *case sensitive*, which means capitalization matters!)

Setting up an account using automatic settings

Outlook is really good at detecting settings and setting up an account without being told a lot of technical details. Most people setting up accounts don't need to adjust any settings, so this method works great for them.

WARNING

If you have an account that could potentially be set up as either POP3 or IMAP and you want POP3, don't use this method, because Outlook will configure it as IMAP. Instead, use the steps in the next section.

To set up an Internet email account and let Outlook detect and configure the right settings, follow these steps:

1. **Click the File tab.**

   The Backstage view appears.

2. **Click the Add Account button near the top of the screen.**

   A dialog box opens for adding a new account, as shown in Figure 7-1.

FIGURE 7-1:
Enter your email address and let Outlook take it from there.

3. **Type the email address for the account you want to set up and click Connect.**

   At this point, Outlook tries to perform an automatic setup based on your email address.

4. **If prompted, type the account's password in the Password box and click Connect.**

   I say *If* here, because if this account has previously been set up in Outlook, you may not have to enter it again.

   A configuration screen briefly appears, and Outlook begins trying to automatically set up your email account. If it succeeds, the Account Successfully Added box appears. If it doesn't, cancel by closing all the dialog boxes and try again using the steps in the next section.

CHAPTER 7 Managing Multiple Email Accounts and Data Files

CHAPTER 7 Managing Multiple Email Accounts and Data Files   **149**

5. **Click the Done button to complete the process.**

Shortly after you finish setting up the account, you will probably get a Microsoft Outlook Test Message in your Inbox. Receiving that confirms that the account is working properly in Outlook.

Setting up an account using manual settings

There are a lot of complicated mail settings you can specify for an account in Outlook, but as you saw in the previous section, Outlook hides those from you in most cases. So if you're able to set up your email account in Outlook and remain blissfully ignorant of all those settings, more power to you.

YAHOO MAIL AND TWO-FACTOR AUTHENTICATION

Two-factor authentication is a security measure that makes accounts more secure. Each time you sign in, you have to authenticate yourself in two different ways, such as entering a password and responding to a code texted to a phone. It greatly increases security, but it can throw a wrench into setting up the account in Outlook. Yahoo Mail is one of the services that offers it as an option.

To set up a Yahoo account that has two-factor authentication enabled, you have to generate an app password for Yahoo and then use that password for your account in Outlook. You sign into the web interface for your Yahoo Mail account, and then choose Account Info ➪ Account Security ➪ Generate App Password. Choose the version of Outlook you are working with (probably Outlook Desktop) and click Generate. You see an app password and instructions for using it in Outlook.

Next, you open up Outlook and choose File ➪ Info ➪ Add Account. Set up your Yahoo email as you learned in the preceding steps, and use your app password instead of your regular password for that account.

If you have some other email service that uses two-factor authentication, a quick web search should turn up the steps to use to set it up in Outlook.

But should that automatic method bomb out on you, here's what to try next:

1. **Click the File tab.**

   The Backstage view appears.

2. **Click Add Account.**

   A dialog box opens for adding a new account (refer to Figure 7-1).

3. **Type the email address for the account you want to set up.**

4. **Click Advanced Options.**

   A Let Me Set Up My Account Manually check box appears.

5. **Select the check box and click Connect.**

   The Advanced setup screen appears, showing icons for several email account types: Microsoft 365, Outlook.com, Exchange, Google, POP, IMAP, and Exchange 2013 or earlier.

6. **Click the type of account you want to set up.**

   Depending on the account type, you might see an Account Settings screen at this point, where you can enter setup details. See Figure 7-2.

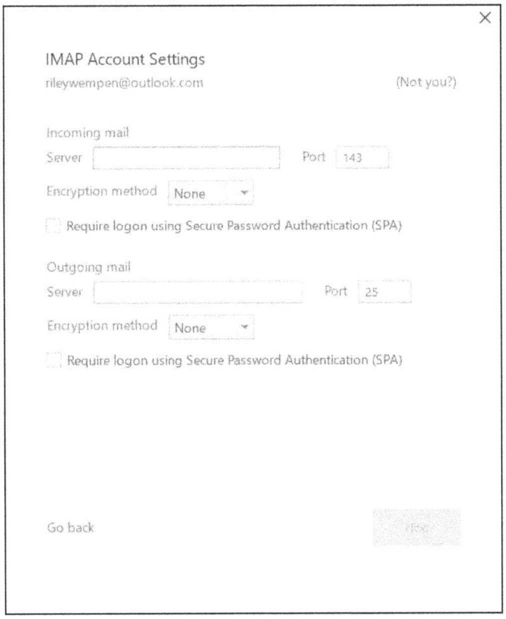

FIGURE 7-2:
Enter mail server settings if prompted for them.

7. **If prompted for account settings, enter them and click Next.**

   This is that information I advised that you get ahold of earlier in the chapter, including the incoming and outgoing mail servers, ports, and encryption methods.

8. **Respond to any other prompts that appear.**

   For example, when setting up certain account types, you might be prompted for offline settings, which specify how much old mail you want downloaded (such as one year's worth).

9. **At the Password prompt (if you see one), type the account password and click Connect.**

   You might not see a password prompt if this account has previously been set up in Outlook.

   The Account Successfully Added screen appears, as shown in Figure 7-3.

FIGURE 7-3:
The account has been successfully set up with custom settings.

10. **Do any of the following:**

- To set up another account, enter its address in the Add Another Email Address box, click Next, and follow the prompts to repeat the process.

- To send a message to your mobile phone with a link for setting up this email address there, select the Set Up Mobile Outlook on My Phone, Too check box. You are redirected to a webpage with instructions for doing that.

- Click Done to finish up.

11. **In the Account Settings dialog box, click Close.**

Sending Messages from Different Accounts

When you have multiple email accounts set up in Outlook, there's a small change to the message composition screen: a From button at the top. Click From to open a drop-down menu, where you can choose the account from which to send the message. See Figure 7-4.

FIGURE 7-4:
Choose which account from which to send the new message.

Each time you start a new email message, the default From account will be which-ever account is set up as the default. The choice of which account to use for this is not necessarily obvious. Some people set it to whichever account they use the most. However, if one account is business and one is personal, and the personal account has something that could be potentially embarrassing if you accidentally used it for business (for example, a flirty account name or signature block), you might get more peace of mind if you set your business account as the default, so that your personal account is only used when you specifically choose it.

To change which account is the default, follow these steps:

1. **Click the File tab.**

   The Backstage view appears.

2. **Click the Account Settings button and choose Account Settings from the drop-down menu.**

   The Account Settings dialog box opens.

3. **Click the Email tab if it's not already selected.**

   The Email Accounts setup page appears. See Figure 7-5.

4. **Click the account that should be the default.**

5. **Click Set as Default.**

6. **Click Close to close the Account Settings dialog box.**

FIGURE 7-5:
Choose which account should be the default from the Account Settings dialog box.

Modifying Mail Account Settings

You can modify the settings for any of the mail accounts set up in Outlook. For example, you might need to change the stored password for the account if you change it on the server (for example, if someone got ahold of it and you need to change it for security reasons).

TIP

You can change most settings, with the exception of account type. If you need to change the account type (such as switch between IMAP and POP3), you must first remove the account and then re-create it in Outlook.

Changing the basic account settings

To modify an account's settings, follow these steps:

1. **Click the File tab.**

   The Backstage view appears.

2. **At the top of the screen, open the drop-down menu and choose the email account for which you want to change the server settings.**

   It might already be selected.

3. **Click the Account Settings button and choose Account Name and Sync Settings from the drop-down menu.**

   The Account Settings dialog box opens for the selected account. Figure 7-6 shows it for an IMAP account; the settings are similar for a POP (just slightly fewer options).

WARNING

   For an Exchange Server account, you get a different dialog box with very few options, because you don't have a lot of local choices for a corporate-managed account. Contact your IT department if you need to make changes that don't appear in the dialog box.

4. **Make any changes to the account details.**

5. **Click Next.**

6. **Click Done.**

7. **Click Back or press Esc to exit from the Backstage view.**

Changing the mail server

If you are having trouble accessing your email account, someone in tech support at your ISP might suggest that you make some changes to the mail server address or the port assigned to it. You can do this for IMAP and POP accounts, but not for Exchange, Microsoft 365, or Outlook.com accounts.

Follow these steps to view and change the mail server information:

1. **Click the File tab.**

   The Backstage view appears.

2. **At the top of the screen, open the drop-down menu and choose the email account for which you want to change the server settings.**

   It might already be selected.

3. **Click the Account Settings button and choose Server Settings from the drop-down menu.**

   An Account Settings dialog box opens. See Figure 7-7 for an IMAP account; POP is similar. The Incoming Mail settings appear first.

4. **Make any changes to the Incoming Mail settings.**

   For example, you might change the mail server or the port number, the password, or the encryption method.

5. **Click Outgoing Mail.**

   The Outgoing Mail settings appear.

6. **Make any changes to the Outgoing Mail settings.**

   For example, you might change the outgoing mail server or port number, the server timeout delay, or whether SMTP requires authentication.

7. **Click Next.**

8. **Click Done.**

Updating your stored email password

If you change your email account's password at some point, you'll need to update the stored copy in Outlook so that Outlook won't prompt you to type the password every time it sends and receives mail. Fortunately, it's super easy. First, change your password with your email provider using its web-based interface. Then the next time you attempt to send or receive mail via Outlook using that account, Outlook will prompt you for the new password.

Managing Outlook Data Files

Outlook data files are not the same thing as email accounts, but they're closely related. When you set up any kind of email account, Outlook automatically creates a new data file just for that account. It holds all the folders that appear in the Folder pane for that account (Inbox, Outbox, Sent Items, and so on).

TECHNICAL STUFF

Outlook data files can have one of two extensions: .pst or .ost. A .pst file is for a POP3 account. It stores all data locally on your computer. An .ost file is a local mirror of online content from your mail server; it's used for all other types of accounts *except* POP3.

Most of the time you don't have to think about data files in Outlook. They're there silently behind the scenes, storing your mail, calendar, and contacts automatically for you. Nevertheless, there are some housekeeping occasions where you have to interact with them, and the following sections explain those processes.

Removing an account from Outlook

You might want to remove an account from Outlook, for a variety of reasons. Maybe the account doesn't exist anymore, or maybe you lost it in your last divorce and your ex-spouse changed the password on it. (Bummer.) Or maybe it's an adult account (freaky4U?) and you don't want to keep it on your home computer anymore now that your inquisitive 13-year-old nephew has come to stay with you. For whatever reason, it's fairly easy to remove an account. Doing so does not delete the account; it just prevents Outlook from communicating with it.

Even if you remove the email account from Outlook, its data file remains behind, so you can continue to access its old messages from within Outlook. If you don't want that, you have to remove the data file from Outlook, too.

Follow these steps to remove an account and its associated data file from Outlook:

1. **Click the File tab.**

   The Backstage view appears.

2. **Click the Account Settings button, and then click Account Settings from its menu.**

   The Account Settings dialog box opens. Refer to Figure 7-5.

3. **If needed, click the Email tab to select it.**

   It probably appears by default.

4. **Click the account you want to remove and click the Remove button.**

   A confirmation dialog box appears.

5. **Click Yes.**

   The account is removed from the list on the Email tab.

6. **Click the Data Files tab.**

   The data file for the removed email account may still be there. If it is, you will want to remove it also. Otherwise the folders for the removed account will still be hanging around in Outlook's Folder pane, even though new mail is not being sent or received with it.

7. **Click the data file associated with the removed account and click the Remove button.**

   A confirmation dialog box appears.

8. **Click Yes.**

9. **Click Close to close the Account Settings dialog box.**

TIP

Here's a shortcut: Instead of steps 1–4, right-click the account in the Folder list and choose Remove *accountname*.

Purging old data files

WARNING

If you're worried about privacy, here's an important warning: Removing a data file from Outlook doesn't delete it; it'll still be there in whatever location Outlook stores its data files, and anyone who knows the steps can add it back into Outlook and peruse its contents (including any sent and received messages). To permanently get rid of a data file so that nobody can access it, you have to take an extra step by deleting the file from your hard drive.

Follow these steps to see what old data files may be lurking around on your hard drive and delete any that you don't want to keep:

1. **Click the File tab.**

   The Backstage view appears.

2. **Click the Account Settings button, and then click Account Settings from its menu.**

   The Account Settings dialog box opens. Refer to Figure 7-5.

3. **If needed, click the Data Files tab to select it.**

   A list of the data files that are currently open in Outlook appears. Check out the locations in the Location column.

4. **Click one of the accounts and then click Open File Location.**

   A File Explorer window opens, showing the location of that data file. Outlook tends to store all data files in the same place by default, so any other data files you might have had on your system will be here.

5. **If you see a data file that you want to get rid of, select it and press Delete on your keyboard.**

   Depending on your Windows settings, a confirmation box might appear. If it does, click Yes.

6. **When you are finished deleting unwanted data files, close the File Explorer window.**

Moving a data file to another computer

So you've got a new computer — congratulations! You could set up your email account on your new computer, but you might lose access to your old email folders, depending on the account type. (IMAP and Exchange accounts will probably be fine, but POP3 accounts . . . not so much.)

If you've got a POP3 email account set up on one computer, you must copy its data file over to the new computer to retain all your old message folder contents. Here's how to do that.

Export from the old computer

On the old computer, follow these steps:

1. **Click the File tab.**

   The Backstage view appears.

2. **Click Open & Export in the navigation pane on the left.**

   Options appear for managing data files.

3. **Click Import/Export.**

   The Import and Export Wizard dialog box opens. See Figure 7-8.

4. **Click Export to a File and click Next.**

   You are prompted for a file type to create.

5. **Click Outlook Data File (.pst) and click Next.**

   You are prompted to select the folder to export from. You can export from an individual folder (such as Inbox) or you can choose the top level of the outline (Outlook Data File) to export everything.

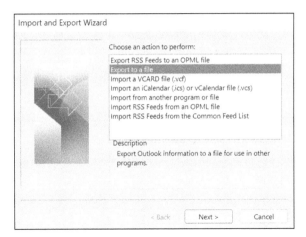

Import and Export Wizard

Choose an action to perform:

Export RSS Feeds to an OPML file
Export to a file
Import a VCARD file (.vcf)
Import an iCalendar (.ics) or vCalendar file (.vcs)
Import from another program or file
Import RSS Feeds from an OPML file
Import RSS Feeds from the Common Feed List

Description
Export Outlook information to a file for use in other programs.

< Back   Next >   Cancel

FIGURE 7-8:
The Import and
Export Wizard
dialog box.

6. **Select the account for which you want to export the data.**

   You can optionally choose just one folder from that account by drilling down in the folder listing, but you'll probably want everything associated with that account (that is, everything in that account's current data file). See Figure 7-9.

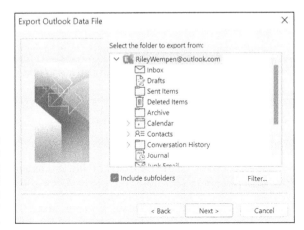

Export Outlook Data File   ✕

Select the folder to export from:

⌄ 📧 RileyWempen@outlook.com
    ✉ Inbox
    📝 Drafts
    📄 Sent Items
    🗑 Deleted Items
    📁 Archive
  > 📅 Calendar
  > 👥 Contacts
  > 💬 Conversation History
    📓 Journal
    📧 Junk Email

☑ Include subfolders   Filter...

< Back   Next >   Cancel

FIGURE 7-9:
Choose which
data file to export
from, and
optionally choose
a certain folder
from it.

7. **Click Next.**

   You are prompted for a filename and location for the exported file.

8. **In the Save Exported File As box, type the path and filename desired, or click Browse to locate the desired location.**

   You can save this on your hard drive locally, but if the old and new computers are both connected to the same network, you might want to save it to a network location that the new computer can access. Alternatively, if you are signed into the same OneDrive account on both computers, you can save it to OneDrive.

9. **Click Finish.**

You are prompted for an optional password.

10. **Click OK to skip assigning a password.**

The data has been exported. Now it's time to move over to the new computer and import it.

Import to the new computer

On the new computer, follow these steps to import data from a data file:

1. **Click the File tab.**

The Backstage view appears.

2. **Click Open & Export in the navigation pane on the left.**

Options appear for managing data files.

3. **Click Import/Export.**

The Import and Export Wizard dialog box opens. Refer to Figure 7-8.

4. **Click Import from Another Program or File and click Next.**

You are prompted for the file type.

5. **Select Outlook Data File (.pst) and click Next.**

You are prompted to locate the file from which to import.

6. **Click Browse and browse to the location and file you exported earlier. Then click Open to select it.**

The selected path and file appear in the File to Import text box.

7. **Click Next.**

You are prompted to select the folder to import from. (You don't have to import everything contained in the exported file, although you will probably want to.)

8. **Select the folder to import from.**

9. **Select where you want to import the data.**

You can import it into the current folder, or you can import it into the same folder in one of your existing data files on the new computer. (Choose which one from the drop-down menu, as shown in Figure 7-10.)

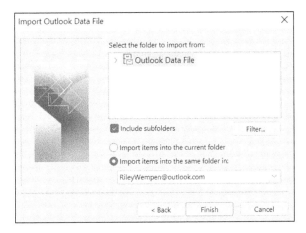

FIGURE 7-10:
Select the folder
to import from.

10. **Click Finish.**

The content is imported into Outlook on the new computer.

TIP

You can use these importing steps to import from any Outlook data file, such as a backup or archive file.

3

Keeping Track of Contacts, Dates, Tasks, and More

Learn how to create and manage your Contacts list, including changing how you view your contacts, attaching photos to them, and sending them to other people, as well as how to sort your contacts and use grouped views.

Explore how to use the Calendar to make and change appointments as well as how to print your calendar and handle multiple calendars.

Stay on track with your to-do list by creating tasks for yourself (or others) in Outlook and then marking them as complete to celebrate your successes.

IN THIS CHAPTER

» **Storing names and addresses**

» **Sorting and rearranging views**

» **Flagging friends in your Contacts list**

» **Finding names in your Contacts list**

» **Sorting people into Contact groups**

Chapter **8**

Your Little Black Book: Managing Your Contacts

You've heard people say "It's not *what* you know; it's *who* you know." Well, how do you keep track of what you know about who you know? You either need a terrific memory or a convenient tool for keeping track of all those whatshisnames and whoziwhatzits out there. Years ago, I had a habit of keeping track of all the people I needed to know by memory. Then, something happened that changed that habit. What was it? I forget. But take my word for it: I don't go around memorizing names and numbers anymore. I put them all into Outlook and let my computer do the memorizing. Now, instead of wasting hours memorizing, I can spend quality time with my dear friends Whatshisname and Whoziwhatzit.

All kidding aside, I work as a university instructor and a freelance writer. The information I need to keep about my academic colleagues and students differs from the information I need for dealing with editors and managers in the publishing business. I'm also on the board of a non-profit, which has its own set of personalities to keep in touch with. But when someone calls on the phone or when I want to do a mailing to a group from one world or another, I need to be able to look up the person right away — regardless of which category the person fits in.

Outlook is flexible enough to let you keep your entire collection of names and addresses in a single place — but you can also sort, view, find, and print it in different ways, depending on what kind of work you're doing. You can also keep lists of family and friends stored in Outlook right alongside your business contacts and distinguish them from one another quickly when the need arises.

Putting in Your Contacts: Names, Numbers, and Other Stuff

Storing lots of names, addresses, and phone numbers is no big trick, but finding them again can take magic unless you have a tool like Outlook. Other programs can store names and related numbers, but Outlook — by far — is the most popular program for doing work that uses names, addresses, and phone numbers.

If you've ever used a little pocket address book, you pretty much know how to use the Outlook Contacts feature. Simply enter the name, address, phone number, and a few juicy tidbits — and there you are!

The quick-and-dirty way to enter contacts

If you want, you can enter scads of details about every person in your Contacts list and choose from literally dozens of options, but if all you want to do is enter the essentials and move on, that's fine.

Entering a new name in your Contacts list is as simple as following these steps:

1. **In the People module, click the New Contact button on the Ribbon (or press Ctrl+N).**

   The Untitled - Contact form opens.

2. **Fill in the blanks on the form.**

   Figure 8-1 shows an example. You don't have to fill in all the fields; just use the fields that are relevant to the contact at hand.

3. **Click the Save & Close button.**

   That's really all there is to it. If you don't enter every detail about a contact right away, it's okay — you can always add more information later.

Click the New Contact button.

Click the Save & Close button.

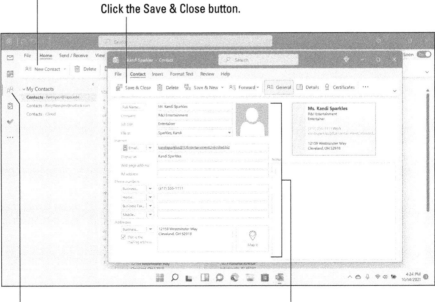

FIGURE 8-1:
The Contact entry
form.

Start in the People module.   Fill out the form.

TIP

Here's a really handy time-saver: To create a new contact in your Contacts list from the information in a received email message, drag that message and drop it on the People module's icon in the navigation bar. A New Contact window opens that pulls all the information Outlook can glean from the email message; you can fill in any missing pieces yourself, and then click Save & Close.

The slow, complete way to enter contacts

If you're more of a detail-minded person, here's the way to enter every little thing about each contact:

1. **In the People module, click the New Contact button on the Ribbon (or press Ctrl+N).**

    The Untitled - Contact form opens. (That's its name when it starts out; it changes to the person's name when you enter their name.) Refer to Figure 8-1.

2. **Click the Full Name button.**

    The Check Full Name dialog box opens, as shown in Figure 8-2.

FIGURE 8-2:
The Check Full
Name dialog box.

3. **Do some or all of the following:**

- Click in the Title box and either type a title here or choose one from the drop-down menu, such as *Mrs.* or *Dr.*

- Click in the First text box and type the contact's first name.

- Click in the Middle text box and type the contact's middle name or initial (if any). If there's no middle name or initial, you can leave this box blank.

- Click in the Last text box and type the contact's last name.

- Click in the Suffix box and either type a suffix here or choose one from the drop-down menu, such as *Jr.* or *III.*

4. **Click the OK button.**

The Check Full Name dialog box closes and back in the contact form, the name you entered is in the Full Name and File As text boxes. The window's title bar now shows the person's name instead of Untitled.

5. **Click in the appropriate box and enter the information requested on the form.**

If you don't have the information for a particular field — for example, if the contact has no job title — leave that box blank. A down arrow button to the right of a box means there's a menu you can select from. If your choice isn't listed, you can type it in the box.

- If you've entered a name in the Full Name box, the File As box will already show that name.

TIP

- If you want this person filed under something other than their name, click in the File As box and type in your preferred designation. For example, you may want to file your dentist's name under the term *Dentist* rather than by name. If you put *Dentist* in the File As box, the name turns up under Dentist in the alphabetical listing rather than under the name itself. The Full Name *and* the File As designations exist in your Contacts list. That way (for example), you can search for your dentist either by name or by the word *Dentist.*

6. **Click in the Email text box and enter your contact's email address.**

   If your contact has more than one email address, click the arrow next to Email, as shown in Figure 8-3, select Email 2, click in the text box, and then enter the second address.

FIGURE 8-3:
You can enter
more than one
email address for
each person in
your Contacts list.

7. **Click in the text box next to Business and type the contact's business phone number.**

8. **Click in the text box next to Home and type the contact's home phone number.**

   For numbers other than business and home phones, click the down arrow beside a number option, choose the kind of number you're entering, and then enter the number.

   The New Contact form has four phone number blocks. You can use any of them for any of the 19 phone number types available in the drop-down menu — as shown in Figure 8-4 — depending on what types of phone numbers your contacts have.

9. **Click the down arrow in the Addresses section to choose the type of address you want to enter.**

   You can choose Business, Home, or Other.

10. **Click the button in the Addresses section.**

    The button's name is whatever you chose in Step 9. For example, if you chose Business in Step 9, click Business now. The Check Address dialog box opens.

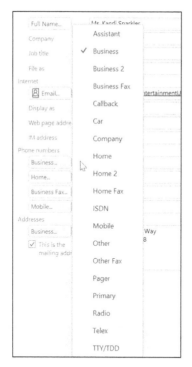

FIGURE 8-4:
You can always
reach your
contact at one of
these phone
numbers.

11. **Enter the following information in the appropriate boxes:**

   - Street

   - City

   - State/Province

   - ZIP/Postal code

   - Country/Region

   See Figure 8-5 for a look at a completed Check Address dialog box.

12. **Click OK.**

   The Check Address dialog box closes.

13. **On the New Contact form, select the This Is the Mailing Address check box if the address you just entered is the one to use for sending mail to the contact.**

   The check box is already marked if this is the first (or only) address you've entered for this contact.

   The Map It button enables you to validate an address (for example, to check whether the ZIP code is correct).

TIP

FIGURE 8-5:
The Check
Address
dialog box.

14. **Click in the Web Page Address text box and type a page's address (its URL) if you want to link to that page directly from the address card.**

    To see a contact's webpage, open the contact record, click the More button on the Contact tab of the Ribbon, and choose Web Page. Your web browser launches and opens the page.

TECHNICAL
STUFF

URL is a fancy name for the address of a page on the World Wide Web. When you see ads on TV that refer to www.discovery.com or www.dummies.com, what you're seeing is a *Uniform Resource Locator* (the even fancier term that *URL* stands for — essentially an Internet address).

15. **Click in the Notes box at the bottom right of the form and type in anything you want.**

    You can enter directions, meeting details, the Declaration of Independence — anything you want (preferably something that can help you in your dealings with the contact).

TIP

    You can format the text in the big text box, as shown in Figure 8-6, by clicking the Format Text tab of the Ribbon and using the buttons on that tab. The tools on the Format Text tab are just like the ones that all other word processing programs use: font, point size, bold, italic, justification, and color. Select the text you want to format. You can change the formatting of a single letter or the whole text box. You can't format the text in the smaller data text boxes in the other parts of the Contact form — only the text in the Notes box.

    If the controls on the Format Text tab are not available, it's probably for one of two reasons: Either the message format is set to Plain Text, or the insertion point isn't in the Notes box.

16. **When you're done, click the Save & Close button on the Contact tab of the Ribbon.**

    After you enter anything you want or need (or may need) to know about people you deal with at work, you're ready to start dealing.

Formatting controls on the Ribbon   Formatted text

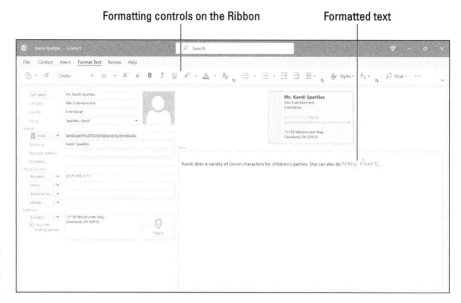

Viewing Your Contacts

After you enter your contact information, Outlook lets you see the information arranged in many different and useful ways, called *views*. Viewing your contact information and sorting the views are quick ways to get the big picture of the data you've entered. Outlook comes with several predefined views in each module. You can easily alter any predefined view, name and save your altered view, and use it just as you would the predefined views.

To change the view of your Contacts list, follow these steps:

If you're using the Simplified Ribbon:

1. **In the People module, click the View tab on the Ribbon.**

2. **Click Change View and then click the view you want.**

   The display changes to use that view. If you choose Business Card view, you get something like what's shown in Figure 8-7. You can also choose Card view, Phone view, List view, or whatever other views are listed.

If you're using the Classic Ribbon:

1. **In the People module, click the Home tab on the Ribbon.**

2. **Click the view you want in the Current View group.**

   The display changes to use that view.

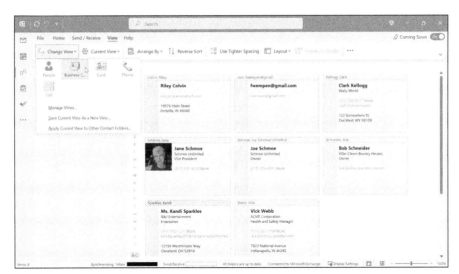

FIGURE 8-7:
Business
Card view.

TIP

You can switch views just like you can switch television channels, so don't worry about changing back and forth. When you change views, you're just seeing different ways to organize the same information.

Sorting a view

Some views are organized as simple lists, such as the Phone view of the People module. Figure 8-8 shows Phone view: a column of names on the left, followed by a column of company names, and so on.

FIGURE 8-8:
Phone view.

If you can't find a certain contact in a view that's arranged in columns, click the column title once to sort by that column. For example, suppose you want to see the names of the people who work for IBM who are entered in your Contacts list. One easy way to see all their names simultaneously is to sort the COMPANY column.

To sort by column name in a view that has column headings (such as Phone or List), follow these steps:

1. **In the People module, choose Phone view or List view.**

   The preceding section explained how to change views. Your Contacts list appears in Phone view or List view. They are similar; both have column headings that you can use for sorting purposes.

2. **Click the heading at the top of the Company column.**

   Your contacts appear in alphabetical order from A to Z (ascending order) according to the name in the Company column. (You can toggle that to descending order, Z to A, by clicking the column heading again.) Now it's easier to find someone — just scroll down to that part of the alphabet. If you sort by company, all the contacts line up in order of company name. If you click the heading a second time, your contacts appear in reverse alphabetical order (descending order).

TIP

In views that don't have column headings (such as People and Business Card), you can only sort by the File As field (usually the name, but sometimes the company name). However, you can reverse the sort to toggle between A-Z and Z-A. To do that, right-click a blank area and choose Reverse Sort from the shortcut menu.

Rearranging views

You can rearrange the appearance of a view that uses column headings simply by dragging the column title and dropping the title where you want it. Here's an example that moves the Country/Region column to the left of the File As column:

1. **If the Contacts list is not already displayed in Phone view, switch to that view.**

   It might already be in Phone view from the preceding set of steps. You could also do these steps from List view.

2. **Click the Country/Region heading and drag it on top of the File As column to its left.**

   You see a pair of red arrows pointing to the border between the two columns to the left of the column you clicked. The red arrows tell you where Outlook will drop the column when you release the mouse button.

3. **Release the mouse button.**

   The column you dragged is now to the left of the other column. You can use the same process to move any column in any Outlook view.

Because the screen isn't as wide as the list, you may need to scroll to the right to see additional columns. You can reorder the columns as desired so that the ones you use most frequently appear at the left, so you don't have to scroll every time you want to see them.

Using grouped views

Sometimes, sorting just isn't enough. Contacts lists can get pretty long after a while; you can easily collect a few thousand contacts in a few years. Sorting a list that long means that if you're looking for something starting with the letter *M*, for example, the item you want to find will be about 3 feet below the bottom of your monitor — no matter what you do.

Groups are the answer — and I don't mean Outlook Anonymous. Outlook already offers you several predefined lists that use grouping.

You can view several types of lists in Outlook: A sorted list is like a deck of playing cards laid out in numerical order, starting with the deuces, then the threes, then the fours, and so on — up through the picture cards. A grouped view is like seeing the cards arranged with all the hearts in one row, then all the spades, then the diamonds, and then the clubs.

Gathering items of similar types into groups is handy for such tasks as finding all the people on your list who work for a certain company when you want to send congratulations on a new piece of business. Because grouping by company is so frequently useful, the List view sorts your contacts by company, and it's set up as a predefined view in Outlook.

To see the grouping by company, switch to List view. You learned how to switch views in the People module earlier, in this chapter.

> In List view, each heading has a company: prefix and represents a different company. Each heading tells you how many items are included under that heading. In Figure 8-9, for example, you can see that two people work for Fizzy Lifting Drinks, Inc.

> The down arrow to the left of the heading expands or collapses the group of contacts under that heading.

FIGURE 8-9:
The List view
applies grouping
by company by
default.

If the predefined group views don't meet your needs, you can group items according to just about anything you want, assuming you've entered the data. To group by another field, follow these steps:

1. **In the People module, do one of the following:**

   - Using the Simplified Ribbon: On the View tab, click Current View and then click View Settings.

   - Using the Classic Ribbon: Click the View tab and select View Settings.

   The Advanced View Settings: List dialog box opens. Notice that Group By is set to Company.

2. **Click Group By.**

   The Group By dialog box opens. Notice that Group Items By is set to Company. See Figure 8-10.

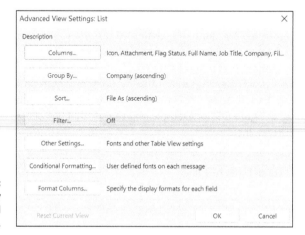

FIGURE 8-10:
Group items by
some other field
if desired.

3. **Open the Company list and select a different field.**

4. **Click Ascending or Descending to specify the sort order.**

   A to Z is ascending, and Z to A is descending.

5. **Click OK to close the Group By dialog box.**

6. **Click OK to close the Advanced View Settings: List dialog box.**

Flagging Your Friends

Sometimes, you need a reminder to do something involving another person — but tying a string around your finger looks silly and doesn't help much anyway. Outlook offers a better way. For example, if you promise to call someone next week, the best way to help yourself remember is to flag that person's name in the Contacts list. A reminder will pop up in your Calendar. Contacts aren't the only items you can flag. You can add reminders to tasks, email messages, and appointments to achieve the same effect.

TIP

If you are still in List view, you might want to change back to Business Card view for these steps.

To attach a flag to a contact, follow these steps:

1. **In the People module, right-click the contact you want to flag.**

   A shortcut menu appears.

2. **Choose Follow Up.**

   The Follow Up menu appears, as shown in Figure 8-11.

3. **Click the date you plan to follow up with the contact you chose.**

   Your choices include Today, Tomorrow, This Week, and Next Week. Sadly, When Heck Freezes Over isn't an option.

   Flagging a contact for a specific day makes that contact's name appear on your Outlook Calendar on the day you chose.

If you want to set a follow-up reminder, continue with the steps:

4. **Right-click the contact again, point to Follow Up with your mouse, and then click Add Reminder.**

   The Custom dialog box opens.

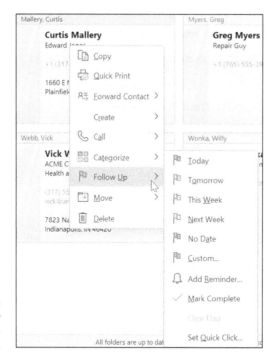

FIGURE 8-11:
Right-click on any
contact to add a
flag.

This is an optional step, but it makes a reminder window open and play a sound at the time you choose.

5. **In the Custom dialog box, open the Date drop-down menu in the Reminder section and choose a reminder date.**

   Clicking the arrow next to the date opens a calendar date picker, as shown in Figure 8-12. Click the desired date.

6. **Open the Time drop-down menu and choose a reminder time.**

   You can customize the sound that plays by clicking the speaker icon to the right of the time.

   TIP

7. **Click OK to set the reminder.**

TIP

Here's a time-saver. If you know you want to flag *and* set a reminder, you can skip directly to Step 4, because creating a reminder also creates a flag.

FIGURE 8-12:
Choose a
reminder date.

Using Contact Information

Call me crazy, but I bet you actually plan to use all that contact information you enter. So I'm sure you'll indulge me while I show you a few ways to dig up and exploit the valuable nuggets you've stashed in your Contacts list.

Searching for contacts

The whole reason for entering people's contact information is so you can find them again. Otherwise, what's the point of all this rigmarole?

Finding names in the People module is child's play. You can browse or search from any view of the People module. To browse, just page through the contacts using the vertical scroll bar. To search, enter a name or any other relevant text in the Search box above the Ribbon and select what you want from the search results.

Here's how to do it from Card view — which you haven't worked with yet officially. It's like Business Card view, except the cards are of different sizes based on the information they contain, and they're arranged in columns.

To find a contact by last name in Card view, follow these steps:

1. **In the People module, switch to Card view.**

You learned how to switch views in the People module, earlier in this chapter.

2. **Click in the white space below any card and begin typing the first few letters of the desired contact's last name.**

The display jumps to the first instance of that name and highlights the card heading.

TIP

Card view has lettered tabs along the left edge. You can browse your contacts by scrolling, but if there are a lot of them, you might find it quicker to click one of those lettered tabs to jump quickly to last names that begin with the chosen letter.

Of course, you may need to base a search for a contact name on something like the company the contact works for. Or you may want to find all the people in your list who live in a certain state — or people who put you in a certain state of mind (now *there's* a useful tidbit to include in their contact records). In such a case, the Search tool takes you to your contact.

To use the Search tool to search for a contact, follow these steps:

1. **In the People module, with your favorite view chosen, type the text you want to find in the Search box above the Ribbon and then press Enter.**

Your Contacts list shrinks to those that contain the information you typed, as shown in Figure 8-13.

If you get no contacts that match your search, check to see whether you correctly spelled the search text you entered.

2. **To remove the search filter, click the X button at the far right end of the Search box.**

REMEMBER

It's hard to be as stupidly literal as computers; close doesn't count with them. If you see *Grg Wshngtn*, you know to look for *George Washington*, but a computer doesn't.

On the other hand, if you have only a scrap of the name you're looking for, Outlook can find that scrap wherever it is. A search for *Geo* would turn up George Washington as well as any other Georges in your Contacts list, including Boy George and George of the Jungle (provided they're all such close personal friends of yours that they're in your Contacts list).

Type the first few letters.   Only one contact matches the search text.

FIGURE 8-13:
Use the Search
box to narrow
down the
displayed
contacts to those
that match your
criteria.

Finding a contact from the Mail module

Want to search for a person, but you're using the Mail module at the moment? No problem. The Search People box on the Home tab on the Ribbon can help you dig up a contact record in a jiffy from either the People or Mail module. Follow these steps:

1. **Switch to the Mail module.**

   You can also try this out from the People module, but since it's a more useful feature when you're *not* already in the People module, let's try it from Mail.

2. **Click the Search People box on the Home tab.**

3. **Type any part of the contact name.**

   A list of items (including contacts) that match the text you type appears. See Figure 8-14.

4. **Click one of the contacts on the list to open the record for that contact.**

   The contact's information opens in a new window.

5. **Close that window by clicking the Close (X) in its upper right corner when you are done with it.**

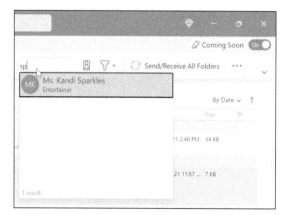

FIGURE 8-14:
Search for a
contact from any
module using the
Search box in the
Find group of the
Home tab.

Forwarding a business card

Outlook can also forward an electronic *business card* to any other person who uses
Outlook (or any other program that understands how to use digital business
cards). It's a handy way to email any contact record in your list to anybody else.

The most obvious thing you may want to send this way is your own contact
information:

1. **In the People module, create a contact record for yourself.**

    It should have all the information you want to send someone.

2. **Double-click the contact record that has the information you want to
    send.**

    The contact record you double-clicked opens.

3. **Click the Forward button on the Contact tab on the Ribbon.**

    A menu offers three choices: As a Business Card, In Internet Format (vCard),
    and As an Outlook Contact.

4. **Choose the format you prefer.**

    If you're not sure, choose As a Business Card. That sends both kinds of
    cards — in Outlook format and Internet format. A new message opens, as
    shown in Figure 8-15, with the contact information attached.

5. **In the To text box, type the address of the person who should get the
    message.**

    Or click the To button and pick a name from the Address Book.

6. **Click the Send button (or press Alt+S).**

    Your message and the attached vCard are sent to your recipient.

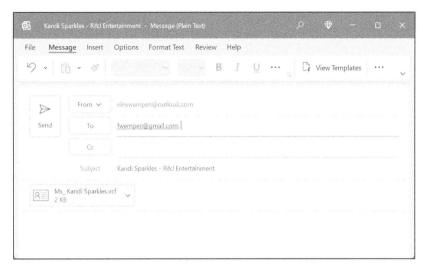

FIGURE 8-15:
Sending a
business card.

When you get a business card in an email message, you can add the card to your Contacts list by double-clicking the icon in the message that represents the business card. Doing so opens a new contact record. Simply click the Save & Close button to add the new name — along with all the information on the business card — to your Contacts list.

You can also forward a business card by clicking the contact record and then clicking the Forward Contact button on the Ribbon. This is a few mouse clicks shorter, but your forwarding options are reduced to sending as a business card or as an Outlook contact.

Gathering People Into Groups

You can create a Contact group in your People module that has more than one person. Organizing people into groups helps when you need to send a message to several people simultaneously. You can also assign categories to your Contact groups (just as you can with individual contacts), and you can send a Contact group to other people as an attachment to an email message so they can use the same list you do if they're also using Outlook.

Creating a Contact group

Creating a Contact group is a simple matter of making up a name for your list and choosing from the collection of names you've stored on your system. A Contact group doesn't keep track of phone numbers and mailing addresses — just email addresses.

To create a Contact group in your People module, follow these steps:

1. **In the People module, do one of the following:**

   - Using the Simplified Ribbon: On the Home tab, click the arrow on the New Contact button and then click Contact Group.

   - Using the Classic Ribbon: On the Home tab, click the New Contact Group button.

   - Keyboard shortcut: Press Ctrl+Shift+L.

   The Contact Group window opens.

2. **In the Name box, type the name you want to assign to the group.**

3. **Click the Add Members button and choose From Outlook Contacts.**

   The Select Members: Contacts dialog box shows the available names on the left side and a blank Members box at the bottom.

4. **Double-click the name of each person you want to add to your Contact group.**

   Each name you double-click appears in the Members box at the bottom of the dialog box. Figure 8-16 shows two people added.

   If you have multiple Contacts lists or address books, you can open the Address Book drop-down menu at the top of the dialog box to switch between lists.

TIP

FIGURE 8-16:
Picking members
for your Contact
group.

5. **If there are addresses you want to include that aren't in your Contacts list, type them manually into the Members box.**

   Separate entries in the Members box with semicolons.

6. **When you're done picking names, click the OK button.**

   The Select Members: Contacts dialog box closes.

7. **Click the Save & Close button (or press Alt+S).**

   The Contact Group dialog box closes and your Contact group appears in your Contacts list.

Editing a Contact group

People come and people go in Contact groups — just as they do everywhere else. It's a good thing you can edit the lists:

1. **In the People module, double-click the name of one of your Contact groups.**

   You see the same screen you saw when you first created the list.

2. **Edit the list in one or more of these ways:**

   - *Remove a member of the list:* Click that name and then click the Remove Member button. Depending on the window width, you might need to click More Commands to access the Remove Member button.

   - *Select a new member from the names already in your Contacts list:* Click the Add Members button and follow the same routine you used when you created the list.

   - *Add a person whose email address isn't listed in your Contacts list:* Click the Add Members button, select New Email Contact, fill in the person's name and email address, and then click the OK button.

3. **Click the Save & Close button (or press Alt+S) to save your changes to the contact group.**

Using a Contact group

Contact groups show up as items in your Contacts list along with people's names — so, as you'd guess, you can use a Contact group to address an email message just as you would with any contact. You can drag the card for a Contact group to your Inbox to create a new email message that goes to contacts in that list. You can also type the name of the Contact group in the To field of an email message and click the Check Names button on the toolbar. When Outlook adds an underline to the name in the To box, you know your message will go to the people in your Contact group.

Adding pictures to contacts

You can include a picture with the contact information you collect — and not just for decoration. Now that many cell phones and other mobile devices synchronize with the Outlook Contacts list, you can make someone's picture appear on your cell phone screen every time they call or text. Those pictures also appear when you pick Business Card view of your Outlook contacts. If you're the type who forgets names but never forgets a face, you can collect names *and* faces.

To add a picture to a contact record, follow these steps:

1. **In the People module, double-click the contact who will get a picture.**

   The contact record opens.

2. **Click the picture icon at the top center of the contact record.**

   The Add Contact Picture dialog box opens.

3. **Browse to the location containing the picture and double-click the picture you want to add.**

   The picture you chose appears in the contact record.

4. **Click the Save & Close button.**

   Another smiling face now adorns your world, as shown in Figure 8-17. Isn't it wonderful? If you're likely to be sending out your own business card, it's probably worthwhile to add a nice-looking picture of yourself to help make a good impression.

FIGURE 8-17:
A picture is
worth a thousand
words —
sometimes.

Chapter **9**

Organizing Your Schedule with the Calendar

Do working people work all day? No. Most working people spend the day going to meetings. It's enough to send anyone to Overmeeters Anonymous. The Outlook Calendar can't halt the relentless tedium of meetings, but it can speed up the scheduling process and help you budget your time for more meetings!

Getting a Good View of Your Calendar

No doubt you've been looking at calendars your whole life, so the Outlook Calendar will be pretty simple for you to understand. It looks like a paper calendar: plain old rows of dates, Monday through Friday plus weekends, and so on. You don't have to think like a computer to understand your schedule.

To get to the Calendar module, click the Calendar icon at the bottom of the Folder pane. It's the one that looks like a little monthly calendar. (You probably figured that out on your own. You're sharp like that.)

Choosing a view

Once you get into the calendar, you can choose how you want to view it. The basic Calendar views are Day, Work Week, Week, and Month. Other views (such as Schedule view) are helpful when you're trying to figure out when you did something or when you'll do something.

Outlook displays buttons on both the Home and View tabs of the Ribbon. You can change Calendar views by clicking the name of the view you want to see. If the view you select doesn't suit you, don't worry — just click a different view. Figure 9-1 shows Work Week view, for example. As time goes by (so to speak), you'll gravitate to the Calendar view that suits you best.

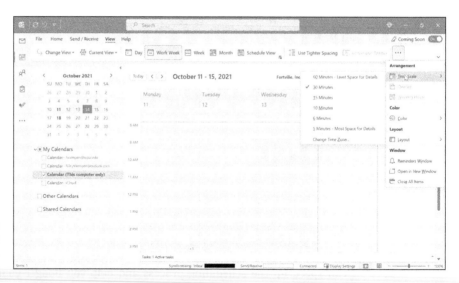

FIGURE 9-1:
Adjust the time
scale from the
View tab.

TIP

For all views *except* Month, you can set a time scale, which are the increment blocks that show on the calendar, such as 30 minutes or 15 minutes. On the View tab, click Time Scale and then make your selection. If you're using the Simplified Ribbon, you might need to click More Commands to access the Time Scale command, as shown in Figure 9-1.

TIP

The Day, Work Week, and Week views all include the Daily Task List pane at the bottom of each day's column. You can turn the Daily Task List pane off like this:

>> Using the Simplified Ribbon: Click More Commands if needed, and then click Layout ⇨ Daily Task List ⇨ Off.

>> Using the Classic Ribbon: Choose View ⇨ Daily Task List ⇨ Off.

Viewing calendar items

Items you've added to your calendar appear as text on the scheduled date, at the appropriate time (if a time was specified). If you want to see more information about something in your calendar, most of the time, you just point to the item with your mouse. A box pops up with the basic info, as shown in Figure 9-2. If that doesn't give you enough information, you can double-click the item to open it in a separate window.

Calendar item

Wednesday	Thursday	Friday	Saturday
25	26	27	28

Staff meeting

Sep 1

10:00am Staff meeting; Conference Room A

🕐 Wednesday, September 1, 2021 10:00 AM-11:00 AM

📍 Conference Room A

🔔 15 minutes before

| 8 | | | |
| 15 | 16 | 17 | 18 |

FIGURE 9-2:
Point to an item on the calendar to see its basic details.

Time Travel: Viewing Different Dates in the Calendar

Time travel isn't just science fiction. You can zip around the Outlook Calendar faster than you can say "Star Trek." Talk about futuristic — the calendar can schedule appointments for you well into the year 4500!

To learn the various ways of moving between dates in your calendar, follow these steps:

1. **Click Calendar in the navigation pane (or press Ctrl+2).**

   The Folder pane shows the Date Navigator (the little monthly calendar) at the top and a list of calendars at the bottom. If you have the To-Do bar open, the Date Navigator also appears there. (Figure 9-2 doesn't show the To-Do bar.)

2. **Switch to Month view if it is not already displayed.**

   To switch views, use the buttons on the View tab.

REMEMBER

3. **Drag the scroll bar to the right of the calendar downward to scroll to the next month, and then back to the current month.**

   This is one way to view different dates. You can drag the scroll box to scroll quickly, or you can click above or below the scroll box to move one screen at a time.

4. **Click the right arrow at the top of the Date Navigator to switch to the next month.**

   This is a quick way to view different dates.

5. **Click the left arrow above the current calendar (the big version, not the Date Navigator) to return to the current month.**

   If you're in Month view, doing this has the same effect as using the arrows on the Date Navigator. If you're in some other view, like Day or Week, the arrows above the calendar move the view one screen forward or back. For example, in Week view, it moves one week at a time.

6. **Click the month and year at the top of the Date Navigator to open a list of months, and then hold down the mouse button while you drag up or down to select a different month. Then release the mouse button.**

   This is a handy way of quickly moving ahead or backward by several months. You can jump up to 3 months ahead or backward using this method. See Figure 9-3.

7. **On the Home tab of the Ribbon, click Today.**

   This is a quick way to return to the current date. You can also click the Today button above and to the left of the calendar.

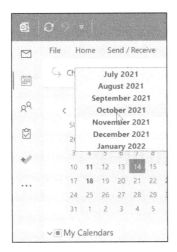

FIGURE 9-3:
Jump ahead or
back 3 months at
a time by clicking
the month and
year above the
Date Navigator.

When you need to access a certain date quickly that's far in the past or future, follow these steps:

1. **Press Ctrl+G.**

   G is short for "go to." The Go To Date dialog box opens with a date highlighted, as shown in Figure 9-4.

FIGURE 9-4:
The Go To Date
dialog box.

2. **To go to another date, type the date you want in the Date box as you normally would, such as *January 15, 2022* or *1/15/22*.**

   A really neat way to change dates is to type something like *45 days ago* or *93 days from now*. Try it. Outlook understands simple English when it comes to dates. Don't get fancy though; Outlook doesn't understand *Four score and seven years ago*. (But who does?)

3. **(Optional) Open the Show In drop-down menu and choose a different view.**

   By default, the desired date appears in whatever calendar view you are already working with.

4. **Click OK.**

No matter which date you land on, you can plunge right in and start scheduling. You can double-click the time and date of when you want an appointment to occur and then enter the particulars, or you can double-check the details of an appointment on that date by double-clicking the date and making changes to the appointment if necessary.

Meetings Galore: Scheduling Appointments

Outlook makes it surprisingly easy to add appointments — and even easier to find items you've entered. It also warns you when you've scheduled two dates simultaneously. (Very embarrassing!)

TIP

Press Ctrl+Shift+A from any Outlook module to create an appointment. The catch is that you won't see the appointment on the calendar until you switch to the Calendar view.

The quick-and-dirty way to enter an appointment

Some appointments don't need much explanation. If you're having lunch with Mom on Friday, there's no reason to make a big production out of entering the appointment:

1. **Make sure the Calendar module is open in a view that shows the hours of the day.**

    For example, Day, Week, and Work Week views do.

2. **Click the box on the calendar for the starting time of your appointment on the desired day.**

    You can also click and drag to create an appointment of a longer duration than the default.

3. **Type a description of the appointment.**

    For example, *Lunch with Mom*.

4. **Press Enter.**

   Your appointment is now part of your official schedule — faster than you can say "Waiter!"

TIP

You can also click in a day on the Month calendar view and type an appointment, but it won't be set for a particular time; it'll be set to All Day. You can then go in later and edit the appointment to assign a certain time or leave it general.

The complete way to enter an appointment

Appointments you set up at work often require you to include a little more information than you'd need for your lunch date with Mom. You might want to add:

>> Details about the location of a meeting

>> Notes about the meeting agenda

>> A category (so you can show the boss how much time you spend with your clients)

When you want to give an appointment the full treatment, use the complete method:

1. **In the Calendar module, click the New Appointment button on the Home tab on the Ribbon (or press Ctrl+N).**

   The Appointment form opens.

   You can also double-click on the calendar at the desired date and time, or drag to select a time block of multiple units (whatever you have the interval set for). These methods have the advantage of filling in the date and time automatically for you.

2. **Set or change the date and time as needed.**

   On the Start Time line, choose the desired date and time; then do the same thing on the End Time line.

   If you started the appointment by double-clicking a date/time block on the Calendar in any view except Month, the starting values for the start time are the date and time where you double-clicked; adjust as needed.

WARNING

   If you started the appointment by double-clicking a date in Month view, the date is filled in, but the time is set to All Day by default (which means no time is specified). To specify a time, you must first deselect the All Day check box.

3. **Click in the Subject box and type something there to help you remember what the appointment is about.**

   For example, type *Dentist appointment* or *Deposit lottery winnings* or whatever. This text shows up on your calendar.

4. **Click in the Location box and enter the location.**

   This step is optional, but it can be helpful information to add to your appointment.

TIP

5. **Add any other information you need to remember about your appointment.**

   The large empty box on the Appointment form is a great place to save driving directions, meeting agendas, or anything else that might be helpful to remember when the appointment time arrives. Figure 9-5 shows a completed appointment.

6. **Click the Save & Close button.**

   The appointment you created appears in your calendar. You may have to change your Calendar view by clicking the Date Navigator on the date the appointment occurs so you can see your new appointment.

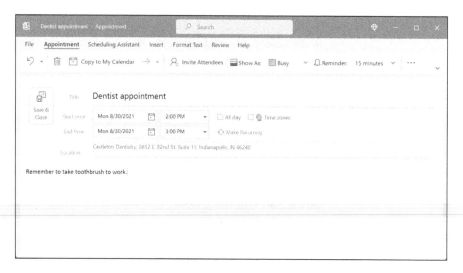

REMEMBER

If you want to see reminders for all your important appointments, you must keep Outlook running so the reminders pop up. You can keep Outlook running in the background if you start a second program, such as Microsoft Word. When the reminder time arrives, you see a dialog box similar to the one shown in Figure 9-6.

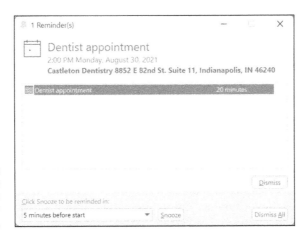

Changing an appointment's date or time

You can be as fickle as you want with Outlook. In fact, to change the time of a scheduled item, just drag the appointment from where it is to where you want it to be.

Moving an appointment by dragging

To change an appointment by dragging it, follow these steps:

1. **Switch to an appropriate view for the change you want to make.**

   The best view depends on whether the appointment is changing its start time or not (in which case you need a view that shows times) and on how far apart the original and revised dates are.

   You'll need to be able to see the original date/time and the new date/time in a single view. If they're both in the same week, Week view will work. If they're in the same month, Month view will work. If they're more than a month apart, this is not the best method for you; see "Moving an appointment using the Appointment form" later in this chapter.

2. **In the Calendar module, click the appointment to change.**

   A dark border appears around the edge of the appointment.

3. **Drag the appointment to the date and time you want it to be.**

   If you're using Month view, you won't be able to set the time by dragging, so the original time will be retained on the new date.

TIP

Technically, there *is* a way to move an appointment by dragging when the dates are far apart, but it involves an extra step. You can set the Date Navigator to the desired month and then drag the appointment from the big calendar to the appropriate date on the Date Navigator. That's a lot of bother, though, and you will probably find the form method easier.

Copying an appointment by dragging

TIP

If you want to copy an appointment for another time, hold down Ctrl while you use the mouse to drag the appointment to another time or date. For example, if you're scheduling a summer intern orientation from 9 a.m. to 11 a.m. and again from 1 p.m. to 3 p.m., you can create the 9 a.m. appointment and then copy it to 1 p.m. by holding down Ctrl and dragging the appointment. Then, you have two appointments with the same subject, location, and date — but with different start times.

If you copy an appointment to a different date by dragging the appointment to a date on the Date Navigator, you keep the hour of the appointment but change the date.

Moving an appointment using the Appointment form

You can also change an appointment by modifying its date and time settings in its own window. This method works best when the new date can't be seen on the calendar at the same time as the original one, or when you want to change other details such as the location or the notes. Follow these steps:

1. **In the Calendar module, double-click the appointment.**

    The Appointment window opens.

2. **Click the Calendar icon in the Start Time box to see the selected month's calendar.**

    A drop-down calendar appears, as shown in Figure 9-7.

3. **Pick the month by clicking the arrow buttons to the left or right of the month's name.**

    Clicking the left arrow moves you one month earlier; clicking the right arrow moves you one month later.

4. **Click the day of the month you want.**

FIGURE 9-7:
The drop-down
calendar on the
Appointment
form.

5. **Click in the Start Time text box and enter the appointment's new time, if needed.**

   You can also use the scroll-down button to the right of the time to select a new start time.

6. **Make any other changes you need in the appointment.**

   Click the information you want to change and type the revised information over it. For example, you might want to change the end time to change the appointment's duration.

7. **Click the Save & Close button.**

Adjusting the length of an appointment

Imagine that your dentist calls to tell you that you *won't* need a root canal after all but that you'll still need a routine checkup.

There are two ways to change the appointment duration: by dragging, or by adjusting the End Time setting in the Appointment form.

To change the length of an appointment by dragging, follow these steps:

1. **In the Calendar module, click the appointment in Day, Work Week, or Week view.**

   The dragging method requires you to work in Day, Work Week, or Week view because you need a view where you can see the time without opening the appointment.

2. **Move the mouse pointer over the handles at the top or the bottom of the appointment.**

   When the pointer is in the right place, it turns into a two-headed arrow. See Figure 9-8.

3. **Drag the line down or up to lengthen or shorten the appointment duration.**

The mouse pointer becomes an arrow.

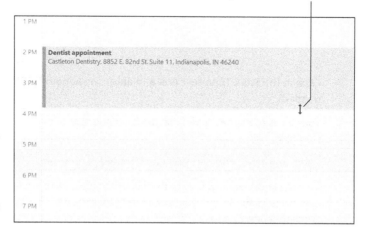

FIGURE 9-8:
Drag the top or
bottom of an
appointment up
or down to
change the
appointment
duration.

You can specify a more precise time than the time intervals on the calendar, but you'll need to use the Appointment form method. Follow these steps:

1. **In the Calendar module, double-click the appointment.**

   The Appointment form opens.

2. **Click the End Time box.**

   You can either type a precise time here or use the drop-down menu on the End Time box to select a time.

3. **Type the end time or select it from the drop-down menu.**

4. **Click the Save & Close button.**

REMEMBER

You can adjust the time intervals shown on the calendar to be more or less precise. For example, if you commonly have appointments that start at 15 or 45 minutes past the hour, set the time interval for 15 minutes. To do this, on the View tab, click Time Scale and choose a different grid interval. (With the Simplified Ribbon, you might need to click More Commands to access the Time Scale command.)

TIP

You can enter times in Outlook without adding colons and often without using a.m. or p.m. Outlook translates 443 as 4:43 p.m. If you plan lots of appointments at 4:43 a.m., just type *443A*. (Just don't call *me* at that hour, okay?) You can also enter time in the 24-hour format — 1643 would be 4:43 p.m. — but Outlook likes normal time better, so the time will display as 4:43.

Cancelling an appointment

Well, sometimes things just don't work out. Sorry about that. Even if it's hard for you to forget, with the click of a mouse, Outlook deletes dates you otherwise fondly remember. Okay, *two* clicks of a mouse.

To delete an appointment (after you've called to break it), you can do any of the following:

>> **Right-click the appointment and choose Delete.**

>> **Select the appointment and press Delete on the keyboard or press Ctrl+D.**

>> **Select the appointment and then on the Appointment tab of the Ribbon, click Delete.**

As far as Outlook is concerned, your appointment is cancelled.

TIP

If you make a mistake, you can immediately undo the deletion by pressing Ctrl+Z (the shortcut for the Undo command). This only works if you haven't done anything else in the interim, though; Undo only goes back one step.

Scheduling a recurring appointment

Some appointments are one-time things, like job interviews and blind dates. Others happen on a regular basis, like staff meetings.

To create a *recurring* (that is, regularly scheduled) appointment, follow these steps:

1. **In the Calendar module, click the appointment you want to repeat.**

    The appointment is highlighted and the Appointment tab becomes available on the Ribbon.

2. **Click the Recurrence button on the Appointment tab.**

    The Appointment Recurrence dialog box opens, as shown in Figure 9-9.

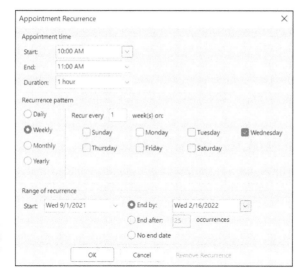

FIGURE 9-9:
The Appointment
Recurrence
dialog box.

3. **Click in the Start box and enter the start time.**

   Outlook assumes your appointment is the same length as the original appointment. Click in the End box and enter an end time if needed.

4. **In the Recurrence Pattern section, click the Daily, Weekly, Monthly, or Yearly option.**

   This is the interval at which the appointment recurs.

5. **Choose how many times the appointment occurs, and on what schedule.**

   The exact names of the boxes here depend on the pattern you chose in the preceding step. For example, in Figure 9-9 you see the options for Weekly.

6. **In the Range of Recurrence section, enter the first occurrence in the Start box.**

7. **Choose when the appointments will stop.**

   You can select from these options:

   - End By (a certain date)

   - End After (a certain number of occurrences)

   - No End Date (infinity)

8. **Click the OK button.**

   The Appointment Recurrence dialog box closes.

In every view except Month, your recurring appointment appears on the Calendar with a symbol to show that it's a recurring appointment, as shown in Figure 9-10. The symbol looks like two little arrows chasing each other's tails — a little bit like people who go to too many recurring meetings. Coincidence? I don't think so.

FIGURE 9-10:
Repeating appointments display the recurrence symbol in the lower-right corner.

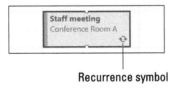

Recurrence symbol

Changing a recurring appointment

Even a recurring appointment gets changed once in a while. Edit a recurring appointment this way:

1. **In the Calendar module, double-click the appointment you want to edit.**

   The Open Recurring Item dialog box opens.

2. **Choose The Entire Series.**

3. **Click the OK button.**

   The appointment appears, displaying the recurrence pattern above the location, as shown in Figure 9-11.

FIGURE 9-11:
A recurring appointment includes a description about how and when the appointment recurs.

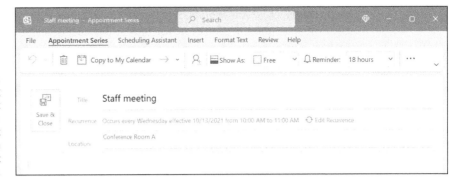

4. **Click Recurrence.**

   The Appointment Recurrence dialog box opens.

SCHEDULING YOUR MAIN EVENTS

You can enter more than just appointments in your calendar. You can also add events (in other words, all-day appointments) by selecting the All Day check box on the Appointment form. You can also start one by clicking the New Items button on the Home tab and choosing All Day Event. Then, follow the same steps you used to create an appointment. (Refer to "Meetings Galore: Scheduling Appointments," earlier in this chapter.)

Events correspond to occurrences that land on your calendar (such as business trips or conferences) that last longer than an appointment — and you can still enter routine appointments that happen during the event. For example, you can create an event called 2022 Auto Show and then add appointments to see General Motors at 9 a.m., Chrysler at noon, Ford at 3 p.m., and the Ghost of Christmas Past at 5 p.m.

5. **Edit the details for the appointment and then click OK.**

6. **Click the Save & Close button.**

TIP

I find it helpful to enter regular appointments, such as classes or reoccurring recreational events, even if I'm sure I won't forget them. Entering all my activities into Outlook prevents me from scheduling conflicting appointments.

Printing Your Appointments

Plain old paper is still everybody's favorite medium for reading. No matter how slick your computer organizer is, you may still need old-fashioned ink on paper to make it really useful.

WARNING

To be brutally honest, Outlook's calendar-printing feature has always been pretty weak. If you can't figure out how to print your calendar the way you want, it's probably not your fault. I'll try to help you out here.

Here's how to print your calendar:

1. **From the Calendar module, switch to the view that you want to print.**

    This isn't critical, but it saves you a step later. (You'll see.)

    For example, to print a Week calendar, switch to Week view.

2. **Select a date within the range of dates you want to print.**

   The range of dates selected to print depends on the view you are in. For a Week calendar, the entire week that the date you selected falls within is the range. For a Month calendar, the entire month will print.

   If you don't like having to select a date range this way, skip it for the moment; you'll see another method for selecting the date range in Step 5.

3. **Click the File tab and choose Print (or press Ctrl+P).**

   The Print controls appear, as shown in Figure 9-12.

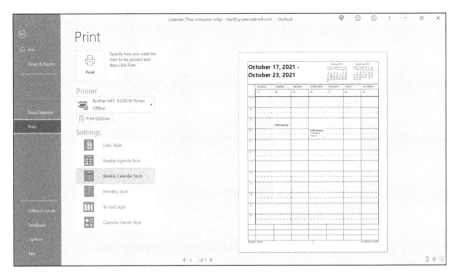

FIGURE 9-12:
Calendar printing
options.

4. **In the Settings section, choose a style.**

   You can skip this step if you switched to the correct view in Step 1, because the current view is the default here.

   Daily, Weekly, Monthly, Tri-fold, and Calendar Details are the basic choices. You can also define your own print styles in Outlook, so you may eventually have quite a collection of choices showing up in this box. Outlook also shows you a preview of the page you're about to print, which eliminates surprises.

5. **(Optional) To check and/or adjust the date range to print, do the following:**

   a. **Click the Print Options button.**

      The Print dialog box opens. See Figure 9-13.

   b. **At the bottom of the dialog box, in the Print Range section, adjust the date range by changing the Start and End dates.**

FIGURE 9-13:
The Print dialog
box when
printing a
calendar.

6. **Click the Print button.**

   If you completed Step 5, the Print button is at the bottom of the Print dialog box; if you skipped Step 5, the Print button is in the upper-left section of Backstage view. They both do the same thing.

   You can also click Preview to return to the print preview and *then* click Print. That's an extra step, but it does allow you to see the preview one last time before you commit to using a sheet of paper.

   Your calendar is sent to the printer.

Adding Holidays

What days are most important to working people? The days when they don't have to work! Outlook can automatically add calendar entries for every major holiday so you don't forget to take the day off. (As if you'd forget!) In fact, Outlook can automatically add holidays from more than 70 different countries and several major religions. Thus, if you have a yen (so to speak) to celebrate Japanese Greenery Day, an urge to observe Estonian Independence Day, or suddenly want to send a gift for Ataturk's birthday, Outlook Calendar can remind you to observe those monumental events.

To add holidays to your calendar, follow these steps:

1. **Click the File tab.**

2. **Choose Options.**

   The Outlook Options dialog box opens.

3. **Click Calendar.**

4. **Click the Add Holidays button (under Calendar Options).**

   You see a list of nations and religions.

5. **Click the holidays you want to add.**

   The countries and religions are mixed in together, so keep scrolling to find the one you want. For example, Jewish religious holidays are between Japan and Jordan on the list. In some countries, the federal holidays at least somewhat correspond with the holidays of a particular religion.

6. **Click OK to add the holidays to your calendar.**

7. **When the holidays have been added, click OK to close the confirmation box.**

8. **Click OK to close the Outlook Options dialog box.**

   Then go check out the calendar to see your holidays there. It's easiest to browse them in Month view.

Handling Multiple Calendars

People who led double lives were once considered thrilling and dangerous. Now they're underachievers. You only have two lives? Well, get busy, pal — get three more. Outlook can manage as many calendars as you have lives. Even if you're a mild-mannered person who just likes peace and quiet, you might want to keep your personal calendar and your business calendar separate by creating two calendars in Outlook.

Creating multiple calendars

To create an additional Outlook Calendar, follow these steps:

1. **From the Calendar module, do one of the following:**

    - Using the Simplified Ribbon: On the Home tab, click Add and then click New Blank Calendar.

    - Using the Classic Ribbon: On the Home tab, click Add Calendar in the Manage Calendars group and then click Create New Blank Calendar.

    The Create New Folder dialog box opens. This is similar to creating a mail folder, but you're creating a special kind of folder that displays as a calendar.

2. **Click the Name box and type a name for your new calendar.**

3. **Make sure that the Folder Contains setting is set to Calendar Items.**

    This tells Outlook what kind of folder you are creating. (Each calendar is considered a folder.)

4. **In the Select Where to Place the Folder section of the dialog box, select the email account with which to associate this calendar.**

    See Figure 9-14. You might create a new calendar just for your workplace appointments and associate it with your work email, for example.

FIGURE 9-14:
Creating a new calendar.

5. Click OK.

The name you've assigned to your new calendar appears in the Folder pane — to the right of a blank check box. If you select the check box, your new calendar will appear side by side with your original calendar — using the same Day, Week, or Month view, as shown in Figure 9-15. If you deselect the check box, the calendar you deselected disappears.

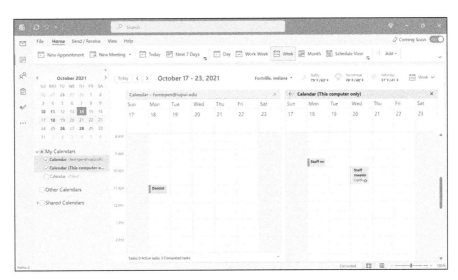

FIGURE 9-15:
Two calendars
side by side.

TIP

If you don't see the new calendar on the My Calendars list in the Folder pane, quit and restart Outlook and then look for it again.

Managing multiple calendars

You can't be in two places at once. Even if you could, you wouldn't want your boss to know that; otherwise, you'd end up having to be everywhere at once for the same pay. That's why you'll like how you can superimpose Outlook Calendars to avoid schedule conflicts.

When you open two calendars side by side, one of the two calendars displays an arrow on the tab of the calendar's name at the top of the screen. By clicking that arrow, you can superimpose the two calendars to see whether any appointments conflict, as shown in Figure 9-16. While they're combined like that, any new appointments you create will be placed on the active calendar. You can tell which one is active because it's selected on the My Calendars list in the Folder pane, and its name appears in bold on the calendar tab above the calendar (pointed out in Figure 9-16). To switch which calendar is active, click its tab.

Calendar tabs

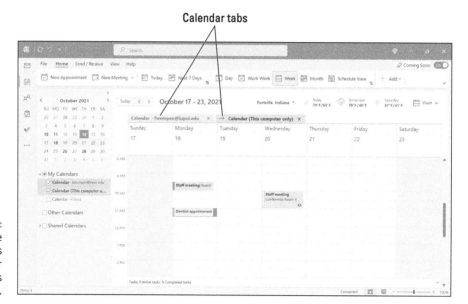

FIGURE 9-16:
Superimpose
two calendars
to keep your
appointments
straight.

Click the arrow again to un-superimpose it so that the calendars are separate again.

Sharing Calendars

Before we start talking about calendar sharing, I want you to check something out. Display any single calendar (not a combined one). If you've got some combined calendars, as in the preceding section, deselect their check boxes in the Folder pane to close all of them but one.

First, switch the Ribbon to Classic Ribbon mode. Then on the Home tab, look at the Manage Calendars group. Does your screen look more like Figure 9-17 or Figure 9-18? This little experiment will tell you whether that calendar is associated with an Exchange account or not. It matters because the calendar-sharing options are different.

If there are multiple calendars in the Folder pane, click each one in turn to display it. (Only display one at a time.) Check the Home tab for each one to see if the options change. Now you've got a baseline of what you're working with, calendar-wise.

TECHNICAL STUFF

An Outlook.com or Microsoft 365 email account has most of the same calendaring options as a regular business Exchange account because they are administered by Microsoft via a cloud-based version of Exchange. You won't see a Groups group (as in Figure 9-17), but nearly everything else will be the same. Chapter 15 talks about some of the special features you'll encounter in Exchange-based servers.

I had you switch to the Classic Ribbon to do this experiment because some of the settings are more readily visible. (You can get to most of them via the Simplified Ribbon, but they're not as obvious.)

Sharing a calendar associated with an Exchange account

When viewing a calendar associated with an Exchange account, you have access to calendar-sharing tools via your Exchange server. Follow these steps to share your calendar with certain people on your company's Exchange network:

1. **Make sure a calendar is displayed that is associated with your Exchange-based email account.**

   If you don't do this, you won't be able to complete the rest of the steps.

2. **On the Home tab, click Share (if using the Simplified Ribbon) or Share Calendar (if using the Classic Ribbon).**

   If you have multiple sharable calendars, a menu will appear that lists them; click the calendar you want to share.

   The Calendar Properties dialog box opens. If your organization has already defined certain sharing properties for your calendar, they appear in the Currently Sharing With list. Figure 9-19 shows an example of a predefined share. Otherwise, that list is blank.

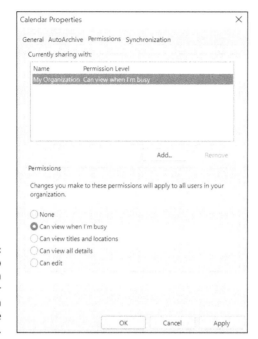

3. **Click Add.**

   The Add Users dialog box opens. The address book that appears depends on the default for your organization. You can open the Address Book drop-down menu at the top of the dialog box to select a different address book.

WARNING

   Keep in mind that while you can invite anyone to share your calendar, only people who use an Exchange server for their email will be able to actually view it when sharing with this method.

4. **Add users to the Add box at the bottom of the dialog box in one of these ways:**

   a. Type email addresses directly into the Add box, as in Figure 9-20. Separate addresses with semicolons.

   b. Double-click the user's name in the Name list.

5. **Click OK.**

   The Calendar Properties dialog box reappears.

6. **In the Permissions section of the dialog box, choose what permission that person (or those people) will have.**

   The choices of sharing permissions you see here may vary depending on the server settings.

7. **Click OK.**

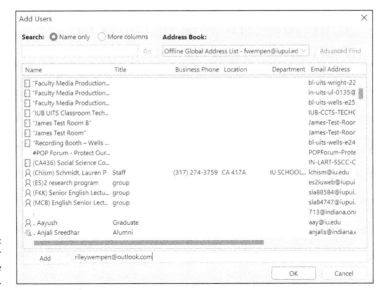

FIGURE 9-20:
Inviting another
user to share
your calendar.

Accepting a calendar-share invitation

The person (or people) who you sent a calendar-sharing invitation to (in the pre-ceding section) will receive an email message with the invitation. After they click the Accept and View button in the email message, and follow any additional prompts that appear (the details of which will vary depending on the server), they will be able to view your calendar.

After that, your calendar will appear in their Calendar module, under the Shared Calendars section of the Folder pane. See Figure 9-21.

FIGURE 9-21:
A shared calendar
appears in the
Shared Calendars
section of the
Folder pane.

Calendar-sharing options for non-Exchange accounts

If your Home tab in Classic Ribbon mode looked like Figure 9-18 rather than Figure 9-17, then you can't share calendars the way the previous sections described it. (There may be a Share Calendar button on the Ribbon, but clicking it doesn't do anything.) However, you have some other calendar-sharing options at your fingertips instead.

One of them is to publish your calendar to a WebDAV server. WebDAV is a rather "mature" (old) technology for sharing data on the web. If you happen to have access to one, you can publish your calendar there by choosing Home ⇨ Publish Online ⇨ Publish to WebDAV Server. I'm not going to get into the nitty-gritty details of this option because it's not common, but now you know it's there.

A more common option is to share your calendar via email. Sending an email calendar creates a static copy of the current calendar to send; it doesn't send a live link that will be updated as you later make changes. To send your calendar via email, follow these steps:

1. **Switch to the Classic Ribbon mode if it's not already displayed.**

    This is one of the few things you actually do need the Classic Ribbon for.

2. **From the Home tab in the Calendar module, click Email Calendar.**

    A new email message starts, and the Send a Calendar via Email dialog box opens.

3. **Open the Calendar drop-down menu and choose which calendar to send.**

4. **Open the Date Range drop-down menu and choose a date range.**

    You can choose Today, Tomorrow, Next 7 Days, Next 30 Days, Whole Calendar, or Specify Dates. If you choose Specify Dates, Start and End boxes appear below the Date Range box, where you can enter custom dates.

5. **Open the Detail drop-down menu and choose the desired level of detail.**

    Your choices are Full Details, Availability Only, or Limited Details.

    Figure 9-22 shows the completed dialog box.

6. **Click OK.**

    A file containing the calendar information is created and attached to the email message.

7. **Enter the recipient's email address in the To box.**

8. **Complete and send the email as you normally would.**

9. **Switch back to the Simplified Ribbon if you prefer it, or if you want your screen to match the figures in this book.**

TIP

Another way to send a static copy of a calendar via email is to save it as a file and then attach that file to an outgoing email. Display the desired calendar and then choose File ⇨ Save Calendar. In the Save As dialog box, pick a name and location and then click Save. Then compose a new email message as you normally would and add that file as an attachment.

Chapter **10**

Staying on Task: To-Do Lists and More

Some people say that work expands to fill the available time — and chances are your boss is one of those people. (Who else would keep expanding your work to fill your available time?) One way of saving time is to keep a list of the tasks that fill your time. That way, you can avoid getting too many more tasks to do.

Outlook makes it easy to remember and monitor your daily work. Organizing your tasks doesn't have to be a task in and of itself. I used to scrawl a to-do list on paper and hope I'd find the list in time to do everything I had written down. Now Outlook pops up and reminds me about the things I'm trying to forget to do just before I forget to do them. It also keeps track of when I'm supposed to have done my daily tasks and when I actually did them. That way, I can use all the work I was supposed to do yesterday as an excuse not to do the drudgery I'm supposed to do today. Sort of. (Outlook still won't *do* the stuff for me; it just tells me how far I'm falling behind. Be forewarned.)

REMEMBER

As I mentioned earlier in the book, the latest version of Outlook (at least at this writing) has two separate modules for managing tasks: one called Tasks and one called To-Do. The bulk of this chapter covers the Tasks module, but I explain the To-Do module at the end of this chapter. The confusing part is that within the Tasks module is a To-Do List that doesn't have anything to do with the To-Do module. Just accept that as "it is what it is" and move forward.

Entering New Tasks in the Tasks Module

I don't mean to add work to your busy schedule; you already have plenty of that. But adding a task in Outlook isn't such a big to-do. Even though you can store gobs of information about your tasks in Outlook, getting them into Outlook is pretty simple.

The quick-and-dirty way to enter a task

When you're viewing your Tasks list, a little box at the top of the list says *Click Here to Add a New Task* (or *Type a New Task*, depending on which view you're using). Do what the box says. If you can't see the box, switch to a different view (like Simple List) or go on to the following section to discover the regular, slightly slower way to enter the task.

To enter a task by using the quick-and-dirty method, follow these steps:

1. **In the Tasks module, click the text that says *Click Here to Add a New Task* (or *Type a New Task*).**

    If you don't see either one, switch to a different view: On the View tab of the Ribbon, click Change View and then switch to a different view, such as Simple List. You'll learn more about views later in this chapter.

2. **Type the subject of your task.**

    Your task subject appears.

3. **Press the Enter key.**

    Your new task moves down to the Tasks list with your other tasks.

Isn't that easy? If only the tasks themselves were that easy to do. Maybe in the next version of Outlook, the tasks will get easier, too (in my dreams).

The regular way to enter a task

The official way to enter a task is through the Task form, which requires a tiny bit more effort but lets you enter much more detailed information. But you don't need to work your fingers to the bone; as long as you enter a subject for the task, you've done all you really must do. If you want to go hog wild and enter all sorts of due dates or have Outlook remind you to actually *complete* the tasks you've entered (heaven forbid!), you just need to put information in a few more boxes.

To add a task to your Tasks list, follow these steps:

1. **In the Tasks module, in the navigation bar under the My Tasks heading, click To-Do List.**

   Later in this chapter I explain the relationship between Tasks and To-Do, and why you might see multiple Tasks folders under My Tasks.

2. **Click the New Task button on the Home tab of the Ribbon (or press Ctrl+N).**

   The Task form opens.

3. **Type the subject of the task in the Subject box.**

   Use a subject that will help you remember what the task is. The main reason to create a task is to help you remember to do the task.

   TIP

   You can finish at this point by jumping to Step 11 (click the Save & Close button or press Alt+S) if you want to add only the subject of the task to your list. If you want to note a due date, start date, reminders, and so on, you have more to do. All the rest of the steps are optional; you can skip the ones that don't interest you.

4. **(Optional) To assign a start date to the task, click the Start Date box and choose a start date.**

   You don't need a start date; it's strictly for your own use.

   TIP

   When you're entering information in a dialog box, such as the Task form, you can press Tab to move from one text box to the next. You can use the mouse to click each text box before you type, but pressing Tab is a bit faster. You can also move in the opposite direction by pressing Shift+Tab.

5. **(Optional) To assign a due date to the task, click the Due Date box and choose a start date.**

   By default it's the same as the start date.

   REMEMBER

   You can enter start dates and due dates in Outlook in several ways. You can type *6/1/2022, the first Wednesday of June,* or *three weeks from Wednesday.* You can also click the button at the right end of the Due Date text box and choose the date you want from the drop-down calendar.

6. **(Optional) Click the Status box and choose the status of the task.**

   If you haven't begun, leave Status set to Not Started. You can also choose In Progress, Completed, Waiting on Someone Else, or Deferred.

7. **(Optional) Click the Priority box and choose the priority.**

   If you don't change anything, the priority stays Normal. You can also choose High or Low.

8. **(Optional) Select the Reminder check box if you want to be reminded before the task is due.**

   If you'd rather forget the task, forget the reminder. But then, why enter the task?

9. **(Optional) Click the date box next to the Reminder check box and choose the date when you want to be reminded.**

   If you entered a due date, Outlook has already entered that date in the Reminder box. You can enter any date you want, as shown in Figure 10-1. If you click the icon on the right of the date box, a calendar appears. You can click the date you desire in the calendar.

TIP

There's no reason that the reminder date you enter has to be the same as the due date of the task. You might consider setting a reminder sometime before the task is due. That way, you avoid that last-minute angst over things you forgot until the last minute. Unless you enjoy last-minute anxiety, you should use reminders.

Save & Close

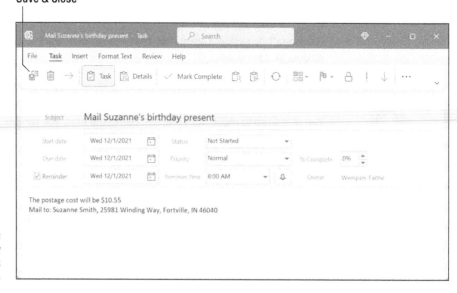

FIGURE 10-1:
Enter your new task in the Task form.

10. **(Optional) Enter the time in the time box for when you want to activate the reminder.**

The easiest way to set a time is to type the numbers for the time. You don't need colons or anything special. For example, if you want to finish by 2:35 p.m., just type *235*. Outlook assumes you're not a vampire; it schedules your tasks and appointments during daylight hours unless you say otherwise. (If you *are* a vampire, type *235a* and Outlook translates that to 2:35 a.m. If you simply *must* use correct punctuation, Outlook can handle that, too.)

11. **(Optional) In the text box, enter miscellaneous notes and information about this task.**

If you need to keep directions to the appointment, a list of supplies, or whatever, it all fits here.

Figure 10-1 shows a completed task example.

12. **Click the Save & Close button to finish.**

Your new task is now included in your Tasks list, waiting to be done by some fortunate person. Unfortunately, that person is probably you.

Working with Tasks Folders

Now that you've got a task (or two) on your list, let's take a step back and admire the Tasks module's interface, shall we? It looks pretty simple at first, but the more you investigate it, the more you'll appreciate the many different options and features available for viewing and managing your tasks.

REMEMBER

When I talk about the To-Do List in this section, I'm referring to the list within the Tasks module. The To-Do module you access from the navigation pane is an entirely separate thing, and I explain it at the end of this chapter.

Tasks vs. To-Do List: What's the difference?

When you are in the Tasks module, in the navigation pane on the left, you probably see a To-Do List, as well as one or more Tasks lists. A *Tasks list* is a folder that holds the tasks you create. A Tasks list is associated with a particular data file, so if you have multiple data files in Outlook, you may have multiple Tasks lists. The Tasks list travels with the data file, so if you move or copy the data file, it rides along.

Tasks lists associated with Exchange, Outlook.com, or Microsoft 365 accounts can be accessed online; they are stored on the Exchange server that hosts the account. In the navigation pane in Outlook, the associated email address appears next to the folder name, so you can keep track of which account it belongs to.

Tasks lists associated with other email accounts are local — that is, they can only be seen and used from the PC on which they were created. Such lists will usually appear with *(This computer only)* to the right of their names to help you remember that. Figure 10-2 shows examples of an Exchange account, an Outlook.com account, and a local Tasks list.

> My Tasks
> **To-Do List**
> Tasks (This computer only)
> Tasks - fwempen@iupui.edu
> Tasks - RileyWempen@outlook.com

REMEMBER

The To-Do List is not an actual folder, but a view that aggregates the content from all the individual Tasks lists. It also includes all the items you have flagged in other modules, such as email messages you have flagged for follow-up.

SETTING THE DEFAULT DATA FILE

If you display the To-Do List and then create a new task, which Tasks list does it end up on? That depends on which email account is set as the default. If you want to do a quick test, display To-Do List, create a phony task, and then look at the different Tasks lists to see where it is. To change which data file is the default, choose File > Account Settings > Account Settings, and click the Data Files tab. Select the desired data file and click Set as Default.

One little gotcha — if you have more than one Exchange-based data file set up in Outlook, you won't be able to choose a non-Exchange data file as the default. You can set it as the default for sending and receiving email (on the Email tab of the Account Settings dialog box), but it can't be the default for tasks and other non-email activity.

Browsing a data file's folders

Some data files will have Tasks folders by default and others won't; it all depends on the account type and how you have set it up.

You can browse the folders associated with each data file from the Folders module. Here's how to access it:

1. **In the navigation pane, click the More button (. . .) to see the additional modules that don't appear by default, and click Folders.**

   The navigation pane is replaced by a Folders pane, showing all the folders for all the data files in separate lists.

2. **Expand the folder list for each data file if it is not already expanded and look for a Tasks folder.**

   Tasks folders have an icon that looks like a clipboard with a red check mark on it. They also usually have the word "Task" in their name. For example, in Figure 10-3, you can see that riley@sycamoreknoll.com has a Tasks (This Computer Only) folder. The phrase "(This Computer Only)" is actually part of the folder name; Outlook added that when it created it. You learn how to rename a Tasks list later in this chapter.

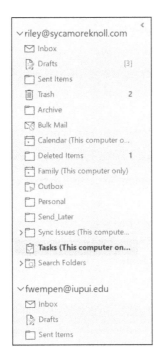

FIGURE 10-3:
The Folders module enables you to browse all the folders within each data file.

Creating new Tasks lists

It's easy to create new Tasks lists any time you want them. After you create them, they appear on the navigation pane in the Tasks module. It is customary for a data file to have just one Tasks list (if any), or one per email account, but it's not a requirement; you could have separate Tasks lists for different projects or clients, for example. (Remember that the To-Do List aggregates all the tasks from all lists, so you don't have to jump around between Tasks lists looking for a certain task.)

TIP

If you create a new Tasks list and it doesn't immediately show up in the navigation pane, close Outlook and reopen it.

To create a new Tasks list, follow these steps:

1. **Open the Folders module.**

    You learned that skill in the preceding section.

2. **Decide which data file into which you want to place the new Tasks list folder.**

    It may be helpful to expand each data file's folder list (by clicking the arrow to the left of its name) so you can see what Tasks lists, if any, are already present.

3. **Right-click the desired data file name and choose New Folder.**

    The Create New Folder dialog box opens.

4. **In the Name box, type a name for the new Tasks list.**

    Try to be a little more creative than *Tasks* for the name. After all, the idea here is to give yourself more options for task storage, and you probably already have a folder named Tasks.

5. **Open the Folder Contains drop-down menu and choose Task Items.**

    This step is important; it is what makes the folder able to hold tasks.

6. **In the Select Where to Place the Folder list, confirm that the desired data file is selected.**

    In Figure 10-4, for example, I'm creating a new Tasks list in my fwempen@ gmail.com account's data file.

7. **Click OK to create the new Tasks folder.**

8. **Switch to the Tasks module.**

    If you don't see the new folder there, exit Outlook and restart it to refresh the list.

FIGURE 10-4:
Creating a new
Tasks folder.

Renaming a Tasks list

If you have multiple Tasks folders that are all named the same, you might want to rename them so it's easier to remember which account each one is associated with. Follow these steps to rename a Tasks list:

1. **In the navigation pane, right-click the Tasks list to rename.**

   A shortcut menu appears.

2. **Choose Rename Folder.**

3. **Type a new name for the Tasks list.**

   This name will not only appear here on the navigation pane but will also be changed in the data file.

4. **Press Enter.**

Moving tasks between lists

If you accidentally create a task on the wrong list, it's a snap to move it. Just drag and drop the task onto the desired list name in the navigation pane.

Switching Up the View

The Tasks module provides several different views you can use to change how your Tasks list appears. (That's not unique; other modules do that too, of course.) But because there's some potential for confusion, I want to point out how things work view-wise before we go any further.

A *view* in the Tasks module is a preset combination of choices made about how the Tasks list will appear. These choices include:

- » **Fields:** Which fields will appear

- » **Sorting:** By which field(s) the tasks will be sorted, and in what order (ascending or descending)

- » **Grouping:** By which field the tasks will be grouped, and in what order

- » **Filtering:** What criteria will be used to include or exclude certain tasks from the list

You can change the view from the View tab's Change View button, shown in Figure 10-5. In Classic Ribbon mode, you can also choose a view from the Home tab's Current View gallery.

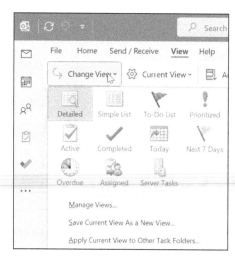

FIGURE 10-5:
Choose a view from the Change View button's menu.

Here's the lowdown on the views Outlook provides:

- » **Simple List** view presents just the facts: the names you gave each task and the due date you assigned (if you assigned one). Simple List view makes it easy to add new tasks and mark old ones as complete. However, you won't see any extra information. If you want details . . .

>> **Detailed** view is a little more chock-full of the fiddly bits than Simple List view. It's really the same information, plus the status of the tasks, the date and time last modified, and the completion date (if completed).

>> **To-Do List** view includes all the tasks you've entered as well as any flagged emails that show up in the To-Do bar. The other Tasks list views only show the items you've added directly to the Tasks list.

>> **Prioritized** view groups your tasks according to the priority that you've assigned to each one. That way, you know what's important as well as what's urgent.

>> **Active** view shows you only the tasks you haven't finished yet. After you mark a task as complete — zap! Completed tasks vanish from Active view, which helps keep you focused on the tasks remaining to be done.

>> **Completed** view shows (you guessed it) tasks you've marked as complete. You don't need to deal with completed tasks anymore, but looking at the list gives you a warm, fuzzy feeling, doesn't it? It's also useful if you need to move a task back to uncompleted status. Just click its flag.

>> **Today** view shows tasks due today and overdue tasks, which are basically tasks due today! It's a great way to start the day — if you like being reminded of how much work you have to do.

>> **Next 7 Days** view is even more focused than Active view. Next 7 Days view shows only uncompleted tasks scheduled to be done within the next 7 days. It's just right for those people who like to live in the moment — or at least within the week.

>> **Overdue** view means you've been naughty. These are tasks that really *did* need to be done yesterday but are still hanging around today.

>> **Assigned** view lists your tasks in order of the name of the person upon whom you dumped, er, I mean, *to whom you delegated* each task.

>> **Server Tasks** view enables you to see tasks assigned via a task server, if your company uses one. It has fields for Assigned To, Custom Status, and Custom Priority, all of which are useful in collaboration situations.

TIP

If you are curious about the details of the different views, here's how to get them. On the Change View button's menu, choose Manage Views. Then select the desired view and click Modify. In the Advanced View Settings dialog box that appears, you can see a full description of the view, including its fields, grouping, sorting, and filtering. (You can also change them, but that's beyond the scope of this chapter.) For example, Figure 10-6 shows the controls for Simple List view.

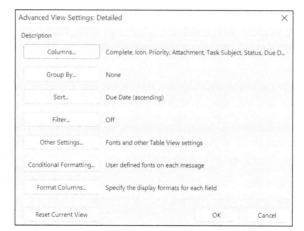

FIGURE 10-6:
View (and
optionally
change) the
details of a view
in the Advanced
View Settings
dialog box.

Editing Your Tasks

No sooner do you enter a new task than it seems like you need to change it. Sometimes, I enter a task the quick-and-dirty way and change some of the particulars later: Add a due date, a reminder, an added step, or whatever. Fortunately, editing tasks is easy.

The quick-and-dirty way to change a task

For lazy people like me, Outlook offers a quick-and-dirty way to change a task — just as it has a quick-and-dirty way to enter a task. You're limited in the number of details you can change, but the process is fast.

If you can see the subject of a task and if you want to change something about the task you can see, follow the steps I describe in this section. If you can't see the task or the part you want to change, use the regular method, which I describe in the next section of this chapter.

To change a task the quick-and-dirty way, follow these steps:

1. **In the Tasks module, highlight and then click the part of the task you want to change.**

    For example, you might click the task's due date or subject. You see a blinking line at the end of the text, a triangle at the right end of the box, or a menu with a list of choices.

2. Select the old information.

The item you clicked is highlighted to show it's selected, as shown in Figure 10-7.

3. Type the new information.

The new information replaces the old.

4. Press Enter.

Isn't that easy? If all you want to change is the subject or due date, the quick-and-dirty way will get you there.

FIGURE 10-7:
You can type
changes to a
task directly
into the list.

Click the field to change, and type or select as needed.

The regular way to change a task

If the information you want to change about a task isn't visible in the view you're looking at, you have to take a slightly longer route.

To make changes to a task the regular way, follow these steps:

1. In the Tasks module, click Simple List from the Current View section on the Ribbon if Simple List view is not already active.

You can choose a different view if you know that the view includes the task you want to change, but Simple List view is the most basic view of your tasks; it's sure to include the task you're looking for.

2. Double-click the task you want to change.

You can double-click any part of the task; it doesn't have to be its subject. The Task form opens. Now you can change anything you can see in the box.

3. (Optional) Change the subject of the task.

The subject is your choice. Remember to call the task something that helps you remember the task. There's nothing worse than a computer reminding you to do something you can't understand.

4. **(Optional) To change the start date or due date, click the Start Date box or the Due Date box and then enter the new date.**

Plenty of date styles work here — *7/4/23, the first Friday in July, 6 weeks from now*, whatever. Unfortunately, *the 12th of Never* isn't an option. Sorry.

5. **(Optional) To change the status, click the Status box and select a different status.**

TIP

If you're using Outlook at work and you're hooked up to a network, the Status box entry is one way of keeping your boss informed about your progress. You'll need to check with your boss or system administrator if this is the case.

If you're using Outlook at home, chances are that nobody else will care, but you may feel better if you know how well you're doing. You can't add your own choices to the Status box. (I'd like to add "Waiting, hoping the task will go away." No such luck.) Figure 10-8 shows the Task box with the Status field menu open.

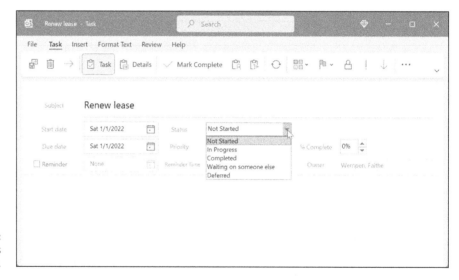

FIGURE 10-8:
Change a task's status.

6. **(Optional) To change the priority, click the Priority box and select a different priority.**

7. **(Optional) Select or deselect the Reminder check box if you want to turn the reminder on or off.**

Reminders are easy and harmless, so why not use them? If you didn't ask for one the first time, do it now.

8. **(Optional) Click the calendar button next to the Reminder check box to enter or change the date when you want to be reminded.**

   You can enter any date you want. Your entry doesn't have to be the due date; it can be much earlier, reminding you to get started. The default date for a reminder is the date the task is due, which isn't very useful. You should make sure the reminder is before the due date.

9. **Change the time in the time box for when you want to activate the reminder.**

   When entering times, keep it simple. The entry *230* does the trick when you want to enter 2:30 p.m. If you make appointments at 2:30 a.m. (and I'd rather not know what kind of appointments you make at that hour), you can type *230a*.

10. **Click the text box to add or change miscellaneous notes and information about this task.**

    You can add detailed information here that doesn't really belong anywhere else in the Task form. Look back at Figure 10-1 for an example. You see these details only when you open the Task form again; they don't normally show up in your Tasks list.

11. **Click the Save & Close button to finish.**

    There! You've changed your task.

Deleting a task

There are two ways to get rid of a task. One is to change its status to Completed, which you will learn about later in this chapter. But sometimes a task just needs to disappear. Maybe it was a bad idea in the first place, or your plans changed, or the project got cancelled . . . whatever. You can also be sneaky and delete uncompleted tasks if you're trying to avoid doing them.

To delete a task, follow these steps:

1. **In the Tasks module, select the task.**

2. **Click the Delete button on the Home tab of the Ribbon.**

   Alternatively, you can press Ctrl+D, or press the Delete key on your keyboard, or right-click the task and choose Delete. Poof! The task is gone. It's like it never existed.

Managing Recurring Tasks

Lots of tasks crop up on a regular basis. You know how it goes — same stuff, different day. To save you the effort of entering a task, such as a monthly sales report or a quarterly tax payment, over and over again, just set it up as a recurring task. Outlook can then remind you whenever it's that time again.

To create a recurring task, follow these steps:

1. **To turn an existing task into a recurring one, open the task by double-clicking it.**

    The Task form opens. Alternatively, you can start a new task and fill in all the usual details.

2. **Click the Recurrence button on the Task tab of the Ribbon.**

    The Task Recurrence dialog box opens.

3. **Choose the Daily, Weekly, Monthly, or Yearly option to specify how often the task occurs.**

    Each option — Daily, Weekly, Monthly, or Yearly — offers you choices for when the task recurs. For example, a daily recurring task can be set to recur every day, every 5 days, or whatever. A monthly recurring task can be set to recur on a certain day of the month, such as the 15th of each month or on the second Friday of every month. Figure 10-9 shows the Weekly option.

FIGURE 10-9:
Set up the schedule for the recurring task.

4. **In the Recur Every box, specify how often the task recurs, such as every third day or the first Monday of each month.**

   For example, if you choose to create a yearly task, you can configure it to recur on the same calendar day each year, or on a certain day of the month (such as the first Friday of June).

5. **In the Range of Recurrence section, enter the first occurrence in the Start box.**

6. **Choose when you want the task to stop (No End Date, End After a certain number of occurrences, or End By a certain date).**

7. **Click the OK button.**

   A banner appears at the top of the Task form describing the recurrence pattern for the task.

8. **Click the Save & Close button.**

Your task appears in the list of tasks once, but it has a different type of icon than nonrecurring tasks so you can tell at a glance that it's a recurring task. Regular tasks look like a tiny clipboard, but recurring tasks add an even tinier circular arrow icon.

Creating a regenerating task

A *regenerating task* is like a recurring task, except it recurs only when a certain amount of time passes after the last time you completed the task. Suppose you mow the lawn every 2 weeks. If it rains for a week and one mowing happens a week late, you still want to wait 2 weeks for the next one. If you schedule your mowings in Outlook, you can use the Regenerating Task feature to enter your lawn-mowing schedule. So far, Outlook can't replace a weather forecaster by telling you whether it's going to rain. (Okay, the weather forecaster usually can't, either.) But Outlook can help you keep track of whether you actually did mow the lawn and adjust your schedule accordingly.

To create a regenerating task, follow these steps:

1. **To turn an existing task into a regenerating one, open the task by double-clicking it.**

   The Task form opens. Alternatively, you can start a new task and fill in all the usual details.

2. **Click the Recurrence button on the Ribbon.**

   The Task Recurrence dialog box opens.

3. **Click the Regenerate New Task option.**

4. **Enter the number of days, weeks, months, or years between regenerating each task.**

   Figure 10-10 shows an example that regenerates every week.

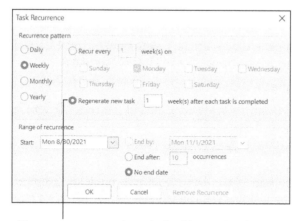

FIGURE 10-10:
Regenerate a task
in the Task
Recurrence
dialog box.

Choose to regenerate the task after it's completed.

5. **Click the OK button.**

   A banner appears in the Task form describing the regeneration pattern you've set for the task.

6. **Click the Save & Close button.**

Your task appears in the list of tasks once, but it has a different type of icon than nonrecurring tasks have so you can tell at a glance that it's a regenerating task. The regenerating task icon looks just like the recurring task icon, including that itsy-bitsy circular arrow icon.

Skipping a recurring task once

When you need to skip a single occurrence of a recurring (but not regenerating) task, you don't have to change the recurrence pattern of the task forever; just skip the occurrence you want to bypass and leave the rest alone.

To skip a recurring task, follow these steps:

1. **In the Tasks module, double-click the recurring task you want to change.**

   The Task form opens.

2. **Click the Skip Occurrence button on the Task tab of the Ribbon.**

   The due date changes to the date of the next scheduled occurrence. If you don't see the Skip Occurrence button, it's not a recurring task.

3. **Click the Save & Close button.**

   Your task remains in the list, with the new scheduled occurrence date showing.

Marking Tasks as Complete

Marking off those completed tasks is even more fun than entering them — and it's much easier. If you can see the task you want to mark as complete in either the To-Do bar or your Tasks list, just right-click on the item and choose Mark Complete. Nothing could be simpler. Except actually there *is* something simpler: You can just click the status flag on the far right to mark it as complete.

REMEMBER

When you mark a task as complete, it remains on the list, but it has a line drawn through it to show that it's done, and it turns gray. In a few views (notably Active and Overdue), completed tasks do not appear at all. They're still there — they're just filtered out of that view. If you want a completed task to not appear at all anymore, you have to delete it, which you learned about earlier in this chapter.

Marking it off

To mark a task as complete, select the check box next to the subject of the task you want to mark as complete, as shown in Figure 10-11. When you select the check box, the subject of the task changes color and gets a line through it.

You can view a list of the tasks you've marked as complete by switching to Completed view. All the jobs you've polished off show up there in a nice, neat list. Ah! How satisfying!

Outlook has more than one place for marking tasks as complete. You can look at the Tasks list I just described as well as certain views of your calendar and also the list of tasks in Outlook Today.

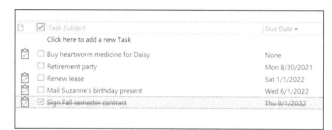

Picking a color for completed or overdue tasks

When you complete a task or when it becomes overdue, Outlook changes the color of the text for the completed tasks to gray and the overdue tasks to red, which makes it easy for you to tell at a glance which tasks are done and which tasks remain to be done. If you don't like Outlook's color choices, you can pick different colors.

To change the color of completed and overdue tasks, follow these steps:

1. **Click the File tab and click Options.**

   The Outlook Options dialog box opens.

2. **Click Tasks.**

   The Task Options page opens, as shown in Figure 10-12.

3. **Click the Overdue Task Color button.**

   A list of colors drops down.

4. **Choose a color for overdue tasks.**

5. **Click the Completed Task Color button.**

   A list of colors drops down.

6. **Choose a color for completed tasks.**

7. **Click the OK button.**

Your completed and overdue tasks will appear in your list in the colors you chose.

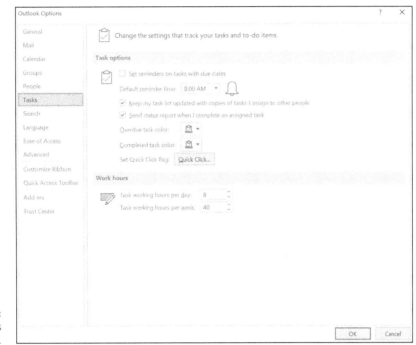

FIGURE 10-12:
The Task Options
page.

Using the To-Do Bar (and List)

As I mentioned earlier, the To-Do List in the Tasks module pulls together all the things you need to do and displays them in a single part of the Outlook screen. The goal of the To-Do List is to let you know what you need to do at a glance rather than making you check your calendar, check your email Inbox, and then check your Tasks list. The items you'll see most often on the To-Do bar include:

>> Tasks you've entered

>> Your next few appointments

>> Email messages you've flagged for action

At first, the To-Do List can seem a little confusing because things turn up there that you may not have put there directly. For example, if you receive an email message on a Monday and apply the flag labeled This Week, it'll turn up for action two Fridays later — when you might have forgotten about it. That's what the To-Do List is for — to prevent you from forgetting.

If you get busy in other modules, you might forget to check the To-Do List in the Tasks module. Fortunately, Outlook has your back. The To-Do List is repeated on a special pane called the To-Do bar, which you can optionally display in any of the other modules.

To display the To-Do bar and show tasks on it, do one of the following:

>> Using the Simplified Ribbon: In the Tasks module, click the View tab, click the Layout button, point to To-Do Bar, and then click Tasks. See Figure 10-13.

>> Using the Classic Ribbon: In the Tasks module, click the View tab, and then in the Layout group, click the To-Do Bar button and then click Tasks.

FIGURE 10-13:
Enable the To-Do
bar from the View
tab on the
Ribbon.

To-Do bar

You can also choose Calendar or People if you want that kind of information displayed, but I think tasks are the most useful information to display on the To-Do bar.

There's a little box at the top of the To-Do bar that says *Type a New Task*. You can use that to create new tasks on-the-fly. Click there, type the task name, and press Enter.

Viewing the Daily Task List

When you are viewing your calendar in Day, Work Week, or Week view, Outlook offers a display of upcoming tasks, a.k.a. the Daily Task List.

To display the Daily Task List on the calendar, do one of the following:

» Using the Simplified Ribbon: From the Calendar module, click the View tab, click More Commands, point to Layout, point to Daily Task List, and then click Normal. See Figure 10-14.

» Using the Classic Ribbon: From the Calendar module, click the View tab, click Daily Task List, and then click Normal.

More Commands

Daily Task List

FIGURE 10-14:
Daily Task List can be displayed in Day, Work Week, or Week view.

REMEMBER

Daily Task List is available only in views that show individual days and their times: Day, Work Week, and Week.

In a strip along the bottom of the screen, you see icons that represent tasks whose due dates fall on each of the days displayed. If you find that you've stacked up more to-do items than can be done in a single day, just drag the task to a day when it can be done. You can even drag a task up to a particular hour in the Calendar and reserve a specific time to get that thing done.

Working with the To-Do Module

The To-Do module (see Figure 10-15) is a recent addition to Outlook 365. It appears as a blue check mark icon in the navigation bar. This module provides an alternative way of creating and managing tasks.

To-Do module icon   Create steps for a task (optional).

      Lists   Create a new task.   Create a reminder.

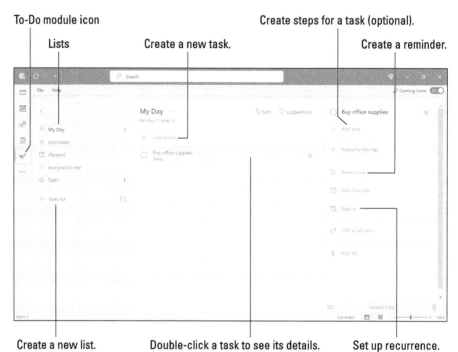

FIGURE 10-15:
Creating a new task in the My Day list in the To-Do module.

Create a new list.   Double-click a task to see its details.   Set up recurrence.

After the full-featured richness of the Tasks module, you might be wondering why the To-Do module is even here in Outlook at all. Surely the Tasks module does everything you want to do, right? Well, sort of. There's one big thing that the Tasks module *doesn't* do: It doesn't integrate with the web-based version of Outlook and its To-Do app (which is basically the online version of the Tasks module). If you sometimes use the web version and sometimes the desktop version, your email carries over just fine, but your tasks don't. So rather than fix it so that your tasks carry over to the Tasks module, Microsoft chose to add the web-based To-Do app into the desktop version of Outlook as a module.

The To-Do module is pretty simple compared to what you've been working with so far in this chapter. You can explore it on your own, or follow these steps to be guided through creating a basic task:

1. **Click the To-Do icon on the navigation bar to display the To-Do module. It starts out without any tasks in it.**

2. **In the Folder pane on the left, click the list on which you want to place the new task.**

   There are several pre-created lists: My Day, Important, and so on. There's even a generic one called Tasks. You can also click New List to create your own.

3. **In the content pane (on the right), click Add a Task and then type the name for the task you want to create.**

4. **Press Enter or click ADD. The task appears on the list and a new *Add a task* line appears.**

5. **Click the newly created task. A task pane appears on the right containing commands for adding more information about it. See Figure 10-15.**

6. **Click any of the buttons in the task pane and follow the prompts to add the information. For example, you can click Remind Me to add a reminder, or click Repeat to set up recurrence.**

7. **In the task pane, click Add Step, and then type a step. This is useful if a task has multiple steps that you need to document. Repeat this as many times as needed to document all the steps.**

8. **To mark a step or task complete, click in the circle to the left of its name.**

9. **To delete a task, right-click the task and choose Delete Task. At the confirmation prompt, click Delete Task.**

   That's pretty much it. As I said, the To-Do module's task list is basic. The main reason to use it is for its connection to the Outlook.com task app, which you will learn about in Chapter 16.

4

Taking Outlook to the Next Level

Discover how to become proficient at creating labels, using mail merge, and setting up form letters, as well as how to print envelopes and create merged email.

Learn how to integrate Outlook with Google and iCloud services for maximum convenience.

Find out how to use Outlook on your mobile devices, including iPads and Android phones and tablets.

Take control of Outlook by customizing how it looks and performs.

IN THIS CHAPTER

» **Creating mailing labels**

» **Making and using a merge template**

» **Compiling form letters**

» **Addressing envelopes**

» **Creating merged email**

Chapter **11**

Merging Mail From Outlook to Microsoft Word

I f you're new to the world of form letters, *mail merge* is the term computer people use to describe the way you can create a letter on a computer and print umpteen copies — each addressed to a different person. You probably get lots of mail-merged letters every day. When you *send* a mass mailing, it's called *mail merge*. When you *get* a mass mailing, it's called *junk mail*.

REMEMBER

Outlook manages the names and addresses and passes them over to Word on request. If your computer doesn't have any version of Microsoft Word installed, you can't run a mail merge from Outlook. (It doesn't work with the free, web-only Word Online.) However, as I write this, you can't buy Outlook as a stand-alone product without buying the whole Office suite, so I assume you have the latest version of both programs.

There are many different merge possibilities when Outlook and Word team up. Here's a quick guide, all of which I cover in the following sections:

>> **Labels:** Create sticky labels to affix to envelopes or packages that will not fit in your printer, or create labels for some other purpose, like inventory tagging or name badges for a conference.

>> **Form letters:** Create the customized letters that will go inside of envelopes.

>> **Envelopes:** Address a set of envelopes that will fit in your printer.

>> **Emails:** Create customized email messages you will send out via Outlook.

REMEMBER

You don't need Outlook to perform mail merges in Word. Mail merge supports a variety of data file types, of which Outlook is just one option. You can also merge from lists from Access, from Excel, or even from a plain text file. For more about Microsoft Word and its myriad mail merge possibilities, take a look at *Word For Dummies* by Dan Gookin (published by Wiley).

Making Mailing Label Magic

By combining the powers of Outlook and Word, you can create mailing labels for everyone in your Contacts list in a flash. The Outlook list connects to Word's Mail Merge feature, which means you don't have to mess around with exporting files and figuring out where they went.

TIP

I like to test a mail merge format before doing an actual merge. You can print the label information on regular paper to see what it looks like. If you make a mistake setting up the merge, it's faster to find out by printing one page of messed-up "labels" on plain paper than by printing 300 messed-up labels.

Make sure you have the right labels in your printer. Then, follow these steps to create mailing labels:

1. **Click People in the navigation bar.**

   Your Contacts list appears.

2. **If you don't want labels for all your contacts, select the contacts you want.**

   Hold down the Ctrl key as you click each one, or hold down Shift to select a contiguous block. Alternatively, you can select a view (or apply a filter) so that only the contacts you want are visible.

3. Do one of the following:

- Using the Simplified Ribbon: On the Home tab, click More Commands and then click Mail Merge.

- Using the Classic Ribbon: On the Home tab, click the Mail Merge button in the Actions group.

The Mail Merge Contacts dialog box opens, shown in Figure 11-1. If you selected contacts in Step 2, the Contacts setting will be Only Selected Contacts; otherwise, it will be All Contacts in Current View.

(Optional) Select only the contacts to include.   More Commands

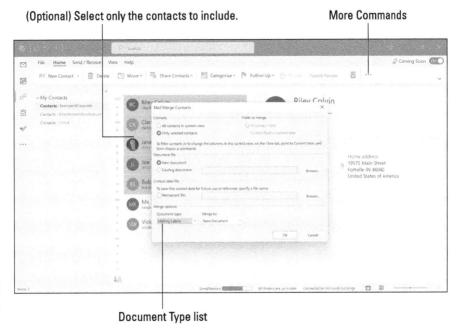

Document Type list

FIGURE 11-1: The Mail Merge Contacts dialog box.

4. In the Merge Options section, choose Mailing Labels from the Document Type list.

5. Choose New Document from the Merge To list.

New Document is usually already chosen, but check to be sure.

6. Click the OK button.

Microsoft Word opens a dialog box that tells you that Outlook has created a Mail Merge document but that you have to click the Setup button in the Mail Merge Helper dialog box to set up your document.

7. Click the OK button.

The Mail Merge Helper dialog box opens, shown in Figure 11-2.

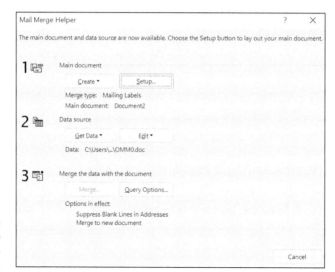

FIGURE 11-2:
The Mail Merge
Helper dia-
log box.

8. **Click the Setup button.**

   The Label Options dialog box opens.

9. **Choose a label brand from the Label Vendors drop-down menu.**

   Avery is one of the most popular label brands; generic labels often list an Avery product number equivalent on their packaging.

10. **Choose the label product number in the Product Number drop-down menu.**

    Check the stock number on your label to make sure it's the same as the one you're choosing. If the stock number isn't available, you can look at the label dimensions in the Label Information section of the Label Options dialog box.

TIP

The product you choose determines the label size, which in turn determines the size of the rows and columns in the table that Word creates to help you space your labels evenly on the page. Figure 11-3 shows the dialog box set up for Avery 5160 Address Labels.

If you don't know the label manufacturer or product number, you can choose New Label and set up a new label based on the dimensions of a single label on the sheet.

11. **Click OK.**

    The Label Options dialog box closes.

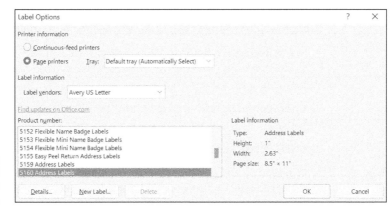

FIGURE 11-3:
The Label
Options
dialog box.

12. Click the Close button in the Mail Merge Helper dialog box.

The Mail Merge Helper dialog box closes and table gridlines appear on the page to show where the labels should go. The insertion point is in the top left label box on the page.

If the dimensions don't look like they match your actual labels, measure the labels and try again, this time clicking New Label and entering a custom label size.

13. Click the Address Block button on the Mailings tab of the Ribbon.

The Insert Address Block dialog box opens, shown in Figure 11-4, to show you what will appear in the labels you're about to create.

TIP

You can page through the previews in the Preview area by clicking the arrow buttons to see how the various entries in your Contacts list will look.

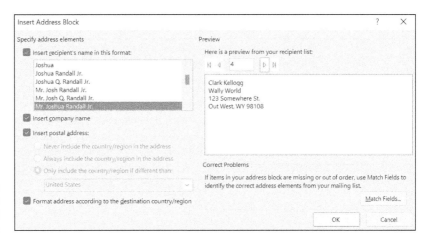

FIGURE 11-4:
The Insert
Address Block
dialog box.

14. **(Optional) Change any of the options as desired in the dialog box:**

- **Insert Recipient's Name in This Format:** You can deselect this check box to omit the people's names (not common), and you can choose the format for the recipient names from the list.

- **Insert Company Name:** Deselect this check box to omit the company name.

- **Insert Postal Address:** Deselect this check box to omit the postal address.

TIP

  If you want a postal address but the fields aren't matching up right, click the Match Fields button to open a dialog box where you can straighten that out.

- **Format Address According to the Destination Country/Region:** Deselect this check box to not take the country/region into consideration when formatting the address.

  Each time you click a choice, an example appears in the Preview box to the right.

15. **Click OK to accept your settings and close the dialog box.**

The Insert Address Block dialog box closes and your document shows a funny-looking code: <<AddressBlock>> in the first table cell and <<Next Record>> in the other table cells. Those are called *merge codes*, and they let Microsoft Word know which information to put in your document.

16. **Click the Update Labels button on the Ribbon.**

Now the <<AddressBlock>> code appears in each cell of the table, along with <<Next Record>>, to show that Word knows how to fill your page of labels with addresses.

17. **Click the Preview Results button on the Ribbon.**

Word shows how your document will look when you print it. If you like what you see, go to the next step.

TIP

If you are using a label type with a short height, and the labels have more than three lines, some of the text might look truncated in the preview. Be glad you noticed this now! To fix it, select the entire table (Ctrl+A) and then on the Home tab, in the Paragraph group, click the Line Spacing button to open its menu, and then click Line Spacing Options. In the Spacing section of the dialog box, set Before and After each to 0 and set Line Spacing to Single. Click OK. Problem solved!

18. Click the Finish & Merge button on the Mailings tab of the Ribbon and choose Edit Individual Documents from the drop-down menu.

The Merge to New Document dialog box opens, allowing you to print all the addresses you see in your document or just part of them. In most cases, you'll choose All to print the whole range.

19. Click the OK button.

You've created your labels.

20. Click the File tab and choose Print to send your labels to the printer.

Making and Using a Merge Template

TIP

If you often print labels, you can reduce your work by saving the blank label document and using it repeatedly. When you've finished creating your labels, follow these steps:

1. Switch back to the document containing your merge fields.

Its name starts with Document, as opposed to the labels output file, which starts with the name Labels. If Preview Results is still enabled, its contents looks a lot like the Labels file; click Preview Results to turn that off, and you should once again see the merge codes <<Next Record>> and <<AddressBlock>> in each cell.

2. Click File, and then click Save As.

The Save As screen of Backstage view appears.

3. Click Browse.

The Save As dialog box opens, where you can specify the file's name and location.

4. Navigate to the desired save location.

This is necessary only if you don't want to save the file in the default location.

5. In the File Name text box, type a name for the document.

Name it something you'll remember, such as the clever *Blank Labels*.

6. Click Save.

The Save dialog box closes and the file is saved.

7. Save the remaining open files as desired, and then close Word.

TIP

You can also create templates for form letters, envelopes, and email messages the same way.

The next time you decide to create labels, use this abbreviated procedure to do your mail merge:

1. **Click People in the navigation bar.**

   Your Contacts list appears.

2. **Do one of the following:**

   - Using the Simplified Ribbon: On the Home tab, click More Commands and then click Mail Merge.

   - Using the Classic Ribbon: On the Home tab, click the Mail Merge button in the Actions group.

   The Mail Merge Contacts dialog box opens (refer to Figure 11-1).

3. **In the Merge Options section, choose Mailing Labels from the Document Type list.**

4. **In the Mail Merge dialog box, select the Existing Document option button.**

5. **Click the Browse button.**

6. **Double-click Blank Labels.**

   That eliminates a lot of the steps in the mail merge process, and lets you get on to more exciting things, such as stuffing envelopes.

TIP

You can also save the address label document as its own file, and then edit the labels before you print them. For example, you could remove your annoying neighbor from your holiday mailing list.

Mastering Form Letter Formalities

Today, I received a personalized invitation — which had my name plastered all over the front of the envelope — to enter a $250,000 sweepstakes. How thoughtful and personal! You don't think that was a form letter, do you? A *form letter* is a letter with standard text that's printed over and over but with a different name and address printed on each copy. You can send form letters too, even if you're not holding a sweepstakes. An annual newsletter to family and friends is one form letter you may want to create.

Follow these steps to create a form letter from Outlook:

1. **Click People in the navigation bar.**

   Your Contacts list appears.

2. **Do one of the following:**

   - Using the Simplified Ribbon: On the Home tab, click More Commands and then click Mail Merge.

   - Using the Classic Ribbon: On the Home tab, click the Mail Merge button in the Actions group.

   The Mail Merge Contacts dialog box opens (refer to Figure 11-1).

3. **Choose Form Letters from the Document Type list.**

4. **Choose New Document from the Merge To list.**

   New Document is probably already chosen, but check to be sure.

5. **Click OK.**

   Microsoft Word opens a blank document.

6. **Type your letter.**

   You might want to type the generic parts of the letter first, the text that will appear the same in every copy, but it's your call. As you go through these steps, type whatever text is needed to have your letter make sense.

7. **(Optional) If you want to insert the recipient's address, position the insertion point where you want it and then click the Address Block button on the Ribbon.**

   An alternative is to not include the recipient's address, or to manually create the address block by inserting the individual fields.

8. **(Optional): To insert a greeting block (such as Dear so-and-so), position the insertion point and click the Greeting Line button on the Ribbon.**

   An alternative is to manually create the greeting line by typing *Dear* and then inserting one or more individual fields, such as First_Name or a combination of Prefix and Last_Name.

9. **To insert an individual merge field, position the mouse pointer where the field should appear. Click the Insert Merge Field button on the Mailings tab of the Ribbon and then click the desired field.**

   For example, I might choose First_Name. Figure 11-5 shows the `<<AddressBlock>>`, `<<GreetingLine>>`, and `<<First_Name>>` fields, all in their places.

FIGURE 11-5:
Several field
codes have been
inserted.

WARNING

When you use Outlook for a mail merge, you get the full list of fields to choose from—and it's a long list. You probably don't have information in every field for every contact, of course, so stick to the basic fields for the most consistent results.

10. **Repeat Step 9 to add other merge fields, and type more text as needed.**

11. **Click the Preview Results button on the Ribbon.**

Word shows how your document will look when you print it. If you like what you see, go to the next step. If not, make the needed adjustments.

TIP

One thing you might want to change is the inter-line spacing in the address block. Select the address block, and then on the Home tab, in the Paragraph group, click Line and Paragraph Spacing, and then click Line Spacing Options. Set the Before and After settings to 0 and the Line spacing to Single, and then click OK.

12. **Click the Finish & Merge button on the Mailings tab of the Ribbon and choose Edit Individual Documents from the drop-down menu.**

The Merge to New Document dialog box opens, allowing you to print all the letters or just part of them. In most cases, you'll choose All to print the whole range.

13. **Click the OK button.**

You've created your form letters.

14. **Click the File tab and choose Print to send your letters to the printer.**

Make sure the correct paper is loaded into the printer at the correct orientation.

Now you don't have to settle for sending impersonal, annoying form letters to dozens of people; you can send a personal, annoying form letters to hundreds of people. (If you're planning to send an annoying form letter to me, my address is 1600 Pennsylvania Ave., Washington, DC 20003.)

Merging to Envelopes

You don't have to print to labels if you're planning a mass mailing of letters; you can print directly on the envelopes you're sending. With luck, your printer has an envelope feeder tray. Feeding envelopes one at a time gets old fast.

To print addresses directly on your envelopes, follow exactly the same steps I describe in the "Making Mailing Label Magic" section earlier in this chapter. The only difference you'll notice is that in steps 8 and 9, instead of choosing a label maker and product number, you choose an envelope size. Pick the type of envelope you're using (usually number 10 — the standard business envelope) and follow the rest of the steps.

TIP

If you've never printed multiple envelopes on your printer before, start small. Try printing four or five, just to make sure your printer feeds envelopes properly. Word and Outlook happily send your printer a command to print hundreds of envelopes in a flash. If your printer chokes on the fourth envelope, however, fixing the problem can take a long time.

TIP

If you're printing only one envelope, that's not really a merge. Your best bet is to go directly to Microsoft Word and click the Envelopes button on the Ribbon. That opens the Envelopes and Labels dialog box, which has a tiny Address Book icon. Click the icon and then choose a name from your Outlook Contacts list to add it directly to an envelope or label.

Merging to Email

Another appealing Mail Merge feature is the ability to create merged email. You don't usually need to use merge email because you can send a single message to as many people as you want, just by entering their addresses on the To: line. However, if you want to send an email message to a bunch of people and customize each message, you can do that with a mail merge to email. That way, you won't send your message to the wrong person.

TIP

To merge to email, follow steps 1–3 in the "Mastering Form Letter Formalities" section. In Step 4, instead of New Document, choose Email from the Merge To list in the Mail Merge Contacts dialog box.

WARNING

If you're sending from an Exchange email account, your document goes right to your recipient as soon as you click the Finish & Merge button. If you've made a mistake, there's no chance to fix it. I recommend testing your email merge by sending an email to yourself first. Click your own name in the Contacts list and then put together your merge message. When you're sure that you've said what you meant to say, select all the people you want to contact and *then* merge. If you use Outlook at home, you can temporarily disconnect your Internet connection before you merge, and then press Ctrl+Shift+O to switch to your Outbox and approve the collection of messages.

GOING PRO WITH HOSTED MAILING SERVICES

When your business goals drive you to launch a campaign of mass mailings and email marketing, Outlook's built-in tools are a good enough place to start, but you may want to consider using one of the fine professional services that specialize in email marketing. In addition to making your campaigns look more businesslike, a professional service can help you grow your mailing list. Many of the best-known email marketing services can import your contacts from Microsoft Outlook.

Also, your email service provider might cut you off when you try to send too many email messages from Outlook at one time. Many of them do that to reduce the amount of spam email that goes out from their service. Their purpose is laudable, but they might be preventing you from emailing important information to legitimate customers. You may be able to find the limit on the ISP's website or on your bill, but most make it difficult to find. Try contacting the service to ask.

A professional email marketing service can also make your whole marketing program more effective, with such features as

- Email list cleanup to remove people who opt out and so on
- Statistics on the success of each campaign
- A/B testing of different versions of email copy to see which is more effective
- Delivery assurance options to make sure your messages don't get blocked as spam
- Technical support

Each service has particular strengths that may or may not suit your specific needs. There's no doubt, though, that for many businesses, email marketing is the most cost-effective way to improve your business and establish long-term relationships with your customers. Some well-known names in the email marketing business include the following:

- Constant Contact at www.constantcontact.com
- Vertical Response at www.verticalresponse.com
- MailChimp at www.mailchimp.com
- AWeber Communications at www.aweber.com
- iContact at www.icontact.com

You can find even more by going to Google and searching for the phrase *hosted email marketing*.

Chapter **12**

Integrating Outlook with Google and iCloud

O utlook is great when you're working on a Windows PC, but it's unrealistic to assume that that's *all* people will use. Especially when you're using a mobile device, you may prefer a Google application or the native apps on your iPhone.

Outlook actually integrates fairly nicely with both Google and Apple products, but it isn't obvious how to set up those connections. You could scour the Internet for hours clicking on articles that supposedly explain how to do it, but many of them are just clickbait for some add-on application that someone wants to sell you.

Alternatively, you could read this chapter, which explains in no-nonsense terms how to set up those connections. And I promise I won't try to sell you anything. Well, except this book.

Integrating Google Calendar with Outlook

If you want items from a Google Calendar to appear in Outlook, you have two choices: You can synchronize the calendar in Outlook or you can import it. If you subscribe to it, the Google Calendar content will automatically synchronize (update) in Outlook whenever it changes. If you import it, there won't be any automatic updates.

TIP

Which is better? That all depends on whether you are planning on continuing to use Google Calendar in the future or not. If you are, subscribing is better. If not, importing is better.

Subscribing to a Google Calendar in Outlook

Subscribing to a calendar is a good thing if you want to maintain the calendar on the Google app but access it via Outlook. The copy in Outlook and the copy online in Google Calendar are constantly kept synchronized (provided Internet service is available).

WARNING

Not all the calendars that appear in the Google Calendar app can be shared with Outlook. The one named Google Calendar generally works fine, though.

Follow these steps to synchronize a Google Calendar in Outlook:

1. **Open your web browser and navigate to** `Calendar.google.com`.

   If prompted, sign in to your Google account.

2. **In the lower left corner of the screen, in the My Calendars section, click the More button (the three dots) next to the calendar you want to subscribe to.**

   The More button appears only when you hover over the calendar you're interested in. A menu appears. See Figure 12-1.

3. **Click Settings and Sharing.**

   A Settings screen appears, with options for configuring the sharing.

WARNING

   If you see a Settings command instead of Settings and Sharing, you can't share this calendar with Outlook because it doesn't support the iCal format.

4. **Scroll down to the Integrate Calendar section near the bottom of the page.**

Click the More button next to the calendar name.

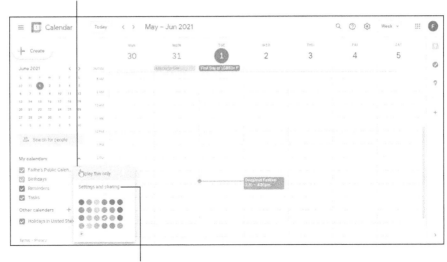

FIGURE 12-1:
Open the menu
for the desired
calendar.

Click Settings and Sharing.

5. **Locate the Secret Address in iCal Format, and click the Copy to Clipboard button to copy it to the Clipboard.**

   See Figure 12-2.

   Depending on your calendar permissions, you might not see this secret address option. You might try a different calendar and see if that makes any difference.

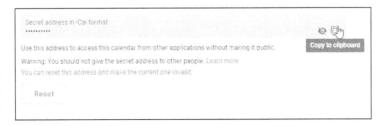

FIGURE 12-2:
Copy the secret
address to the
Clipboard.

6. **At the security warning that appears, click OK.**

7. **Open Outlook, or switch to it if it is already open, and display the Calendar module.**

8. **On the Home tab, click Open Calendar, and then click From Internet.**

   A New Internet Calendar Subscription dialog box opens.

9. **Paste the content into the dialog box, as in Figure 12-3, and click OK.**

   Use Ctrl+V as a paste shortcut. A confirmation box appears asking if you want to add the calendar to Outlook and subscribe to updates.

FIGURE 12-3:
Paste the secret
address into the
New Internet
Calendar
Subscription
dialog box.

10. **Click Yes.**

    The calendar appears on your calendars list in the Other Calendars section.

Importing a Google Calendar into Outlook

If you have decided not to use Google Calendar anymore (Outlook all the way from here on!), but you already have a bunch of appointments set up in Google Calendar, you can import the calendar into Outlook. With this method, the Google Calendar is not synchronized with Outlook.

To import a Google Calendar, follow these steps:

1. **Open your web browser and navigate to `Calendar.google.com`.**

   If prompted, sign in to your Google account.

2. **In the lower left corner of the screen, in the My Calendars section, click the More button (the three dots) next to the calendar you want.**

   A menu appears. Refer to Figure 12-1.

3. **Click Settings and Sharing.**

   A Settings screen appears.

4. **Click the Export Calendar button.**

   A Downloads pane appears telling you that the calendar has been downloaded. It was placed in the default download location for your web browser (probably the Downloads folder for the signed-in Microsoft account).

   Some browsers might prompt you for a location.

5. **In File Explorer, navigate to the Downloads folder (or whatever folder the file was downloaded into).**

The easiest way is to click the Downloads shortcut in the Quick Access list in the navigation pane, but you can also navigate to C:\Users*username*\ Downloads.

6. **Double-click the downloaded .ical.zip file to open it.**

It opens as if it were a folder.

7. **Select the calendar file and press Ctrl+C to copy it.**

8. **Navigate to any location where you want to store the file temporarily and press Ctrl+V to paste it there.**

You can delete the file after you import it, so it doesn't matter much where you put it. You can put it in the Downloads folder or on the Desktop, for example.

9. **Open or switch to Outlook, and choose File ⇨ Open & Export ⇨ Import/ Export.**

The Import and Export Wizard dialog box opens. See Figure 12-4.

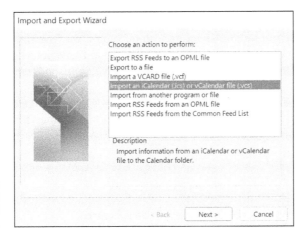

Import and Export Wizard

Choose an action to perform:

Export RSS Feeds to an OPML file
Export to a file
Import a VCARD file (.vcf)
Import an iCalendar (.ics) or vCalendar file (.vcs)
Import from another program or file
Import RSS Feeds from an OPML file
Import RSS Feeds from the Common Feed List

Description
Import information from an iCalendar or vCalendar file to the Calendar folder.

< Back   Next >   Cancel

FIGURE 12-4: The Import and Export Wizard dialog box.

10. **Choose Import an iCalendar (.ics) or vCalendar File (.vcs) and click Next.**

The Browse dialog box opens.

11. **Navigate to the folder where you put the calendar file in Step 8, and select the calendar file.**

12. **Click OK.**

A dialog box asks how you want to open it: Open as New or Import.

13. **Click Import.**

Importing the items into an existing calendar is usually the best way to go because that way you have fewer calendars to manage separately. You can choose Open as New if that sounds like a better plan to you, though — for example, if you want to keep the appointments and events on the imported calendar separate.

The imported items appear on your default calendar.

Remember, the default calendar is the calendar in your default data file. You set the default data file by choosing File ⇨ Account Settings ⇨ Account Settings ⇨ Data Files. Choose the data file that should be the default and click Set as Default.

Accessing Gmail Contacts in Outlook

Just like with the calendars, you can either synchronize or import Gmail contacts. Unfortunately, Google and Outlook do not share a common contact synch protocol. In other words, they don't speak a common language between them when synchronizing. So in order to synchronize the contacts, you have to use a third-party utility to function as an interpreter. Some are free and some you pay for. I am not going to recommend one because I don't have a favorite, but if you read the online reviews, they should lead you to a legit app, and maybe even a free one.

Things get a lot simpler if you don't need to keep your contact lists synchronized between the two apps. If you just want to import your Gmail contacts into Outlook, it's pretty straightforward to do. Follow these steps:

1. **Open your web browser and navigate to** `Contacts.google.com`**.**

If prompted, sign in to your Google account.

2. **In the navigation bar on the left, click Export.**

The Export Contacts dialog box opens. See Figure 12-5.

3. **In the Export As section, click Outlook CSV.**

4. **Click Export.**

A Downloads pane appears telling you that the contacts have been downloaded to a file called contacts.csv. It was placed in the default download location for your web browser (probably the Downloads folder for the signed-in Microsoft account).

FIGURE 12-5:
Exporting
contacts from
Google Contacts.

5. **Open or switch to Outlook, and choose File ⇨ Open & Export ⇨ Import/ Export.**

   The Import and Export Wizard dialog box opens. Refer to Figure 12-4.

6. **Choose Import from Another Program or File and click Next.**

   The Import a File dialog box opens.

7. **Click Comma Separated Values and click Next.**

8. **Click the Browse button, browse to the download location, select contacts.csv, and click OK.**

9. **Choose how you want the contacts to be imported, as shown in Figure 12-6. Your choices are:**

   - Replace Duplicates with Items Imported

   - Allow Duplicates to Be Created

   - Do Not Import Duplicate Items

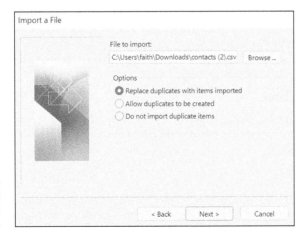

FIGURE 12-6:
Specify how the
contacts should
be imported.

10. **Click Next.**

    The Select a Destination Folder list appears.

11. **Select the location where you want the contacts to be stored.**

    The folders for each data file are shown separately. I recommend using the existing Contacts folder for the email account you use the most. See Figure 12-7.

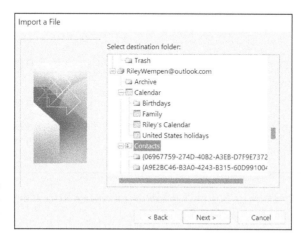

FIGURE 12-7:
Choose where to put the imported contacts.

12. **Click Next.**

    A summary screen appears letting you know what actions will be performed. In this case it's to import the contacts.

TIP

    If you get an import error at this point, open the contacts.csv file in Excel and check the fields to see if there is anything that an import tool might balk at. When I did this, I found that Excel was showing the phone numbers in Scientific Notation format. I selected the phone number column, and then on the Home tab, I opened the drop-down menu in the Number group and chose Number. Then I saved and closed the file and re-tried these steps and it all worked. Don't forget to close Excel before you try to continue the import.

13. **Click Finish.**

    Outlook imports the contacts.

Integrating Outlook with iCloud

iCloud is the cloud environment for Apple apps and services. That includes many of the apps that come preinstalled on Apple operating systems for the iPhone and iPad (iOS) and desktop and laptop Macs (macOS), including the Calendar and Notes apps. iCloud is the storage system where your data resides from all your Apple devices, such as iPhone, iPad, or iMac. So when you synch with the apps on those devices, what you are *really* synching with is the cloud storage system — in other words, iCloud.

The good news is it's a one-stop shop for all your Apple-related data. You just set up iCloud once to synch on your PC, and all available data is automatically set up to be accessible in Outlook.

Installing the iCloud app on your PC

To synch Outlook with iCloud, you must first install the iCloud app. If you have previously connected an iPhone or iPad to your computer, you might already have it. To check, click Start and type *iCloud* and see if an app appears. If it does, you're all set.

If not, you can get it from the Microsoft Store by following these steps:

1. **Close Outlook.**

   Some parts of the iCloud setup may require Outlook to be closed.

2. **Open the Microsoft Store app in Windows.**

   Click Start, type *Store*, and then click Microsoft Store.

3. **In the Microsoft Store app, click Search.**

   A Search box appears in the top right corner of the Microsoft Store window.

4. **In the Search box, type *icloud* and press Enter.**

   Search results appear.

5. **Click the iCloud app in the search results.**

   A page appears for the app.

6. **Click the Get button.**

   The app is downloaded and installed. It will take a few minutes, so be patient.

7. **Launch the iCloud app from the Start menu in Windows.**

   The iCloud app finishes setting itself up, and then opens.

8. **When prompted, enter your Apple ID and password and click Sign In.**

   See Figure 12-8. You may be prompted to enter a verification code sent to your other Apple devices, such as your iPhone. You may also see some other prompts, such as asking whether you want to send diagnostic and usage information to Apple. Respond to the prompts as needed.

FIGURE 12-8:
Sign in to iCloud.

Setting up Outlook to work with iCloud

After you've installed the iCloud app, you can set up Outlook using the iCloud app. The app may even already be configured correctly, and all you need to do is check on it.

Follow these steps to confirm that iCloud is set up to integrate with Outlook, and to make it so if needed:

1. **Make sure Outlook is not running.**

2. **Start the iCloud app if it is not already running.**

3. **If it is not already selected, select the check box next to Mail, Contacts, and Calendars.**

   See Figure 12-9. After you select the check box, respond to any prompts that appear to complete the setup.

FIGURE 12-9:
If needed, select the Mail, Contacts, and Calendars check box.

4. **Click Apply.**

   If you have the Google Chrome browser installed, you may see a prompt that iCloud Passwords extension for Chrome is required.

5. **If you see a prompt to enable the iCloud Passwords extension for Chrome, choose Download ⇨ Add to Chrome ⇨ Add Extension. Then close the Chrome browser window.**

6. **If you see a prompt asking if you want to merge bookmarks with iCloud, click Merge or click Cancel — your choice.**

   Follow the prompts that appear if you click Merge; there may be an extra step or two.

7. **Wait for Outlook Setup for iCloud to complete, and then click Done.**

   The iCloud window reappears.

8. **In the iCloud window, click Close.**

Using iCloud content in Outlook

When you start up Outlook after installing iCloud, you will notice new items in the different modules. For example, in the Calendars module, there is now an iCloud calendar item under My Calendars. This calendar will automatically synch with your calendar on your other Apple devices.

In the Tasks module, you'll find a Reminders list, which is iCloud's version of Tasks. This list stays in synch with your Reminders from your Apple devices.

In the People module, you'll see a Contacts – iCloud list. This list stays in synch with your Contacts list on your Apple devices. Figure 12-10 shows the iCloud content in each of those three modules.

FIGURE 12-10:
iCloud content in the Calendars, Tasks, and Contacts modules in Outlook.

IN THIS CHAPTER

» **Understanding how mobile Outlook works**

» **Reading, replying to, and composing email on your mobile device**

» **Archiving, scheduling, and deleting email**

» **Dealing with groups of messages**

» **Checking your mobile calendar**

» **Adding new appointments**

Chapter **13**

Outlook for iOS and Android Devices

" Mobile first" is the current rallying cry at Microsoft. The company's CEO, Satya Nadella, has declared that the company will give mobile computing its top priority. And with good reason: Mobile device sales are growing wildly, while sales of traditional desktop and laptop PCs are shrinking. Billions of people now use a mobile phone as their primary computing device, and millions use a phone as their only computing device. That's why the availability of Microsoft Outlook on mobile platforms is good news for everyone.

The Android and iOS app called Outlook is different in many ways from the desktop version, and lacks some of the features and customization options, but that's to be expected. There's no way anyone could ever shoehorn all the features and functions of desktop Outlook on a tiny smartphone screen, so these products pare the features down to the ones that matter most.

TIP

Outlook does not come preinstalled on Android or Apple devices (for obvious reasons, because Microsoft is a competitor). You can download the mobile version of Outlook from the app store for your device.

WARNING

The mobile version of Outlook on an iPad or iPhone requires iOS or iPadOS 13 or later. Some old iPads (basically anything older than the iPad Air Version 2) won't update past version 12.5, so if you've got one of these old models, you can't install the latest version of Outlook on your iPad. Sorry.

Understanding the Mobile Difference

Back in 2011, a Pew research study showed that 35 percent of Americans owned a smartphone. Since then that number has doubled to more than 81 percent. At that rate, if you're reading this and you don't already own a smartphone, odds are that you're on your way out the door to buy one right now.

So, I think it's fair to guess that you've already experienced how smartphones work and how different they are from laptops and desktop computers. The biggest difference, of course, is that they don't come with an actual physical keyboard — you do everything on a smartphone or tablet by touching the screen with your fingers. It's a little like finger painting — but without the mess.

In this chapter, I describe what to touch, tap, or swipe with your finger in order to do what you're trying to do — make some version of Outlook work on your phone.

VERSION DIFFERENCES

As examples, I've included figures from an iPhone, because that's what I happen to have. For the most part, the versions of Outlook available for the iOS and Android platforms are equivalent. One or two major features of each aren't available on the other. The bigger version differences you may encounter aren't between Android and Apple, though, but due to updates. By the time you read this, Microsoft may have made changes to the mobile Outlook app that create some differences between what you read here and what you see on your device.

Accessing Mobile Email

The biggest benefit you get from a mobile version of Outlook is the ability to do something useful with your incoming email when you're away from your desk and only have a phone to work with. The design philosophy behind mobile Outlook versions is to make it faster and easier to rapidly process your email, sorting, filing, and marking messages for later action. Nobody's pretending that you're going to compose messages proposing marriage or multimillion-dollar deals on a mobile device. (Although I'm sure both have been done more than you might think!) But you can use mobile Outlook as a convenient, rapid-response tool just to let people know you're on top of things. Or possibly to make them think you're toiling away at your desk when you're really frolicking at the beach. Don't worry — your secret's safe with me.

Setting up Outlook on a mobile device

When you install Outlook on your mobile device and then run it for the first time, prompts appear for setting up your email account. They're nearly identical to the steps for setting up an account on the desktop version of Outlook, and self-explanatory. Just follow along with the prompts.

Reading email

The first thing you'll probably want do with Outlook on your phone or tablet is to check your incoming email.

The iPad screen shows you a layout of email messages that might remind you of desktop Outlook. It shows a list of messages on the left side and a reading pane on the right that displays the content of one message, as shown in Figure 13-1. To view a different message, tap the message you want to view in the list on the left and the contents of that message will appear.

If you're using Outlook on an iPhone or Android phone, you'll only see the message list. To see the body of a message, tap the message in the list and the message opens up. To go back to the message list, just swipe your finger from left to right across the body of the message. Android devices also feature a back button at the bottom of the device that does the same thing.

GETTING IN FOCUS

At the top of the message list, you'll see a few words: Focused, Other, and Filter. Focused view shows only messages that are addressed directly to you as well as messages that Outlook thinks matter most to you. If you tap Other, you'll see a different set of messages that Outlook guesses are less important to you. It makes that guess based on the content of each message and what you've done with messages like that in the past. As time goes on, it learns what you find useful and gradually tries to make increasingly accurate guesses as to what's useful to you. That's especially valuable when you're working on a tiny smartphone screen because you don't want your view cluttered with random stuff you don't need.

It also has a Filter feature, which you can access by tapping Filter at the top of the message list. Filter enables you to show only messages with certain attributes: Unread, Flagged, Pinned, Attachments, or Mentions Me.

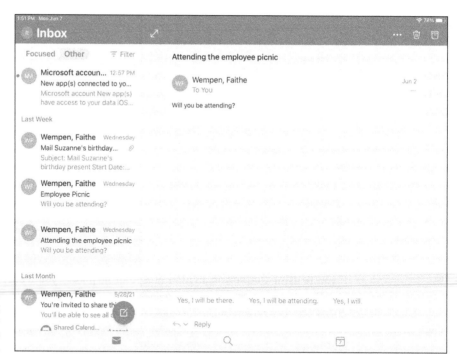

FIGURE 13-1:
You can view an email message by tapping it in the message list.

Replying to email

Replying to an email message is almost as easy as reading one. On the bottom of the message is an icon that looks like a bent arrow. Tap it to see a menu of reply options, as shown in Figure 13-2, and then choose the desired option.

FIGURE 13-2:
Mobile Outlook
makes replying
to emails quick
and easy.

The message reply form opens. If you choose Reply All or Reply, the message is already addressed to your intended recipients. If you choose Forward, you need to add the recipient's address. Edit Recipients enables you to edit the recipient list.

WARNING

The great thing about replying to messages on a smartphone is that you probably have dictation capabilities, so you don't need to type. The scary thing about that is the unspeakable errors that speech-to-text software can produce. I've seen Siri come up with some real whoppers — phrases much too impolite to include in this book. Siri has a real potty mouth sometimes! So, if you dictate email messages that aren't addressed to sailors and stevedores, I have one word of advice: Proofread!

Composing email

What could be more convenient than dashing off a quick email while sitting in the park or riding in a taxi? It's so much better than being stuck at the office. The scenery is a lot nicer, and the coffee even tastes better.

To compose an email message in mobile Outlook, follow these steps:

1. **Tap the New Email icon at the bottom of the message list pane.**

   On an iPad or iPhone, that icon looks like a square with a pencil in it. On the Android version, it's a circle with a plus sign in it. That opens a New Message form, along with the on-screen keyboard, and there's a blinking cursor in the To: box of the message form.

2. **Type the first few letters of an email address or the first letters of the name of the person you're emailing.**

   As soon as Outlook sees a name or address beginning with the letters you type, it shows a list of matching names and email addresses. In many cases, the person you want to email is listed there. If they are, just tap the name and then that person's name and address are automatically entered into the To: box. If the name doesn't appear, type in the entire email address.

3. **Tap the Subject line and enter a subject.**

   A subject line isn't absolutely mandatory, but it's a good idea.

4. **Tap the main part of the message box and enter your message.**

   Because you may be typing on a glass screen, you may want to be brief, but that's up to you. Figure 13-3 shows a completed message, ready to go.

5. **Tap the Send icon.**

   You'll find the Send icon in the upper right corner of the message pane. It looks like an arrowhead pointing to the right. Tap it to send your message on its way.

Send

FIGURE 13-3:
The New Message
form in Outlook
on an iPad.

Forwarding a message is very similar to composing a new message in that you have to enter an email address, but other than that, it requires the same steps as a reply.

Archiving, scheduling, and deleting email messages

Mobile Outlook includes a clever little trick that's not available on desktop Outlook: It allows you to swipe a message right or left as a way of quickly processing the message. As you slide a message to the right or left, a colored background appears, displaying the name of the thing you're about to do.

You can control what swiping left and swiping right do, but you can only have two active actions at a time: one for each direction of swipe. Here are some of the options you have (which may vary depending on your accounts):

TIP

>> **Schedule:** This says "I'll think about that later." Swiping right to schedule a message hides the message until you want it to reappear. When you schedule a message, you get a menu of choices that range from a few hours in the future to tomorrow. You can also choose a specific time.

The first time you use Schedule you will be prompted to choose a folder in which to store your scheduled emails. You might want to create a folder for this purpose. The same goes for Archive.

>> **Delete:** This means just what it says — poof! It's gone. (Although you might be able to retrieve the message from the trash, depending on your mail server.)

>> **Archive:** This choice sends your message to a folder that you've chosen in advance. The trick to this one is that you need to have chosen an archive folder or it doesn't work. Fortunately, it offers to set up an archive folder if you haven't done so. Once you set up an archive folder, everything you archive goes there from then on.

>> **Flag/Unflag** or **Mark Flagged:** This puts a flag on a message so you can remind yourself to get back to it — exactly the same way you'd flag messages on the desktop, as I describe in Chapter 5.

>> **Pin/Unpin:** This choice pins an item to the top of the list, and then unpins it.

>> **Mark Read** or **Mark Read/Unread:** Outlook marks every message once you've read it. You may want to mark things as read without reading them, so this is an easy way to do that. You can also mark them as unread, which resets the read flag so you will notice it again.

>> **Move:** Just like Archive, this choice moves your message to a folder, but it asks you which one each time.

>> **Mark Read and Archive** or **Read & Archive:** Just as its name implies, this combines the Mark Read and Archive functions into a single command.

>> **None** or **No Action:** This disables the swipe so it doesn't do anything at all.

To change swiping options, follow these steps:

1. **Tap the word Inbox in the top left corner of the screen to open a menu.**

   This menu is the equivalent of the File menu in the desktop version of Outlook. It doesn't have an official name in the mobile version, so let's just call it the File menu here, for simplicity's sake. See Figure 13-4.

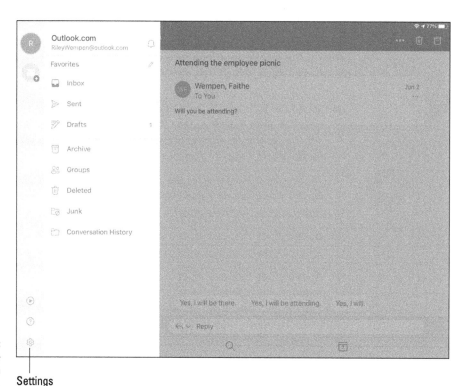

FIGURE 13-4:
Display the File
menu and then
choose Settings.

Settings

2. **Tap the Settings icon in the bottom left corner.**

   The icon looks like a gear. The Settings dialog box opens.

3. **Scroll down to the Mail section and tap Swipe Options.**

   To scroll down with your finger, drag upward. The Swipe Options screen
   appears.

4. **Tap anywhere in one of the two areas labeled Swipe Right or Swipe Left.**

   A menu appears, showing the range of choices listed earlier. See Figure 13-5.

5. **Choose the options you prefer.**

6. **Tap the Back arrow (<) in the upper left corner of the screen to return to
   the Settings screen.**

7. **Tap the Close (X) button in the upper left corner of the screen to close the
   Settings screen.**

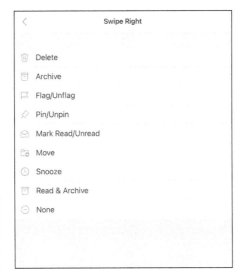

FIGURE 13-5:
The Swipe Right
screen lets you
choose what
happens when
you swipe right.

Deleting messages

To keep your Outlook app tidy, move any items to the trash that you no longer need. Nothing could be easier than deleting a message in mobile Outlook. At the top of the message screen is a little icon that looks like a trash can. Tap the trash can and that's where your message goes. If you don't see the trash can, you don't have a message selected.

Depending on your mail server and your Outlook settings, the trash can may be automatically emptied at a certain interval or deleted messages may sit there forever, or until you empty the trash. You can retrieve any items from the trash that you might have accidentally deleted.

Managing groups of messages

Mobile Outlook is designed to help you process and read email more than to help you create it. You're still better off composing email with a desktop or laptop. But it does offer a clever way to deal with several messages at one time. With the message list open, hold your finger on one message for a second or two and an option button will appear to the left of every message, as shown in Figure 13-6. Tap the option button for every message you want to process and a check mark will appear in the circle. If you tap the trash can icon now, all the messages you checked will be deleted. If you tap the flag icon, they all get flagged. You can also tap the More button (. . .) in the top right corner of the message list to choose other options, including Move or Mark Unread.

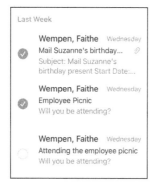

FIGURE 13-6:
Hold your finger
on a message for
a second or two
to make option
buttons appear
for multiple
selection.

Using Your Mobile Calendar

Mobile Outlook also offers a slick, slimmed-down version of the Calendar you've seen on the desktop version of Outlook. It doesn't include every bell and whistle — just the features you're most likely to use and that work well on a phone or a tablet. Tap the Calendar button at the bottom of the Outlook screen to access it.

WARNING

You might not have a calendar if the email service you use doesn't also include a calendar. Such services as Microsoft Office 365, Microsoft Exchange, and Gmail from Google all include a calendar, so if you use one of those, you'll have access to a calendar. I've had accounts at Mail.com for many years, but its service doesn't include a calendar. But I also keep a calendar on Gmail, so it's okay.

Navigating the mobile calendar

You can get to the calendar from nearly anywhere in mobile Outlook by tapping the Calendar icon at the bottom of the screen.

You can change calendar views using the View icon in the upper right corner of the screen. Tapping it opens a menu, as shown in Figure 13-7. The view options are different depending on the screen size. On an iPad, you can choose Week, Agenda, Day, or Month. On a phone, your choices are Agenda, Day, 3-Day, and Month.

Creating a new appointment

You'll find a prominent plus sign in the lower right corner of the screen — that's the New Event button. Tap it to open the New Event form, as shown in Figure 13-8. To set specific details about the appointment you have in mind, tap each line of text on the form to reveal settings for that detail. You can set date, time, location, and more by going through the form and setting each item to what you want.

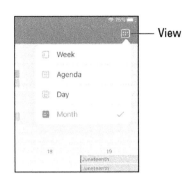

FIGURE 13-7:
Choose the
calendar view
(iPad version
shown here).

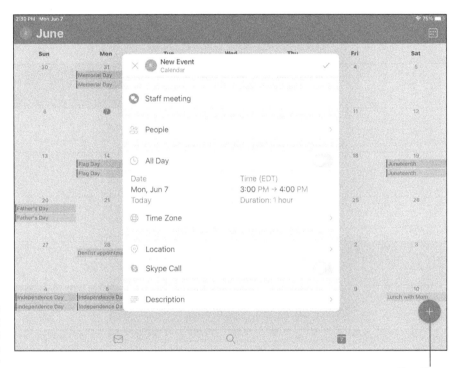

FIGURE 13-8:
The New Event
form is where
you record all the
details for your
calendar.

New Event

TIP

Frankly, if you create a lot of appointments and you have a choice between using desktop Outlook and mobile Outlook, pick the desktop. Mobile Outlook gives you a super-handy way to review your calendar when you're out and about, but it's a bit cumbersome in the way it leaves you fussing with details that are hard to handle on a mobile device — where you can only use taps and swipes with your finger. When you compare how quickly you can enter an appointment in desktop Outlook with how long it takes to enter one in mobile Outlook, you'll agree that the desktop version is easier. Remember, though, that mobile apps get updated every month or so, which makes it likely that the process will be much different (and simpler) by the time you read this.

Chapter **14**

Seeing It Your Way: Customizing Outlook

U ser interface is a fancy term for the arrangement of screens, menus, and doodads on your computer. The people who write computer programs spend lots of time and money trying to figure out how best to arrange stuff on the screen to make a program like Outlook easy to use.

But one person's dream screen can be another person's nightmare. Some people like to read words on the screen that say what to do; other people like colorful icons with pictures to click. Other people prefer to see information in neat rows and columns; still others like to see their information arranged more, shall we say, informally.

Outlook lets you display your information in an endless variety of arrangements and views. There's even a button labeled Organize that shows you what choices are available for slicing and dicing the information you've saved in Outlook. This chapter shows you many of the best steps you can take after you click the Organize button.

Customizing the Quick Access Toolbar

Did you ever notice how about 80 percent of your results come from about 20 percent of the work you do? The famous 80/20 rule applies to more things than you might expect. The Quick Access Toolbar (QAT) takes advantage of that idea by letting you keep a few icons for your favorite functions at the top of the screen so you can use them anytime.

The QAT might or might not already appear. (It used to appear by default in Outlook, but recently Microsoft made a change to the Outlook interface and disabled it by default.)

If it does appear, it might be either above the Ribbon or below it. Figure 14-1 shows the two possible placements; compare your screen to these samples to figure out what you've got now.

QAT above Ribbon

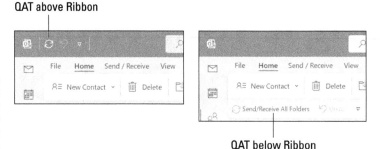

FIGURE 14-1:
The Quick Access Toolbar above the Ribbon (left) and below it (right).

QAT below Ribbon

Notice that when the QAT is above the Ribbon, it's compact, with just an icon for each command. (There's actually just one command in both of these examples — Send/Receive All Folders.) In contrast, when it's below the Ribbon, it's not so compact, with the full name and icon for each command. (You can change that, though, so that it is compact in both places.)

Displaying and positioning the QAT

If the QAT doesn't already appear, here's how to enable it and choose where it should be:

1. **Click the File tab and click Options.**

   The Outlook Options dialog box opens.

2. **In the navigation bar on the left, click Quick Access Toolbar.**

   Here you can not only enable the QAT, but also customize it in various ways. See Figure 14-2.

3. **If the Show Quick Access Toolbar check box is not selected, click it to select it.**

4. **Open the Toolbar Position drop-down menu and choose Below Ribbon or Above Ribbon.**

5. **If you want the command labels to appear when the QAT is below the ribbon, make sure the Always Show Command Labels check box is selected.**

   If you deselect this check box, only the icons will appear on the QAT.

6. **Click OK to close the dialog box.**

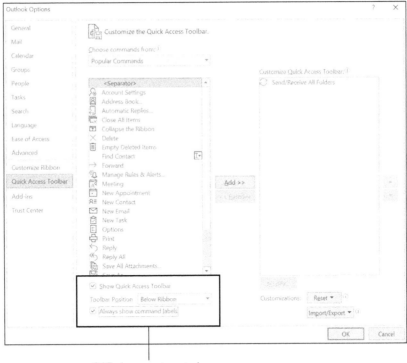

FIGURE 14-2:
Enable and
position the QAT.

QAT placement controls

Once the QAT is visible (in either location), you can control it via its menu. Notice the little down arrow at the right end of the QAT? Click it to open a menu, as shown in Figure 14-3. From here you can switch the position (Show Below the

Ribbon or Show Above the Ribbon), hide it (Hide Quick Access Toolbar), and customize it by adding and removing commands from it. (More about that coming up soon.)

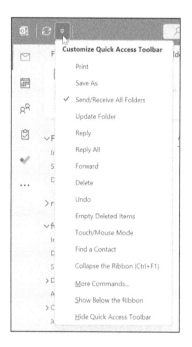

FIGURE 14-3:
Manage the QAT from its menu.

Adding and removing commands from the QAT

There are several ways to add and remove commands on the QAT. The easiest is to select commands from the QAT's menu, shown in Figure 14-3. This menu contains a dozen or so of the most popular commands, like Print, Reply, Delete, and so on. If a command already appears on the QAT, selecting it here removes it; it's a toggle.

Another way is to right-click any command on any tab of the Ribbon and choose Add to Quick Access Toolbar. To remove a command from the QAT, right-click its icon on the QAT and choose Remove from Quick Access Toolbar.

Yet another way is to add and remove commands from the Quick Access Toolbar section of the Outlook Options dialog box (refer to Figure 14-2). Since that method involves a few more steps than the others, let's break it down:

1. **Click the Customize Quick Access Toolbar icon and choose More Commands from its menu.**

    The icon is at the right end of the Quick Access Toolbar. The Outlook Options dialog box opens to the Quick Access Toolbar section (refer to Figure 14-2).

2. **To add a command:**

    a. **Select a command in the list on the left.**

    By default, the most popular commands are listed, but you can open the Choose commands from drop-down menu above the command list and choose All Commands to see the full list.

    b. **Click the Add button.**

    The command is copied to the Customize Quick Access Toolbar list on the right.

3. **To remove a command:**

    a. **Select a command in the list on the right.**

    These are the commands that are already on the QAT.

    b. **Click the Remove button.**

4. **Repeat Steps 2 and 3 as needed, then click OK to close the dialog box.**

Customizing the Ribbon

TIP

Because the Ribbon is the nerve center of Microsoft Office, you have good reason for wanting to make it your own. You can customize the Ribbon in a number of ways, including turning certain tabs and sections on or off, adding new tabs, and adding buttons for commands and macros.

However, you can't just modify the Ribbon willy-nilly, deleting and adding commands anywhere. That would be chaos! Instead, Outlook requires you to create a custom group in which to place commands. You can place a custom group on an existing tab, or you can create a new tab.

But wait, you might be thinking, *the Simplified Ribbon doesn't have groups. So how can I create a custom group to add commands to?* I'm going to let you in on a little secret: The Simplified Ribbon actually does have groups. They just aren't obvious. Take a closer look at any of the tabs, like the one in Figure 14-4, and you'll notice little vertical lines that separate groups of buttons from one another. Everything between a set of vertical lines is actually a group. You don't see the group names in Simplified Ribbon mode, but they're there.

FIGURE 14-4:
The buttons on
each tab are
divided by vertical
lines into groups.

Vertical dividers between groups

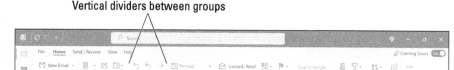

In this section, first I'll show you how to create a new tab, and then I'll show you how to add a custom group and add commands to it.

REMEMBER

When you open the interface to customize the Ribbon, it customizes whichever Ribbon mode you are working with at the moment. If you want to customize the Classic Ribbon, you will need to display the Classic Ribbon before you start customizing. Ditto for the Simplified Ribbon. The two are customized separately; making changes to one does not make the changes to the other.

Creating a new tab and group

If you have a lot of commands to add to the Ribbon, you might want to create a special tab for them. Creating a tab for your customizations can also make it easier to remember where those custom icons are; you don't have to recall which of the existing tabs you put them on.

Follow these steps to create a new tab on the Ribbon and two custom groups for it. (One group is created automatically when you create the tab, and the other we'll generate manually, just so you can see how it's done.)

1. **Make sure that the Ribbon mode you want to customize is displayed (Simplified or Classic).**

   If you need to switch Ribbon modes, click the down arrow at the far right end of the Ribbon and choose the desired mode.

2. **Right-click any area on the Ribbon.**

   A shortcut menu appears.

3. **Choose Customize the Ribbon.**

   The Outlook Options dialog box opens to the Customize the Ribbon section.

4. **In the list on the left, select the main tab that the new tab should appear after.**

   For example, to put it to the right of the Home tab, select the Home tab.

5. **Click the New Tab button.**

   A new tab is created named New Tab (Custom). A single group is created in it, called New Group (Custom). See Figure 14-5.

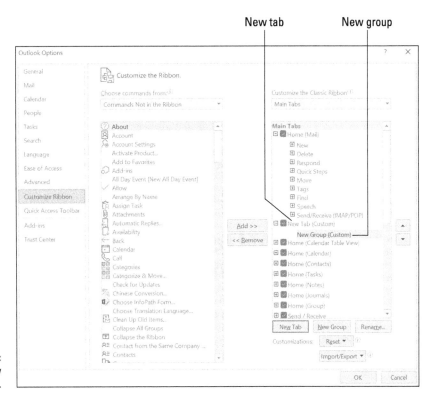

New tab   New group

FIGURE 14-5:
Creating a new
tab and group.

REMEMBER

(Custom) is not part of the name; it's a descriptor. It shows up here so you will remember which tabs and groups are custom ones (and can therefore be deleted and modified). Any tabs and groups that do not have (Custom) after their names cannot be modified.

6. **Click the new tab and then click Rename.**

   The Rename dialog box opens.

7. **Type a name for the new tab and click OK.**

   The tab's new name appears on the list.

8. **Make sure that the new tab's name is selected, and then click the New Group button.**

   A new group appears under the tab name.

9. **Click one of the new groups and click Rename.**

TECHNICAL
STUFF

In the Rename dialog box for a group, you can optionally select a symbol for the group. The icon will appear when the window width is so narrow that not all the groups can display, and each group instead appears as an icon with a drop-down menu showing its content. When this happens, whatever icon you pick here will be that button's icon.

10. Type a name for the new group (and, optionally, choose a symbol) and click OK.

11. Repeat Steps 8 and 9 to rename the other new group.

12. Click OK.

Admire your new tab on the Ribbon. Click it to see what it contains. Nothing, right? It's completely blank at this point, because you haven't placed any commands on it. You don't even see the groups, because empty groups don't appear.

To place commands in the new groups, see the next section.

Adding and removing commands on the Ribbon

Now that you have the structure in place, you can add commands to your custom tab and group(s). Follow these steps:

1. Right-click any area on the Ribbon.

A shortcut menu appears.

2. Choose Customize the Ribbon.

The Outlook Options dialog box opens to the Customize the Ribbon section (refer to Figure 14-5).

3. In the list on the left, open the Choose Commands From drop-down menu and select the command set you want to work with.

You can choose to see just the commands on a certain tab, Just Popular Commands, Commands Not on the Ribbon, and so on. For experimental purposes, you might want to choose Commands Not on the Ribbon so you can see what you might be missing out on with the standard Ribbon commands.

4. In the list on the left, select the command you want to add to the Ribbon.

The sky's the limit! Pick any command you want.

5. In the list on the right, select your custom tab.

Technically, you can add commands to a non-custom tab, as long as you add a custom group to that tab first. But for this example, we'll use the custom tab you created in the previous section.

6. In the list on the right, select the custom group where you want to place the command.

7. **Click Add.**

   The command appears beneath the selected custom tab.

8. **Repeat Steps 4–7 to add other commands if desired.**

9. **Click OK.**

Admire your tab again on the Ribbon. This time you see at least one group and at least one command.

WARNING

Outlook won't let you add just any command anywhere. If you are adding a command to an existing tab (after creating a custom group there, of course), you can only add a command that is suitable to the module in which that tab appears. For example, you can't add the Mark Complete command for tasks to a tab that's specific to the Calendar module — that command isn't useful in that location.

Reordering Ribbon tabs

You can reorder the ribbon tabs any time you like. The order from left to right on the Ribbon corresponds to the order from top to bottom in the Outlook Options dialog box. You can reorder any of the tabs, not just custom ones.

To reorder the tabs, follow these steps:

1. **Right-click any area on the Ribbon.**

   A shortcut menu appears.

2. **Choose Customize the Ribbon.**

   The Outlook Options dialog box opens to the Customize the Ribbon section (refer to Figure 14-5).

3. **In the list on the right, click the tab you want to move.**

4. **Do one of the following:**

   • Click the up or down arrow buttons to the right of the list.

   • Drag and drop the tab to a higher or lower position on the list.

5. **When you are finished reordering the tabs, click OK.**

Check your work on the Ribbon. If you don't like it, make more changes.

Resetting Ribbon customization

If you get carried away and customize Outlook beyond recognition, you can undo all your customizations by clicking the Reset button at the bottom of the Customize the Ribbon screen in the Outlook Options dialog box (refer to Figure 14-5). Then on the menu that appears, click Reset All Customizations. That wipes out all your customizations, but it makes Outlook look normal again.

Hiding or deleting a Ribbon tab or group

To hide a Ribbon tab, deselect its check box in the list of tabs on the right side of the Customize the Ribbon section in the Outlook Options dialog box (refer to Figure 14-5). Alternatively, you can right-click it on the list and choose Show Tab to toggle its check box off. You can hide any tab, not just the custom ones.

To delete a Ribbon tab (and it has to be a custom one), select it on the list in the Outlook Options dialog box and then right-click it and choose Remove. However, there's a gotcha — you can't remove a tab unless it is empty. So first you have to remove each of its groups. Right-click a group and choose Remove to get rid of it.

Playing with Columns in Table/List Views

Every Outlook module has its own selection of views as well as its own set of Ribbon tabs. The Calendar module has (among others) a view that looks like a calendar. The Contacts module includes a view that looks like an address card.

All modules enable you to use at least one type of Table view, which organizes your data into the old-fashioned row-and-column arrangement. Table views show you the most detailed information about the items you've created; these views also help you organize information in the greatest number of ways with the least effort. Table views look a little dull, but they get you where you need to go.

REMEMBER

The names of Table views often contain the word *list*, as in Simple list, Phone list, or just list. The word *list* means that they form a plain vanilla table of items — just like a grocery list. That's not always the case, though, because both Detailed and Simple List views in the Tasks module are tabular views but don't have "list" in their names.

TIP

Table views are organized into columns and rows, as shown in Figure 14-6. Each row shows information for one item: one appointment in your calendar, one task in your Task list, or one person in your Contacts list. Adding a row is easy: Just add a new item by pressing Ctrl+N and then filling in the information you want for that item. Getting rid of a row is easy, too: Just delete the row by clicking the item with your mouse and then pressing Delete on your keyboard.

FIGURE 14-6:
The Tasks module
in Table view
(Detailed view).

The columns in Table view show you pieces of information about each item. Most Outlook modules can store far more data about an item than you can display on-screen in a row-and-column format. For example, the Contacts list holds more than 90 pieces of information about every person in your list. If each person were represented by one row, you'd need more than 90 columns to display everything.

Adding a column

Outlook starts you out with a limited number of columns in the Phone view of your Contacts list. If you want more columns, you can easily add some. You can display as many columns as you want, but you may have to scroll across the screen to see the information you want to see.

To add a column in any Table view, follow these steps:

1. **Right-click on any column title.**

   A shortcut menu appears.

2. **Select Field Chooser from the shortcut menu.**

   The Field Chooser box opens.

3. **Drag the desired field into the table.**

   If the field you want doesn't appear in the Field Chooser pane, open the drop-down menu at the top of the list and select All Contact Fields.

   Be sure to drag the new item to the table's top row — where the heading names are, as shown in Figure 14-7.

   Notice that each name in the Field Chooser is in its own little gray box. Two red arrows show you where your new field will end up when you drop it off.

TIP

4. **(Optional) Click Close (X) on the Field Chooser pane to close it when you are finished using it, or leave it open to add more fields later.**

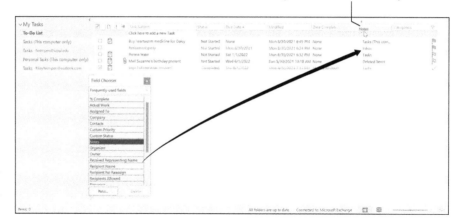

Drag the field to the desired position.

FIGURE 14-7:
The Notes field is
being dragged to
the top row
of the table.

Moving a column

Moving columns is even easier than adding columns. Just drag the column heading to where you want it. Two little red arrows appear as you're dragging the heading to show you where the column will end up when you release the mouse button, just like the ones you saw in Figure 14-7.

Widening or narrowing a column

Widening or narrowing a column is even easier than moving a column. Here's how:

1. **Move the mouse pointer to the right edge of the column you want to widen or narrow until the pointer becomes a two-headed arrow.**

   Making that mouse pointer turn into a two-headed arrow takes a bit of dexterity. Once you get a little bit of practice, you'll find it's fast and easy.

2. **Drag the edge of the column until it's the width you desire.**

   The two-headed arrow creates a thin line you can drag to resize the column. (Figure 14-8 shows a column being widened.) What you see is what you get.

TIP

If you're not really sure how wide a column needs to be, just double-click the right edge of the column header. When you double-click that spot, Outlook does a trick called *size to fit*, which widens or narrows a column to exactly the size of the widest piece of data in the column.

Drag to reposition the column's right edge.

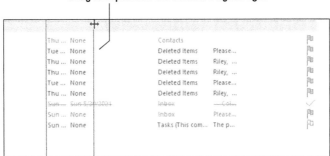

FIGURE 14-8:
Widening the
Modified column.

Removing a column

You can remove columns you don't want to look at. To remove a column, follow these steps:

1. **Right-click on the heading of the column you want to remove.**

A menu appears.

2. **Choose Remove This Column.**

Zap! It's gone!

Don't worry too much about deleting columns. When you zap a column, the field remains in the item. You can use the column–adding procedure (which I describe earlier in this chapter) to put it back. If you're confused by this whole notion of columns and fields, see the earlier sidebar, "Columns = Fields."

Sorting Items

Sorting just means putting your list in order. In fact, a list is always in some kind of order. Sorting just changes the order.

You can tell how your list is sorted:

>> A heading with a triangle in it means the entire list is sorted by the information in that column.

>> If the column has numbers in it and if the triangle's large side is at the top, the list goes from largest to smallest number.

>> Columns that have text get sorted in alphabetical order. *A* is the smallest letter, and *Z* is the largest.

Sorting from Table view

This is by far the easiest way: When sorting from Table view, click the heading of a column you want to sort. The entire table is sorted according to the column you clicked: by date, name, or whatever. Not all fields can be sorted on (for example, Task Subject can't be sorted on in the To-Do List), but most can.

Sorting from the Sort dialog box

Although clicking a column is the easiest way to sort, doing so enables you to perform a sort on only one column. You may want to perform a sort on two or more columns.

To perform a sort on two or more columns, follow these steps:

1. **Choose the View tab on the Ribbon and then click the View Settings button.**

   The Advanced View Settings dialog box opens.

2. **Click the Sort button.**

   The Sort dialog box opens.

3. **From the Sort Items By list box, choose the first field you want to sort by.**

   Choose carefully; a much larger list of fields is in the list than is usually in the view. It's confusing.

4. **Choose Ascending or Descending sort order.**

   That means to choose whether to sort from smallest to largest (*ascending*) or vice versa (*descending*).

5. **Repeat Steps 3 and 4 for each field you want to sort.**

   As the dialog box implies, the first column you select is the most important. The entire table is sorted according to that field and then by the fields you pick later — in the order in which you select them. For example, if you sort your Phone list by company first and then by name, your list begins with the names of the people who work for a certain company, displayed alphabetically, followed by the names of the people who work for another company, and so on.

6. **Click OK.**

   Your list is sorted.

Grouping Items

Sorting and grouping are similar. Both procedures organize items in your table according to columns. *Grouping* is different from sorting in that it creates bunches of similar items you can open or close. You can look at only the bunches that interest you and ignore all the other bunches.

For example, when you balance your checkbook, you probably *sort* your checks by check number. At tax time, you *group* your checks: You make a pile of checks for medical expenses, another pile of checks for charitable deductions, and another pile of checks for the money you invested in *For Dummies* books. Then, you can add up the amounts you spent in each category and enter those figures on your tax return.

The quickest way to group items is to right-click on the heading of the column you want to group by and then choose Group By This Field. The Group By box automatically appears, and the name of the field you chose automatically appears in the Group By box. Isn't that slick? Figure 14-9 shows my To-Do List grouped by Status, for example.

After you've added grouping to a view, you might decide you don't like it. To remove grouping for a view that doesn't have it by default (such as Phone view), click the View tab on the Ribbon and click Reset View.

FIGURE 14-9:
Grouping the
To-Do List by
Status.

Saving Custom Views

If you're used to saving Word documents, you're familiar with the idea of saving views. When you make any of the changes to a view I describe earlier in this chapter, you can save the changes as a new view or save the changes to the current view. If you plan to use a certain view repeatedly, it's worth saving.

TIP

You can save any view you like:

1. **Click the View tab.**

2. **Click the Change View button.**

3. **Choose Save Current View as a New View.**

4. **Name your view.**

5. **Click OK.**

   The new view appears on the Change View button's list, along with the standard views.

Using Categories

There's a lot of value in a good collection of information. However, you can't squeeze full value from a list of contacts or tasks if you can't get a quick handle on which items are important and which aren't. The Categories feature in Outlook is designed to help you tell what's urgent from what can wait.

Assigning a category

You can find out what categories are available by clicking the Categorize button on the Home tab (in the Mail module only). The Categorize button looks like a small, multicolored tic-tac-toe square, as shown in Figure 14-10. Clicking the Categorize button opens a list of (surprise!) categories — each named after a color. If you simply want to color-code your items from the default, the process is pretty simple.

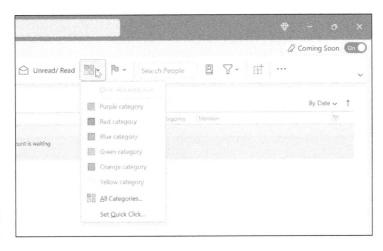

FIGURE 14-10:
The Categorize
button.

Follow these steps to assign a category to an item:

1. **Click the mail item you want to categorize.**

   The item is highlighted.

2. **Click the Categorize button and choose from the list.**

   A colored block appears in the item to indicate which category you chose.

You can assign multiple categories to each item, although putting too many on an item may be more confusing than assigning no categories at all.

Renaming a category

You can memorize what each Outlook category color means to you, but I would rather have a name associated with each color so I know why I'm assigning a certain category to a certain item.

TIP

The first time you use a category, a dialog box appears to let you rename it. If you miss that opportunity, use the following steps to rename it:

1. **Click the Categorize button and choose All Categories.**

    The Color Categories dialog box opens.

2. **Click the category you want to rename.**

    The category you select is highlighted.

3. **Click Rename.**

    The category you chose is surrounded by a box to show that you can edit it.

4. **Type the new name you want to assign to that category.**

    The name you type appears in place of the old name. See Figure 14-11.

5. **Click OK.**

    The Color Categories dialog box closes.

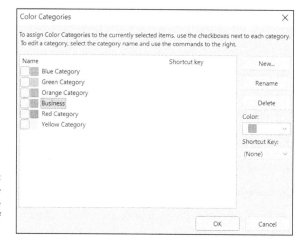

FIGURE 14-11: Rename the categories more meaningfully if you like.

If you change the name of a category you had already assigned to some Outlook items, that category name automatically changes on those items.

Changing a category color

You can change the color of a category as well as its name. Assigning memorable colors can give important clues about how your work is going or how well you're keeping up with current projects.

Follow these steps to change the color of a category:

1. **Click the Categorize button and choose All Categories.**

   The Color Categories dialog box opens (refer to Figure 14-11).

2. **Click the category to which you want to assign a new color.**

   The category you select is highlighted.

3. **Click the Color button.**

   A drop-down menu appears, showing the colors you can choose.

4. **Click the color you want to assign.**

   The color you chose appears in place of the old color.

5. **Click OK.**

   The Color Categories dialog box closes.

TIP

You can choose None and create a colorless category. That's kind of drab, but if it fits your mood, go for it. One possible reason for creating colorless categories is that Outlook only offers 25 colors and you may have more than 25 categories. But after you get past 25 categories, you might consider cutting down on the number of categories to reduce confusion from having two or more categories with the same color.

Assigning a category shortcut key

You can give each category a shortcut key, which enables you to assign a category without touching your mouse. That's very handy when you want to zoom through a screen full of email messages or tasks and set everything into some kind of order.

To assign a shortcut key to a category, follow these steps:

1. **Click the Categorize button and choose All Categories.**

   The Color Categories dialog box opens (refer to Figure 14-11).

2. **Click the category to which you want to assign a shortcut key.**

   The category you select is highlighted to show you selected it.

3. **Click the Shortcut Key drop-down menu box button.**

   A list of shortcut keys appears.

4. **Click the shortcut key you want to assign.**

   The name of the shortcut key you chose appears to the right of the category.

5. **Click OK.**

   You can't assign more than one shortcut to a category; that would be confusing. However, you can assign more than one category to an item.

5

Outlook at Work

IN THIS CHAPTER

» Making meeting planning easy with Outlook

» Allowing coworkers to help you do your work

» Giving permissions to a delegate

» Displaying two calendars side by side

» Setting up your out of office message

» Understanding all those address books

Chapter **15**

Outlook on the Job

icrosoft is a big company that writes big programs for big companies with big bucks. As you'd expect, some parts of Outlook were originally meant for people at big companies. But these days, people in small organizations also need tools to improve teamwork and collaboration. That's especially true in a world of far-flung virtual teams whose members communicate almost exclusively via phone and email.

Companies that use Outlook often have a network that's running a program called Microsoft Exchange Server in the background. If you're working with an Exchange-based account in Outlook, you have access to extra features and capabilities. Outlook users with Exchange can look at another employee's calendar, for example, or give someone else the power to answer email messages on that person's behalf — any of a host of handy tasks right from a single desktop.

REMEMBER

If you have multiple email accounts set up in Outlook, as you learned about in Chapter 7, you might notice the commands on the Ribbon changing when you select a different account. That's because Outlook shows you only the commands that you can actually execute for the selected account. If you don't see a particular command that this chapter discusses, it's probably because you don't have an Exchange-based account selected at the moment. (It could also be that you're in the Classic Ribbon mode, rather than the default Simplified Ribbon mode. Click the down arrow at the right end of the Ribbon to switch.)

TIP

Outlook.com and Microsoft 365 email addresses are also Exchange accounts. If none of your regular email accounts are on Exchange servers, and you want to play around with the features covered in this chapter, consider creating a free email account at Outlook.com.

Planning Meetings with Outlook

If your company is like many others, you spend a lot of time in meetings — and even more time figuring out when to hold meetings and agreeing on what to do when you're not having meetings. Outlook has some tools for planning meetings and making decisions. Although some of these features are available to all Outlook users, they work much better when you're also using Exchange.

Organizing a meeting

Suppose you want to set up a meeting with three coworkers. You call the first person to suggest a meeting time and then call the second — only to find out that the second person isn't available when the first one wants to meet. So, you agree on a time with the second person — only to discover that the third person can't make this new time. You might want to invite a fourth person, but heaven knows how long it'll take to come up with an appropriate time for that one.

If you use Outlook, you can check everyone's schedule, pick a day, and suggest a meeting time that everyone can work with in the first place — with a single message.

To invite several people to a meeting, follow these steps:

1. **Click Calendar in the navigation bar (or press Ctrl+2).**

   Your calendar appears.

TIP

If you have more than one email account, you might also have more than one calendar; make sure the desired calendar is displayed. You can choose among the different calendars in the lower left corner of the Outlook window. It makes a difference if you have an Exchange email account set up in Outlook because the Exchange account's meeting scheduling will give you access to conference rooms and other resources for your company.

2. **On the Home tab of the Ribbon, click the New Meeting button (or press Ctrl+Shift+Q).**

    If you're in Simplified Ribbon mode, make sure you click the face of the button, not its drop-down arrow.

    The New Meeting form opens.

3. **Click the Scheduling Assistant tab on the Ribbon.**

    The Attendee Availability page appears, as shown in Figure 15-1.

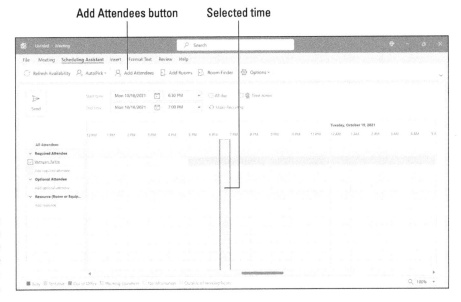

Add Attendees button   Selected time

FIGURE 15-1:
Use the Attendee
Availability page
to invite
coworkers to a
meeting.

4. **Click the Add Attendees button on the Ribbon.**

    The Select Attendees and Resources dialog box opens.

5. **Click the name of a person you want to invite to the meeting.**

    The name you click is highlighted to show that you've selected it.

6. **Click either the Required or Optional button, depending on how important that person's attendance is to the meeting.**

    The name you select appears in either the Required or Optional box, depending on which button you click.

7. **Repeat Steps 5 and 6 until you've chosen everyone you want to add to the meeting.**

    The names you choose appear in the Select Attendees and Resources dialog box, as shown in Figure 15-2.

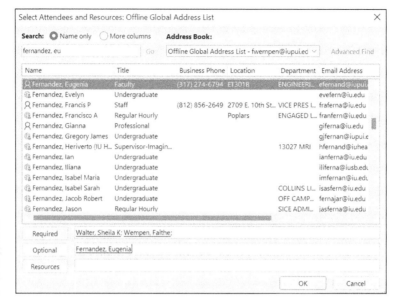

You can also invite people who don't appear in the address list that appears by typing their email addresses in manually. However, if you don't have access to their calendar through your Exchange server, you won't be able to see their availability, so there's not much point in doing it here.

8. **Click OK.**

The Select Attendees and Resources dialog box closes, and the names you chose appear on the Attendee Availability page. If Outlook connects with an Exchange server, the Attendee Availability page also diagrams each person's schedule so you can see when everyone has free time. Depending on how Outlook connects to the Exchange server, it might take a few moments for Outlook to get everyone's schedule.

9. **Enter the meeting start and end times in the boxes at the top of the Attendee Availability page.**

Try to find a time where none of the attendees have conflicts. For example, in Figure 15-3, I've found that we can all meet at 12 p.m.

10. **Click the Meeting tab on the Ribbon.**

A form appears where you can enter the details about the meeting.

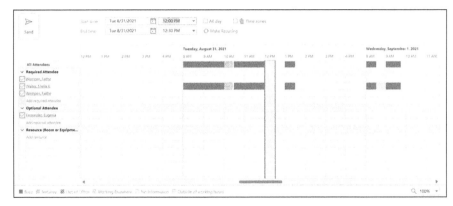

FIGURE 15-3:
Find a time when
all invitees can
attend.

11. **Type the subject of the meeting in the Title box and then add details about where the meeting will be held in the Location box.**

TIP

Many people also use Outlook to set up times for telephone conference calls. The Location box is a good place to enter the dial-in number and conference code when you set up conference calls. Not only does that make the information easier for your attendees to find, but the next time you organize a call, you can also click the arrow in the Location box to pull your codes up again.

12. **In the Message area at the bottom of the form, type information you want attendees to know about your meeting.**

13. **Click Send.**

Your meeting request is sent to the people you've invited, and the meeting is added to your calendar.

TIP

If your system administrators see fit, they can set up Exchange accounts for resources, such as conference rooms. If they do, you can figure out a location and its availability for your meeting while you're figuring out who can attend. A Room Finder pane appears to the right of the appointment window. You can turn Room Finder on or off with the Room Finder button on the Meeting tab of the Ribbon.

Responding to a meeting request

Even if you don't organize meetings and send invitations, you may get invited to meetings now and then, so it's a good idea to know how to respond to a meeting request if you get one. ("Politely" is a good concept to start with.)

When you've been invited to a meeting, you get a special email message that offers the following buttons. Each of these buttons has its own drop-down menu with additional options, as shown in Figure 15-4.

FIGURE 15-4:
Select your response to the meeting request from the Meeting tab on the Ribbon.

>> **Accept:** Outlook automatically adds the meeting to your schedule and creates a new email message to the person who organized the meeting, telling that person your decision.

>> **Tentative:** The meeting's automatically added to your schedule. A new email message goes to the person who organized the meeting.

TIP

>> **Decline:** Just can't make it? If you click Decline, Outlook sends a message to the meeting organizer to let them know. It's good form to add a business reason to explain why you're missing a meeting — "Sorry, I have a deadline" rather than "I have to wash my aardvark" or "Sorry, I plan to be sane that day."

>> **Propose New Time:** If the meeting organizer chose an inconvenient time, you can suggest another by clicking Propose New Time. Outlook gives you two ways to propose a new time:

- Choose Decline and Propose New Time if the original time is simply impossible.

- Choose Tentative and Propose New Time if you're not sure whether the original time will work and you'd like to suggest an alternative time.

>> **Other Actions:** This is the ellipsis (. . .) button, and it opens a menu of additional commands, including Reply, Reply All, Forward, and Calendar. The latter shows your complete calendar in a separate window so you can get a bigger picture of what your schedule looks like.

From the Accept, Tentative, or Decline button menu, you can choose Edit the Response Before Sending if you want to include an explanation to the message, or just select Send the Response Now to deliver your message.

When a recipient gets a meeting invitation, if they are also set up on the Exchange server, the message shows a preview of their calendar for the date and time of the meeting — giving them a quick snapshot of their availability.

Checking responses to your meeting request

Each time you organize a meeting with Outlook, you create a small flurry of email messages inviting people to attend, and they respond with a flurry of messages either accepting or declining your invitation. You may have a good enough memory to recall who said *Yes* and *No*, but I usually need some help. Fortunately, Outlook keeps track of who said what.

To check the status of responses to your meeting request, follow these steps:

1. **Click Calendar in the navigation bar.**

   Your calendar appears.

2. **Double-click the item you want to check.**

   The meeting opens.

3. **Click the Tracking tab.**

   The list of people you invited appears, listing each person's response to your invitation, as shown in Figure 15-5.

Responses received

FIGURE 15-5:
See the RSVPs
from your VIPs.

Sad to say, only the meeting organizer can find out who has agreed to attend a certain meeting. If you plan to attend a certain meeting only because that special someone you met in the elevator might also attend, you'll have to go to the meeting to find out if that person is there. You can tell who was invited to a meeting by checking the names on the meeting request you got by email.

Taking a vote

Management gurus constantly tell us about the importance of good teamwork and decision making. But how do you get a team to make a decision when you can't find most of the team members most of the time? You can use Outlook as a decision-making tool if you take advantage of the Outlook voting buttons.

Voting is a special feature of Outlook email that adds buttons to an email message sent to a group of people. When they get the message and if they're also using Outlook, recipients can click a button to indicate their response. Outlook automatically tallies the responses so you can see which way the wind is blowing in your office.

To add voting buttons to an email message you're creating, follow these steps while creating your message:

1. **From the Mail module, click New Email on the Home tab to start creating a new message.**

    A new Message form opens.

2. **Enter the recipients, subject, message body, and other fields as usual.**

3. **Click the Options tab on the Ribbon and then click the Use Voting Buttons button.**

    A list of suggested voting buttons appears. The suggested choices include the following:

    - Approve;Reject

    - Yes;No

    - Yes;No;Maybe

    - Custom

    If you choose Custom, the Properties dialog box opens. Type your own choices in the Use Voting Buttons text box. Follow the pattern of the suggested choices; just separate your options with a semicolon. If you want to ask people to vote on the lunch menu, for example, include a range of choices, such as *Pizza;Burgers;Salad*. Don't use any spaces after the semicolons.

4. **Click the set of voting buttons you want to use.**

    The message You Added Voting Buttons to This Message now appears at the top of your message. If you're adding your own custom choices, however, you'll need to click the Close button in the Properties dialog box when you're done to return to your message.

5. **Click the Send button.**

And there you are! Democracy in action! Isn't that inspiring?

Casting your vote

When your recipients get your message, here's what they need to do to vote:

1. **On the Message tab, click the Vote button.**

The voting options appear. Figure 15-6 shows two possible versions your recipients might see, depending on their email server.

2. **Click the desired vote.**

What happens next depends on what kind of voting prompt your recipients got. If they got a voting prompt like the one on the left in Figure 15-6, a reply message is created with text as the reply. (No special button functionality.) At that point they just send the message normally.

If they got a voting prompt like the one on the right in Figure 15-6, they then see a dialog box asking whether Outlook should send the response now or edit it before responding. For the sake of these steps, let's say they want to edit the response.

FIGURE 15-6:
Two possible ways that recipients will be invited to vote.

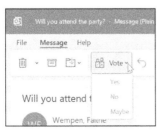

3. **Click Edit the Response Before Sending, and click OK.**

If you choose Send the Response Now, you can skip the rest of these steps.

4. **(Optional) Type any comments in the Message area at the bottom of the box.**

5. **Click Send.**

The message is sent.

When the replies arrive, you'll see who chose what by looking at a reply's Subject. Messages from people who chose Approve, for example, start with the word *Approve*; rejection messages start with the word *Reject*.

Assigning tasks

Anything worth doing is worth getting someone else to do for you. You can assign a task to another person and then keep track of that person's progress.

To assign a task to someone else, follow these steps:

1. **Click Tasks in the navigation bar.**

The Task list opens.

2. **Right-click on an item in your Task list.**

A shortcut menu appears.

3. **Choose Assign Task.**

A Task form appears. It's basically an email message with the task information.

4. **Type the name of the person to whom you're assigning the task in the To box, just as you would with an email message.**

The person's name appears in the To box, as shown in Figure 15-7.

5. **Click the Send button.**

The task is sent to the person to whom you've assigned it.

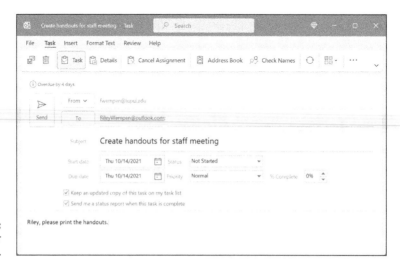

FIGURE 15-7:
Send your
assigned task.

The person to whom you addressed the task gets an email message with special buttons marked Accept and Decline — much like the meeting request message I discuss earlier in this chapter. When the person clicks Accept, the task is automatically added to their Task list in Outlook. If the person clicks Decline, they are fired. Okay, just kidding — the person isn't actually fired. Not yet, anyway.

Sending a status report

People who give out tasks really like the Assign Task feature. People who have to do those tasks are much less enthusiastic. If you're a task getter more often than you're a task giver, you have to look at the bright side: Outlook on an Exchange network can also help the boss stay informed about how much you're doing — and doing and doing!

You may have noticed that the Task form has a box called Status and another called % Complete. If you keep the information in those boxes up to date, you can constantly remind the Big Cheese about your valuable contributions by sending status reports.

To send a status report, follow these steps:

1. **Click Tasks in the navigation bar.**

   The Task list opens.

2. **Double-click the task you want to report on.**

   The Task form opens.

3. **Click the Send Status Report button on the Ribbon.**

   A Message window appears, and the name of the person who assigned the task appears in the To box.

4. **Enter any explanation you want to send about the task into the text box at the bottom of the form.**

5. **Click Send.**

You can send status reports as often as you like — weekly, daily, hourly. It's probably a good idea to leave enough time between status reports to complete some tasks.

Enabling Coworkers to Help You with Your Work

REMEMBER

I focus the rest of this chapter on the features that work only if you have Outlook *and* Exchange Server. Why confuse non-Exchange users by describing features they can't use?

If you use Outlook at home or in an office without Exchange, you can't use the features I describe in the rest of this chapter. But take heart: Little by little, Microsoft is finding ways to make Exchange-only features available to all Outlook users, so you can look over this section as a preview of things to come.

Giving delegate permissions

Good managers delegate authority. (That's what my assistant, Igor, says, anyway.) Extremely busy people sometimes give an assistant the job of managing the boss's calendar, schedule, and even email. That way, the boss can concentrate on the big picture while the assistant dwells on the details.

WARNING

When you designate a delegate in Outlook on an Exchange network, you give certain rights to the delegate you name — in particular, the right to look at whichever Outlook module you pick. Bear in mind, that person will see everything that appears in that module — no matter how personal; always choose a delegate you can trust with your deep, dark secrets. Oh, and try not to have too many deep, dark secrets; it's very stressful trying to remember all of them.

To name a delegate, follow these steps:

1. **Click the File tab, and then click the Account Settings button.**

   A drop-down menu appears.

2. **Click the Delegate Access command.**

   The Delegates dialog box opens.

   If you don't see the Delegate Access command, make sure that your Exchange-based email address is selected from the drop-down menu at the top of the Account Information page.

3. **Click the Add button.**

   The Add Users dialog box opens.

4. **Double-click the name of each delegate you want to name.**

   The names you choose appear in the Add Users dialog box.

5. **Click the OK button.**

   The Delegate Permissions dialog box opens, where you can choose exactly which permissions you want to give to your delegate(s).

6. **Make any changes you want in the Delegate Permissions dialog box.**

REMEMBER

   See Figure 15-8. If you make no choices in the Delegate Permissions dialog box, by default, your delegate is granted Editor status for your Calendar and Tasks, which means the delegate can read, create, and change items in those two Outlook modules.

Delegate Permissions: Walter, Sheila K   ✕

This delegate has the following permissions

Calendar   Editor (can read, create, and modify items)   ⌄
☑ Delegate receives copies of meeting-related messages sent to me

Tasks   Editor (can read, create, and modify items)   ⌄

Inbox   None   ⌄

Contacts   None   ⌄

Notes   None   ⌄

☐ Automatically send a message to delegate summarizing these permissions
☐ Delegate can see my private items

            OK   Cancel

FIGURE 15-8:
Set up the
delegation
permissions.

7. **Click OK.**

   The Delegate Permissions dialog box closes. The names you chose appear in the Delegates dialog box.

8. **Click OK.**

   The Delegates dialog box closes.

Opening someone else's folder

It's fairly common for a team of people who work closely together to share calendars or Task lists; not only can they see what other team members are doing, but they can also enter appointments on behalf of a teammate — for example, if you work in a company that has sales and service people sitting side by side. As a service person, you may find it helpful if your partner on the sales side is allowed to enter appointments with a client in your calendar while you're out dealing with other clients. To do that, your partner needs to open your Calendar folder.

You can't open another person's Outlook folder unless that person has given you permission first, as I describe in the preceding section. After you have permission, you can open the other person's folder by following these steps:

1. **Click the File tab and click the Open & Export button in the navigation pane on the left.**

2. **Click the Other User's Folder button.**

   The Open Other User's Folder dialog box opens, as shown in Figure 15-9.

3. **Click the Name button.**

   The Select Name dialog box opens.

4. **Double-click the name of the person whose folder you want to open.**

   The Select Name dialog box closes; the name you double-clicked appears in the Open Other User's Folder dialog box.

5. **Click the triangle on the Folder Type box.**

   A list of the folders you can choose appears.

6. **Click the name of the folder you want to view.**

   The name of the folder you choose appears in the Folder Type box.

7. **Click OK.**

   The folder you pick is now accessible to you, but it might not be obvious where to find it. For example, if you want to see the other person's calendar, click the Calendar button and then open the Folder pane. The other person's calendar appears in the Folder pane as a shared calendar.

Viewing Two Calendars Side by Side

It's pretty common for an executive to give an assistant the right to view the executive's calendar. That way, the assistant can maintain the executive's schedule while the executive is busy doing other things. Sometimes, when you're working as someone's assistant, you need to see the boss's calendar and your own calendar simultaneously. If you have the required permission (see the section "Giving Delegate Permissions," earlier in this chapter), Outlook can display both calendars side by side — and you can compare schedules at a glance.

After you've gone through the steps to open someone else's calendar, you'll see a section labeled Shared Calendars when you click the Calendar button and open the Folder pane. There, you'll see the names of people whose calendars you've opened. If you select the check box next to one of those names, that person's calendar appears on-screen right next to yours. You can change the date displayed in either calendar by clicking on the date you want to see, exactly in the same way you do it when you're viewing only one calendar.

Your screen might look pretty cluttered when you put two busy schedules side by side, so you may need to switch to a one-day view to keep the screen comprehensible. When you're done viewing two schedules, click the box in the Folder pane next to the other person's name to go back to viewing one calendar.

Setting access permissions

Many times, a busy executive gives their assistant the right to view and even edit the executive's entire Outlook account right from the assistant's desk. That way, the assistant organizes what the executive does and the executive just goes out and does the job. This is known as *granting access permissions*, which is a lot like naming a delegate, which is described in the section "Giving Delegate Permissions," earlier in this chapter.

WARNING

When you grant access permissions, the power you're giving is broader than simply delegating permissions; you're giving the assistant permission to use the entire account.

Before someone can access your account, you have to give them permission by following these steps:

1. **In the Mail module, right-click on your account name in the Folders list.**

   Your account name is above the Inbox icon. When you right-click on your account name, a shortcut menu appears.

2. **Choose Folder Permissions.**

   The Permissions tab of the Properties dialog box opens, as shown in Figure 15-10.

3. **Click the Add button.**

   The Add Users dialog box opens.

FIGURE 15-10:
You can grant
permission to
view your folders
to anyone on
your network.

4. **Double-click the name of the person to whom you want to give access.**

   The name you double-click appears in the Add box at the bottom of the Add Users dialog box.

5. **Click OK.**

   The Add Users dialog box closes, and the name you chose appears in the Name box in the Permissions dialog box.

6. **Click the name that you just added to the Name list in the Properties dialog box.**

   The name you click is highlighted to show that you've selected it.

7. **Open the Permission Level drop-down menu and choose a permission level.**

   Assigning a permission level gives a specific set of rights to the person to whom the level is assigned. For example, an Editor can add, edit, or remove items from your Outlook folders, whereas a Reviewer can only read items. If you want to see exactly which rights you're assigning when you choose a permission level, look at the check boxes below the name of the Permission Level box. You'll see check marks in the boxes representing the rights associated with the selected permission level.

8. **Click OK.**

   Now that you've given a person permission to see your account as a whole, you must give permission to see each folder in the account individually. You can grant permission to another person to see almost every folder in Outlook — even your Deleted Items and Junk Email folders if you want, but not your Contacts folder.

9. **Right-click on the folder you want to let someone see.**

   A shortcut menu appears.

10. **Choose Properties and select the Permission tab.**

11. **Follow Steps 3–7.**

    You can either follow these steps for each icon in the Folders list, or you can read the section "Giving Delegate Permissions," earlier in this chapter, and then follow those steps to grant access to another person.

However, you have no way of knowing whether people have given you permission to view their data unless you try to open one of their folders (or unless they tell you), which prevents nasty hackers from breaking into several people's data by stealing just one password.

Viewing two accounts

If your boss gives you permission to view their entire Outlook account, you can set up your copy of Outlook so *your* folders *and* the boss's folders show up in your Outlook Folders list.

REMEMBER

When you want to see your calendar, click your Calendar folder; when you want to see the boss's calendar, click the boss's Calendar folder.

To add a second person's account to your view of Outlook, follow these steps:

1. **Right-click your account name in the Folders list.**

   Your account name is located above the Inbox icon, and when you right-click on it, a menu appears.

2. **Choose Data File Properties.**

   The Data File Properties dialog box opens, showing the General tab.

3. **Click the Advanced button.**

   The Microsoft Exchange dialog box opens.

4. **Click the Advanced tab.**

   The Advanced tab in the Microsoft Exchange dialog box opens, as shown in Figure 15-11.

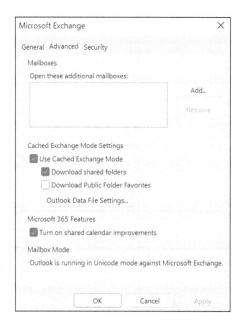

FIGURE 15-11:
Add someone else's folders to your Outlook collection.

5. **Click the Add button.**

   The Add Mailbox dialog box opens.

6. **Type the *username* of the person whose account you want to add.**

   You have to type the person's username, as assigned by the Exchange server administrator. The dialog box doesn't offer you a list of users to pick from. If you don't type the person's username correctly or if the username you typed doesn't exist, you get an error message indicating that the name you entered couldn't be matched to a name in the Address list. If that happens, check to make sure you have the correct spelling of the person's username.

TIP

If you have to make a blind guess at the username, try whatever is before the @ sign in the person's email address.

7. **Click the OK button.**

   The Add Mailbox dialog box closes, and the person's username appears in the Mailboxes list on the Advanced tab of the Microsoft Exchange dialog box.

8. **Click OK.**

   The Microsoft Exchange dialog box closes.

9. **Click OK.**

   The Data File Properties dialog box closes.

After you add another person's account to Outlook, use the Folder pane to see the new person's items. Select Mail from the Folder pane and you'll see a new section in your Folders list called Mailbox, followed by the new person's username; that's where that person's Mail-related items are located, such as their Inbox. Select Calendar from the Folder pane and you'll see a new calendar entry listed in the My Calendars section, followed by the new person's username; that's where that person's calendar is located. And so it goes for each module that the person has given you permission to view.

Managing Your Out of Office Message

What's the best part of anyone's job? Vacation! But it's tough to enjoy your tropical vacation if you keep having to answer pesky emails from work rather than guzzling colorful tropical beverages. Tell all your esteemed colleagues that you're away from work by turning on your out of office message. When you do that, every time someone sends you an email, Outlook will automatically reply with the details you specify.

To turn on Automatic Replies, follow these steps:

1. **Click the File tab and choose Automatic Replies (Out of Office).**

   The Automatic Replies dialog box opens.

2. **Click Send Automatic Replies and set up your reply.**

   The text box at the bottom of the Automatic Replies dialog box turns from gray to white, and so does the check box labeled Only Send During This Time Range. That tells you that you can type an outgoing message into the text box, which will be sent to everyone who emails you while you're gone. You can also enter the times and dates of your absence so Outlook will automatically stop sending automatic replies after the end of your scheduled absence.

   Of course, you don't have to do any of that. You can leave your message mysteriously blank, but that would defeat the purpose of automatic replies. Thus, type a message in the box.

3. **Click OK.**

   Now go have a wonderful vacation. And don't forget to come back. Aloha!

MAILTIPS

Wouldn't it be great if Outlook were psychic and could tell you that the person you want to send a message to is out of the office even before you started writing the message? If you're lucky enough to be working in an office that uses a recent version of Exchange Server, Outlook might have access to a new feature called MailTips. MailTips doesn't give you advice on how to put pithier prose in your emails, but it does give you automatic information about your intended recipients as soon as you add the names to the To box. If you want to send a message to John Doe but John has turned on his Automatic Replies (Out of Office) setting, you'll see a MailTip at the top of your message displaying John's out of office message.

The Automatic Replies (Out of Office) setting is a nifty feature that automatically notifies anyone sending you a message when you aren't reachable via email — assuming you don't want to be bothered by work emails while you're on the beach sipping margaritas. It's activated when you turn on the Automatic Replies (Out of Office) feature.

MailTips can tell you other things, such as when you're addressing a message to a large group of recipients or when an intended recipient's mailbox is full and they can't receive the message you want to send. Most of the MailTips are limited to information about your colleagues within your organization, so don't expect to see a MailTip telling you that Aunt Petunia is on holiday in the south of France.

You might also notice that there's a separate tab for messages to people outside your organization. You can set Outlook to send different messages to outsiders than to fellow employees or not to send anything at all to outsiders and only reply to your coworkers.

Managing Your Address Books

Outlook uses several different address books that are really part of Microsoft Exchange Server, in addition to your regular Contacts list in the People module. The address books have several separate, independent lists of names and email addresses, so it can be pretty confusing.

The Outlook Contacts list (what you see when you click on the People button in the navigation bar) contains all kinds of personal information, whereas an address book (what you see when you click the To button in a new message) focuses on just email addresses. An address book can also deal with the nitty-gritty details of actually sending your message to people on your corporate email system, especially if that system is Microsoft Exchange Server.

Here's the lowdown on your plethora of address books:

» **The Global Address List:** If you're using Outlook on a corporate network, the Global Address List, which your system administrator maintains, normally has the names and email addresses of everyone in your company. The Global Address List allows you to address an email message to anybody in your company without having to look up the email address. If you're not connected to the Exchange server at the moment, it might be called the Offline Global Address List (refer to Figure 15-2).

» **The Contacts Address Book:** The Contacts Address Book contains the email addresses from the Contacts list. Outlook automatically populates the Contacts Address Book so you can easily add people to a message you're sending when you click the To button.

» **Additional address books:** If you create folders for Outlook contacts, those folders also become separate address books. Your system administrator can also create additional address books.

If you're lucky, you'll never see the address book. All the addresses of all the people you ever send email to are listed in the Global Address List that somebody else maintains, such as on a corporate network. Under those circumstances, Outlook is a dream. You don't need to know what an address book is most of the time; you just type the name of the person you're emailing in the To box of a message. Outlook checks the name for spelling and takes care of sending your message. You'd swear that a tiny psychic who knows just what you need lives inside your computer. Unless your Uncle Bob works for your company or is a regular client, however, it's doubtful that his email address will be found in the Global Address List.

Under less-than-ideal conditions, when you try to send a message, Outlook either complains it doesn't know how to send the message or can't figure out whom you're talking about. Then, you have to mess with the address. That situation happens only when the address isn't in one of the address books or isn't in a form that Outlook understands. For these cases, you must either enter the full address manually or add your recipient's name and address to your Contacts list.

OUTSOURCING MICROSOFT EXCHANGE

Even if you're allergic to buzzwords, the term *outsourcing* still has its appeal. If you're an entrepreneur or freelancer, you know how distracted you can get with the details of running your business; you simply don't have time to fuss with the details of running such an email system as Microsoft Exchange.

If you think you need the power of Microsoft Exchange but don't have time to deal with the details, plenty of companies are ready to provide Microsoft Exchange services at the drop of a hat. Microsoft itself offers just such a service through the Microsoft 365 program, and plenty of others are standing by with Microsoft Exchange servers you can log on to for pennies per person per day. If you'd like to shop around, you can search the Internet for other companies; type *hosted exchange service*.

IN THIS CHAPTER

» Finding out about Outlook on the Web

» Getting around the Outlook on the Web interface

» Reading and sending Web email

» Managing contacts

» Viewing and entering appointments

» Creating a to-do list

» Adjusting Outlook on the Web settings

Chapter **16**

Using Outlook on the Web: Your Outlook Away From Outlook

The desktop version of Outlook is the gold standard, with all the features, bells, and whistles. It's the version you want to use whenever you have access to your desktop or laptop PC. The trouble is, you might not always have that access. If you have a mobile device, you can use the mobile app version when you're on the go. The mobile version isn't particularly feature-rich, though, as you saw in Chapter 13.

Somewhere in-between those two extremes is Outlook on the Web (which used to be known simply by its URL, Outlook.com). Outlook on the Web is a moderately equipped web-based version of Outlook that you can access from any PC that has Internet access. That means you can access Outlook from hotel business centers, Internet cafes, and anyplace else that provides computer access when you don't have your own computer with you.

WHATEVER HAPPENED TO THE OUTLOOK WEB APP?

Until recently, organizations running Exchange Server could offer a web-based version of Outlook to their remote employees called the Outlook Web App. It was something like Outlook on the Web but had more features. The Outlook Web App has been discontinued, and organizations that used it are migrating to Outlook on the Web for desktop and laptop PCs, and to the mobile versions of Outlook for iPad, iPhone, and Android devices (which you learned about in Chapter 13).

TIP

Even though it has fewer features, many businesses actually prefer that employees access their company email from Outlook on the Web rather than setting it up in their desktop Outlook app. That's because the web-based version allows system administrators more security and control.

WARNING

Fair warning: The screenshots you see in this chapter may not exactly match what you see, because Microsoft is constantly tweaking and updating the Outlook online interface.

Signing In to Outlook on the Web

Outlook on the Web is a free web-based email service provided by Microsoft. (It used to be called Outlook.com, and that's still its URL, but it has a friendlier name now.) Outlook on the Web is somewhat like Google's Gmail service, but with a twist — it has a link to your desktop Outlook data.

You will need a Microsoft account to sign in to Outlook on the Web. You probably have one that you use to sign in to Windows, for example, or perhaps OneDrive or Xbox LIVE. To create a Microsoft account using an existing email address, start at https://account.microsoft.com/account. The email address associated with your Microsoft.com account must be the same one as the account you use in the desktop version of Outlook in order for the two versions to be synchronized.

WARNING

When you sign in to Outlook.com with your Microsoft account, you enter the email address and password you specified when you set up the Microsoft account. This is a separate password from the mail server password for that email address. You could make them the same, but it's better security to make them different.

The first time you sign in to Outlook.com, a few setup screens may appear. You might be prompted for your language, time zone, a theme color, a signature default, and a phone number. Enter any of that information as you like, and click through the setup to the end.

WARNING

In the past, Microsoft allowed you to send and receive mail from multiple email addresses using Outlook on the Web, similar to the way you do it in the desktop version of Outlook. This feature was discontinued in May 2021, so now you can only work with the data for one specific email address you signed in with. If you have multiple email addresses and you want to be able to check your mail for all of them in Outlook.com, you must create a separate Microsoft account for each of them and then sign out/sign in to switch among them.

TECHNICAL STUFF

If you're going to be jumping back and forth between the desktop Outlook app and Outlook on the Web, you should set up that email account as IMAP (which stands *for Internet Mail Access Protocol*; look back at Chapter 7 if you are confused about what that means). Doing so enables the online mail server to keep control of your incoming and outgoing mail when you use the desktop version of Outlook, so it can share it with Outlook on the Web.

Exploring the Outlook on the Web Interface

Outlook on the Web is similar to the desktop version of Outlook in function, so you won't need to figure out a whole new bunch of tricks and techniques, but it does look slightly different. Because Outlook on the Web is a web application, the screens may change, but Figure 16-1 gives you an idea of what you'll see after you sign in.

There are two versions of the Outlook on the Web interface. If you have a Microsoft 365 subscription, you get the ad-free, enhanced Outlook on the Web shown in Figure 16-1. (It might look slightly different if your company has an Exchange server and your Exchange administrator has customized the Outlook on the Web app. For example, my work email appears with a red bar across the top rather than a blue one. But that's pretty minor stuff, really.)

If you just have a regular free Microsoft account, you get one that's similar, but with an ad pane on the right side of the screen.

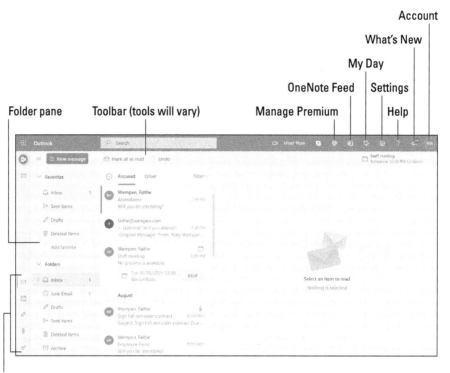

Account

What's New

My Day

OneNote Feed | Settings

Manage Premium | Help

Folder pane | Toolbar (tools will vary)

FIGURE 16-1:
The Outlook on
the Web screen
offers toolbars
and buttons to
help you get
around.

Navigation buttons

TIP

If you have a Microsoft 365 account but it isn't tied to the particular email address you are using for this activity, you can extend your Microsoft 365 privileges to the other account so the ads are removed from it, too. Sign in to your Microsoft account using the email address that has the subscription, go to Office.com, and choose to share your subscription with the other email address. Different subscription levels allow different numbers of people sharing the same account.

Here are some of the noteworthy features shown in Figure 16-1:

>> The **Folder pane** is the area along the left side of the screen that has the default Folders list of Inbox, Sent Items, Drafts, Junk Email, Deleted Items, and Archive.

>> The **Favorites list** is a section at the top of the Folder pane. The items in it are actually just shortcuts to some of the folders under the Folders heading. You can customize which folders appear here, for quick access to the folders you use most often.

>> The **navigation buttons** along the far-left edge enable you to switch to the other modules in Outlook on the Web. The modules, from top to bottom, are Mail, Calendar, People, Attachments, and Tasks. (Notice that there's no Notes module in Outlook on the Web.)

>> Instead of a ribbon across the top, there's a **toolbar.** The commands on the toolbar change depending on what's selected at the moment.

>> **Icons** in the upper right corner of the screen offer the following (from left to right):

- **Manage Premium:** Available only if you have the Premium version of Outlook on the Web (that is, if you have a Microsoft 365 subscription), opens a screen for working with Premium-only tools and checking your storage usage.

- **OneNote Feed:** Opens a pane where you can browse notes you have stored in OneNote.

- **My Day:** Opens a pane where you can browse your calendar and any upcoming meetings and tasks.

- **Settings:** Enables you to change some common settings, such as theme, conversation view, sorting, grouping, and the Reading pane.

- **Help:** Opens a help system for Outlook on the Web.

- **What's New:** Opens a pane of timely tips for using the latest features.

- **Account**: Enables you to edit your profile, view your account, or sign out.

As I noted at the beginning of this chapter, Microsoft is constantly making changes to the Outlook online interface, so you may see more or fewer icons than these and they may be arranged differently.

Getting Caught Up on Web Email Basics

Whether you're catching up on juicy office gossip or deleting spam from exiled Nigerian royalty, you can log on to Outlook on the Web from any browser to keep yourself in the loop.

Reading messages

Reading your incoming messages is probably going to be your first stop in Outlook on the Web. To read your messages in Outlook on the Web, follow these steps:

1. **Click Inbox in the Folders list.**

   Your list of messages appears.

2. **Click the message you want to read.**

    The message text appears in the Reading pane on the right side, or bottom, of the screen. As you click each message in the Message list, the contents show up in the Reading pane.

TIP

You can use the arrow keys to move from one email message to the next.

Click the Settings icon (it looks like a gear) in the upper right corner of the screen to adjust your mail settings, see a list of Reading pane options and Ribbon color options, and get online help. You can have the Reading pane open on the right or on the bottom of the screen, or have it closed entirely. If you close the Reading pane, you'll need to double-click each message to see it in a separate window, or single-click it to display it in the same window (replacing the email list).

Sending a message

When you feel the urge to dash off a quick email from your favorite Internet cafe, you can do that in a jiffy with Outlook on the Web. You'll probably have your message finished before your barista finishes mixing that high-octane mocha latte supremo. After your caffeine jitters die down, follow these steps:

1. **Click Inbox in the Folders list.**

    Your list of messages appears.

2. **Click the New Message button on the Ribbon.**

    The New Message pane opens, as shown in Figure 16-2.

3. **Fill out the New Message pane.**

    Put your recipient's address in the To box, a subject in the Add a Subject box, and the message in the main box.

    If you want to use Cc or Bcc, click the Cc or Bcc hyperlink in the upper right corner of the message composition pane.

TIP

4. **Click the Send button on the Ribbon.**

    Your message is on its way.

TIP

If you're not ready to send your message right away, click Save Draft. If you don't see Save Draft on the toolbar above the message composition pane, click the More button (. . .) to see more commands, including Save Draft. (You can see that menu coming up in the next section, in Figure 16-3.) You can continue working on your message later by clicking the Drafts folder in the Folder pane and then clicking the message.

New message button   Compose new message here.

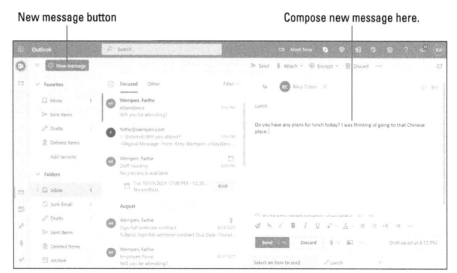

FIGURE 16-2:
The New Message
screen.

More button

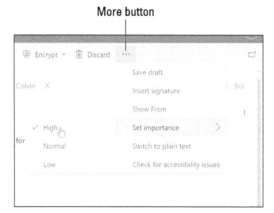

FIGURE 16-3:
You can prioritize
outgoing
messages by
setting their
importance.

Setting message importance

As you are composing a message with Outlook on the Web you can assign a priority of High, Normal, or Low. To set the importance for a message you are composing, click the More button (. . .) on the toolbar above the message composition pane and select Set Importance from the drop-down menu (see Figure 16-3).

WARNING

Don't overuse the High Priority option. Setting all your messages to High eventually leads people to ignore your priority markings. ("Oh, she thinks everything is urgent; just ignore her.") In fact, sometimes it's wise to mark a message as low priority. That tells the person you're contacting that you respect their time but that you also want to keep them informed. A little courtesy goes a long way. For a full explanation of message options, see Chapter 4.

Flagging messages

You can flag a received message to give it added attention. To set a flag, select the message and then click the More button (. . .) on the toolbar above the message (see Figure 16-4). On the menu that appears, click Flag. Flags are more basic in Outlook on the Web than they are in the desktop version of Outlook; you can't add dated reminders for flags here, for example.

FIGURE 16-4:
Flag your message to move it to the top of your Inbox.

Organizing Contacts

The whole point of Outlook on the Web is to let you see your collection of information from anywhere — and what's more important than keeping track of the people in your Contacts list? Practically nothing, so I show you the basics in the following sections.

Sorting your contacts

REMEMBER

Some people see their Contacts list as pure gold. They ogle and admire it whenever they're not busy playing Candy Crush. To see your Contacts list, click the People icon in the navigation bar on the left. (Refer to Figure 16-1.)

To control how the contacts appear, click the Sort drop-down menu in the upper right corner of the Contacts List pane to open the menu shown in Figure 16-5. Generically, this is the Sort list because it allows you to sort by different fields, but the actual name of the command you click will be whatever the current sort order is. In Figure 16-5, it's By First Name. Then choose the sort option you want.

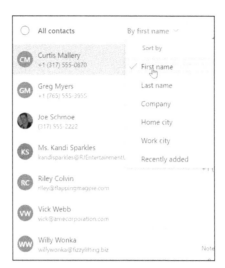

FIGURE 16-5:
Choose how you
would like to sort
your contacts.

A good Contacts list is precious; it's even more valuable than that snazzy office chair you covet or even that enviable cubicle near the coffee station. Outlook on the Web can help you keep your Contacts list up to date from wherever you are. For example, if you go to a conference or convention and exchange business cards with lots of people, you probably want to add those names to your Contacts list as soon as possible. Whether you're using a laptop, tablet, or smartphone (or the nearest public library or Internet cafe), you can log on to your account remotely to enter all those new addresses before you go home.

To add a new contact through Outlook on the Web, follow these steps:

1. **From the People module, click the New Contact button in the upper left corner of the screen.**

   The New Contact form opens.

2. **Fill in the blanks in the New Contact form.**

   The information you type appears in the New Contact form, as shown in Figure 16-6.

3. **Click Create.**

   The New Contact form closes and the name you entered appears in your Contacts list.

If you want to edit a contact you've entered, just open a contact record, click Edit on the toolbar at the top, and follow the same steps. (For a full explanation of Outlook contact entries, see Chapter 8.)

Using Your Calendar

The Calendar module in Outlook on the Web is much simpler than what you're accustomed to in the desktop Outlook app, but it does all the basic things. You can view it in different ways, and create, edit, and delete appointments.

Viewing your calendar

Time management gurus insist that you manage your schedule for the long term, medium term, and short term. The Outlook on the Web Calendar lets you view your appointments in different ways depending on what you want to see (or avoid seeing). To access it, click the Calendar icon on the navigation bar (refer to Figure 16-1).

Click to open the View drop-down menu in the upper right corner of the screen. Depending on the current view, it could be named Day, Week, and so on. Figure 16-7 shows it set to Month. Choose the desired view:

>> **Day** shows one day's appointments. Or, click the arrow to the right of the Day button and choose a number of days from the menu (1 day to 7 days).

>> **Week** shows a week.

>> **Work week** shows a Monday through Friday period.

>> **Month** shows a month.

Entering an appointment

If you're a heavy-duty road warrior, you probably keep your calendar on a smart-phone for your own reference, but for everyone else, those appointments and meetings are very likely on an Outlook Calendar. The appointments and meetings you post in Outlook are linked to Outlook on the Web, so from any web-enabled device, you can see where you should be and with whom. Now you'll know when you're available for meetings, lunches, and random tongue lashings.

WARNING

If you want your Outlook desktop data and your Outlook on the Web data to sync automatically, you must be using the same email address on both systems. Your calendar data won't be the same if you sign up for an Outlook on the Web email account but use a POP account from another service on desktop Outlook. You can have multiple email accounts on Outlook on the Web; just create a new one and then link it to the preferred account you're using on the desktop version of Outlook.

To enter an appointment, follow these steps:

1. **Switch to the Calendar module by clicking the Calendar button on the navigation bar.**

    The Calendar shows your appointments, as shown in Figure 16-8.

2. **Click the New Event button on the toolbar at the top left corner of the screen.**

    A pop-up window appears for creating a new appointment. See Figure 16-9.

3. **Click in the Add a Title placeholder and type a title.**

    Enter something that describes your appointment, such as *Meeting with Bambi and Godzilla*. Or, if you're going to be all boring about, it, something like *Pediatrician*.

4. **Click the Location box and enter a location for your appointment.**

    Hmmm, perhaps central Tokyo? Or the pediatrician's office?

New Event button

FIGURE 16-8:
Your calendar
displays your
appointments.

Calendar button

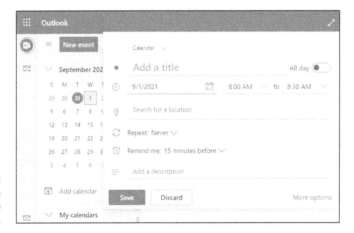

FIGURE 16-9:
Add an
appointment title
and other details.

5. **In the bar at the top of the pop-up window, you see the calendar name (such as My Calendar). If you have multiple calendars, open the bar's drop-down menu and choose the right calendar.**

   You can link multiple calendars to Outlook on the Web.

6. **Click the date on the event and choose a different date if needed.**

   If the pop-up calendar doesn't have the date, click the arrows next to the name of the month in the small calendar until the date appears.

7. **Click the down arrow on the first Time box and choose the start time of your appointment.**

   Or, if it's an all-day thing, click the All Day switch to on and skip ahead to Step 9.

8. **Click the down arrow on the second Time box and choose the end time of your appointment.**

9. **Set any other options as desired, such as recurrence (Repeat) and reminders.**

10. **Click Save.**

   By default, your Outlook on the Web Calendar will send you email notifications about upcoming appointments for the day. Click the link in the email message to see appointment details.

TIP

An even quicker way to enter an appointment is to switch the calendar to Day or Week view (use the Month drop-down menu in the upper right corner of the screen) and then double-click the line that corresponds to the day and hour of your appointment. The Add an Event form appears, showing the date and time you chose.

Moving an appointment

You can change an appointment time by simply dragging the appointment to the date and time you choose. If you need to change anything other than the date and time of your appointment, follow these steps:

1. **Double-click the appointment.**

2. **Select the information you want to change.**

3. **Enter the updated information.**

4. **Click Save.**

   To delete an appointment, click the appointment to select it and then click Delete to zap it. (You can find out more about the power of the Outlook Calendar in Chapter 9.)

Creating a To-Do List

As I pointed out near the end of Chapter 10, Outlook has a To Do module that mirrors the one in Outlook.com. Click the To Do icon in the navigation bar at Outlook.com to check out the app. (It's the icon that looks like a check mark.) Even though you are already signed in at Outlook.com, you might be asked to sign in again at this point.

Once you get signed in, the online interface for the To Do app is nearly identical to the one you saw in Chapter 10 in the desktop version of Outlook. If you created a task in Chapter 10 as you were going through the steps there, and you're signed into Outlook.com using the same Microsoft account, you will see that task here now. And any tasks you create here will automatically appear in the desktop version of Outlook as well. See Figure 16-10.

FIGURE 16-10:
The To Do module at Outlook.com is the same as (and linked to) the To Do module in the desktop version of Outlook.

Exploring Your Options

You can adjust a limited number of options through Outlook on the Web. To see what options are available, click the Settings button (it looks like a gear) in the upper right corner of the screen.

There are two levels of options you can set. The most basic and popular ones appear in the Settings task pane when you click the Settings button, as shown in Figure 16-11. These options change depending on which module you are in. If there are more options than you can see at once, you can scroll down to see the others.

For a lot more options, click View All Outlook Settings at the bottom of the pane, which opens the Settings dialog box shown in Figure 16-12. You can move between the options for different modules by clicking a category in the navigation pane on the left, just like in the Outlook Settings dialog box in the desktop version.

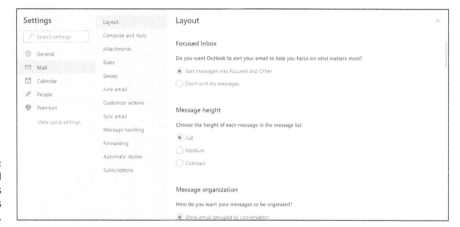

Automated vacation replies/out of office message

With the desktop version of Outlook (and an Exchange email account), you can set your out of office message to let coworkers know when you'll be out of town (or just plain unavailable). You have a similar tool in Outlook on the Web — only it's called the Automated Vacation reply. It's a great way to let all your friends know when you're on vacation (and make all of them envious). Just follow these steps:

1. **From the Outlook on the Web Mail module, click the Settings icon at the top of the screen.**

2. **Scroll down to the bottom of the pane and click View All Outlook Settings.**

   The Settings dialog box opens. Make sure Mail is selected in the navigation pane on the left.

3. **In the middle pane, click Automatic Replies.**

   The Automatic Replies settings appear.

4. **Click the Turn On Automatic Replies control to enable it.**

5. **(Optional) Select the Send Replies Only During a Time Period check box and then enter the start and end dates and times.**

6. **Click the Add a Message Here placeholder and type your out of office message that should be sent.**

   Figure 16-13 shows an example.

7. **Click the Save button.**

   The setting is saved.

8. **Click the Close (X) button to close the Settings dialog box.**

Now you can stop feeling guilty about ignoring all those emails. (Well, okay, maybe you'll still feel a teeny bit guilty, but you've done your part.) Try to remember to turn Automatic Replies off when you get back. Otherwise, everyone will think you're still having fun without them. To turn the feature off, repeat steps 1–3, and then click Automatic Replies On to turn the feature off. Click Save and then close the Settings dialog box.

Creating a signature

You get to decide when to include the one signature you're allowed to create in Outlook on the Web. Your signature for business might be very grand and official — the better to impress lackeys and sycophants as well as to intimidate rivals. In that case, you might prefer to leave it off the messages you send to your friends — unless, of course, your only friends are lackeys and sycophants. Then, lay it on thick, Your Royal Highness!

Create a signature in Outlook on the Web by following these steps:

1. **From the Outlook on the Web Mail module, click the Settings icon at the top of the screen.**

2. **Click View All Outlook Settings.**

   The Settings dialog box opens.

3. **In the left pane, click Mail, and then in the middle pane, click Compose and Reply.**

   An Email Signature box appears.

4. **Type your signature text in the box.**

   Use the formatting tools above the box to format your text as desired. Figure 16-14 shows an example.

FIGURE 16-14: Create a signature for Outlook on the Web.

5. **Click Save.**

   The Settings dialog box closes.

After you create a signature, it goes in every email message you send. Of course, you can always delete the signature before you send an email.

REMEMBER

The signature you created in the desktop version of Outlook won't automatically appear when you send messages from Outlook on the Web, and vice versa. You have to enter your signature in both places.

6

The Part of Tens

Learn about ten worthwhile shortcuts that will help boost your productivity, including turning a message into a meeting and resending messages.

Explore the reasons behind ten things you can't do with Outlook, including not being able to have a unified Inbox and not being able to create a distribution list from an email.

Discover ten actions you can take once you become a super Outlook user, such as simultaneously viewing multiple calendars and inserting symbols and art into Outlook messages.

Chapter **17**

Ten Shortcuts Worth Taking

E ven though computers are supposed to save you time, some days, this just doesn't seem to be the case. Juggling buttons, keys, and Ribbons can seem to take all day. This chapter offers ten (plus one extra!) shortcuts that can save you time and stress.

Using the New Item Button

To create a new item in whatever module you're in, just click the tool at the far-left end of the Ribbon. The name and appearance of that icon changes when you change modules, so it becomes a New Task icon in the Tasks module, a New Contact icon in the People module, and so on.

Depending on the module, that button might have a drop-down menu associated with it, as in Figure 17-1. If there is one, you can open that menu and choose some other type of content to create. That's the case in the Mail and People modules.

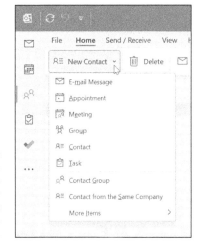

FIGURE 17-1:
The New Item
menu enables
you to create new
items in modules
other than the
active one.

If the leftmost button doesn't have a drop-down menu (which is the case in the Calendar, Tasks, and Notes modules), then there will be another button immediately to its right that *does* have a drop-down menu, and enables you to choose new content to create in other modules.

Sending a File to an Email Recipient

You can send a file via Outlook email with only a few mouse clicks, even if Outlook isn't running. When you're viewing files in File Explorer, you can mark any file to be sent to any email recipient. Here's how:

1. **Find the file in File Explorer.**

2. **Right-click on the file that you want to send.**

    A menu appears.

3. **If you're using Windows 11, click Show More Options.**

    This step isn't necessary in Windows 10.

4. **Choose Send To.**

    Another menu appears.

5. **Choose Mail Recipient.**

    A New Message form appears. An icon that represents the attached file appears in the Attached box.

6. **Type the subject of the file and the email address of the person to whom you're sending the file.**

    If you want to add comments to your message, type them in the message area of the window.

7. **Click Send.**

    Your message goes to the recipient.

WARNING These steps work only if Outlook is your default email application.

In Windows 10 it is fairly easy to check and change the default mail application. Choose Start ➪ Settings ➪ Apps ➪ Default Apps. Under Email, make sure that Outlook appears. If it does not, click the app that *does* appear there and then choose Outlook from the menu. See Figure 17-2.

Windows 11 has made it more difficult to set a default email app in general; its settings are far more granular, and somewhat confusing. Choose Settings ➪ Apps ➪ Default Apps ➪ Mail, and then make sure that all the available email-related file types are set to default to Outlook. If that still doesn't work, see the next section.

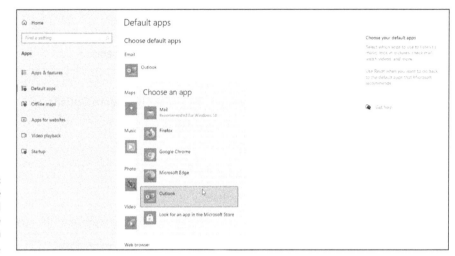

FIGURE 17-2:
Outlook must be
the default email
app in order to
send files from
File Explorer.

Sending a Link to a File

In Windows 11, if the preceding steps don't work, you may find it easier to circum-vent the whole thing and use these steps instead to send a link to the file from your OneDrive storage. You can also use these same steps in Windows 10.

1. **Find the file in File Explorer. If it is not saved to OneDrive, copy it to your OneDrive storage.**

2. **Right-click on the file that you want to send.**

    A menu appears.

3. **Click OneDrive, and then click Share.**

4. **(Optional) To make the link read-only, click Anyone with the Link Can Edit. Deselect the Allow Editing check box and click Apply.**

5. **Fill out the Send Link dialog box, entering the recipient's email address and a message.**

    See Figure 17-3.

6. **Click Send.**

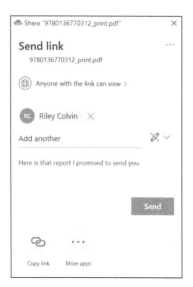

FIGURE 17-3:
Sharing a link to a
file stored on
your OneDrive.

Sending a File From a Microsoft Office Application

You can email any Office document from the Office application itself without using the Outlook email module. Here's how:

1. **With an Office document open in the application that created it, click the File tab.**

2. **Choose Share.**

The Share dialog box appears.

3. **Click Send a Copy.**

4. **On the menu that appears, click the desired format.**

The format choices depend on which app you are in. For example, in Word, your choices are Word Document and PDF.

Use whichever format is most appropriate for the share at hand. Use the default Office app format (such as Word) if you want the recipient to be able to edit the file easily, and use PDF if you don't want that.

A New Message form appears in Outlook.

5. **Edit the subject of the message, if desired.**

By default, it is the filename.

6. **In the To box, enter the email address of the person to whom you're sending the file.**

   You can type it in directly or choose it from a list by clicking the To button, the same as when you send any other message in Outlook.

7. **(Optional) Add a comment in the message body.**

   The message body is the blank area below the file attachment.

8. **Click the Send button.**

   Your message is sent.

Turning a Message Into a Meeting

Sometimes, after you've exchanged umpteen email messages about a topic, you realize it would be faster to just talk for a few minutes. You can turn an email message into a meeting by selecting the message in the Inbox and then clicking the Reply with Meeting button in the Respond group on the Home tab. That opens a New Meeting form so you can set up a meeting based on the contents of the email.

Finding Something

It doesn't take long to amass quite a large collection of items in Outlook, which can then take a long time to browse through when you want to find one specific item. Outlook can search for items at your command if you type what you're seeking in the Search box at the top of every screen. That starts a quick search so you can get to what you want in a flash.

Undoing Your Mistakes

If you didn't know about the Undo command, it's time you heard the good news: When you make a mistake, you can undo it by pressing Ctrl+Z or by clicking the Undo button on the Quick Access Toolbar in the upper left corner of the screen. So, feel free to experiment; the worst you'll have to do is undo! Make sure you undo right away, though, because it only undoes the last thing you did.

Not everything can be undone. For example, you can't un-send a message that you've accidentally sent. Much to the chagrin of anyone who has ever clicked Send too quickly and sent something really embarrassing.

Using the Go to Date Dialog Box

You can use the Go to Date dialog box, shown in Figure 17-4, in all Calendar views. To access it, click the Properties button in the lower right corner of the Go To group on the Home tab. Alternatively, you can press Ctrl+G as a shortcut.

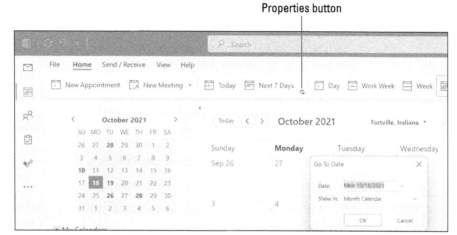

FIGURE 17-4:
The Go to Date dialog box.

You can enter a specific date here, or you can specify a date in a variety of other ways. For example, if you want to skip ahead 60 days, press Ctrl+G and type *60 days from now*. The Calendar moves forward 60 days from the current date.

Adding Items in List Views

Many Outlook lists have a blank field at the top where you can type an entry and create a new item for that list. When you see the words Click Here to Add a New Task, that's exactly what you do. Just click in the field and type your new item.

Sending Repeat Messages

I have one or two messages I send out repeatedly, so I've stored the text as Quick Parts to save time. Quick Parts enables you to save blocks of text and then recall them later, pasting them into new messages.

For example, when I'm writing an article about Outlook accessories, I send a message to every company I encounter that makes things for Outlook. The message says something like this:

> *I'm currently writing an article about Microsoft Outlook, and I'd like to evaluate your product, XXX, for discussion in my article. Could you please send me a press kit?*

I have saved this boilerplate text as a Quick Parts item, so I can re-use it.

To take advantage of Quick Parts, you must first store the text blocks you want to be able to recall later. Follow these steps:

1. **In an email message, appointment, contact record, meeting, or task, type and select the text you want to repeatedly use.**

2. **Click the Insert tab.**

3. **Click the Quick Parts button located in the Text group.**

4. **Click Save Selection to Quick Part Gallery.**

    You can create groups of Quick Part text for different purposes. For example, you could generate introductory text or closing text for different types of messages and then store this text in the gallery under Intro or Closings.

Then, when I find a new Outlook accessory vendor on the Internet, I follow these steps to create a new message to them that uses my saved boilerplate text:

1. **Start a new message, and fill in the recipient's address in the To box.**

2. **Click the Insert tab.**

3. **Click in the message body area, and then click the Quick Parts button.**

4. **Choose the AutoText item you saved.**

    It is pasted into the email body. Change any placeholders to the actual data. For example, I will change XXX to the name of the product.

5. **Click the Send button.**

    I can have a request out in less than 30 seconds and get on to my next task.

Resending a Message

Sometimes, you need to remind someone who forgot to do something you asked them to do. You could draft a whole new message reminding that person how many times you've reminded them already. But it's faster and easier to do this:

1. **Go to your Sent Items folder.**

2. **Double-click the message you sent last time.**

3. **Click Actions.**

4. **Choose Resend This Message.**

    You might also add a sentence saying "In case this didn't reach you, here's another copy."

» Put a phone number in your calendar

» Open a message from the Reading pane

» Print on two sides

» Search and replace area codes

» Print a list of meeting attendees

» Enlarge the type in the Calendar location box

» Create a distribution list from one email

» Track time zones for meetings

» Safely back up Outlook data

Chapter **18**

Ten Things You Can't Do with Outlook

Maybe I sound crabby listing the things Outlook can't do, considering all the things it *can* do. But it takes only a few minutes to find out something a program can do, and you can spend all day trying to figure out something a program *can't* do. I could easily list *more* than ten things that Outlook can't do (walk the dog, deflect incoming asteroids — the usual). This chapter lists just the first big ones I've run into.

Bear in mind that Outlook can't do these ten things when you first get it. I've been informed by geeky programmer types that it's possible to reprogram Outlook with

Visual Basic in order to make Outlook do many of these things by creating shortcut macros. That's not only beyond the scope of this book, but it's also something normal, sensible people don't do. But if you cook up a way to do one of these, let me know and I'll take it off the list next time.

Create a Unified Inbox

Many people have more than one email address; it's pretty common to separate business and personal email accounts. And almost everyone uses email on more than one device today — typically, a computer and a mobile phone. But your desktop version of Outlook 2021 can't create a single unified Inbox if you use the kind of email made for multiple devices — also known as IMAP. (Refer to Chapter 7 if you don't know what that is.) The Android and iPad versions of Outlook offer a unified Inbox, but not the huge, venerable desktop version. That would be very convenient, but it's not happening in this version.

TIP

If it's really important to have a single Inbox for all your accounts, here's a workaround. Configure all your email accounts for POP access when you set them up in Outlook, and choose to manually configure the account (advanced settings). When prompted whether to create a new data file or use an existing one, choose an existing one (such as outlook.pst). Do this with the same existing data file for each mail account.

Insert a Phone Number Into Your Calendar

When you enter an appointment, it would be nice if Outlook could look up the phone number of the person you're meeting and insert that number into the appointment record. Many smartphones can do this through an address lookup feature, but you can't get Outlook to follow suit. Maybe some other time.

Open a Message From the Reading Pane

Let's say you are viewing a message in the Reading Pane, and then you scroll your Inbox pane to check on a different message. So now the Reading Pane shows a message that you can't see in the Inbox pane at the moment.

Now let's say you decide to open the Reading Pane's message in its own window, while still looking at your current spot in the Inbox. How are you going to do that? You can't, because you have to scroll back in the Inbox to the message's location and double-click it.

It doesn't seem like it would be terribly difficult for Microsoft to include a right-click command to open the message in the Reading Pane, but it isn't there.

Perform Two-Sided Printing

Some people like to print their schedule and keep it in a binder to look just like one of those old-fashioned planner books. I guess they're just sentimental for the good ol' paper-and-pencil days. The only problem with that is that Outlook doesn't know how to reorganize printed pages according to whether the page is on the left side or the right side of the book when you look at it. This is a very small quibble, but if it's important to you, sorry — you'll have to live with one-sided printing. That, or print one page, flip the paper over and reload it, print the next page, and so on.

Search and Replace Area Codes

It seems like the people at the phone company change area codes more often than they change their socks these days. If you need to change all your 312s to 708s, Outlook can't do that automatically; you'll have to change them one by one. Microsoft did offer a utility for changing Russian area codes, but as for area codes in the United States — *nyet!*

Print a List of Meeting Attendees

Sometimes, when you're preparing for a big meeting you organized via Outlook, especially if it's a conference call, it's nice to keep a list of attendees handy. Yes, you can keep the meeting item open on your calendar, but that won't work if you're running the meeting and doing a presentation.

Enlarge the Type in the Calendar Location Box

Conference calls are frequently organized in Outlook these days, and it's common to put the dial-in numbers in the location box of the Calendar form. Unless you have eyes like a hawk, those teeny-weeny numbers can be tough to decipher, especially when you're dialing in a hurry — right after getting off your last conference call. I recommend a magnifying glass.

Create Contact Records for All Recipients of an Email

When you get an email message addressed to a whole group of people, you can create a distribution list from that message by copying all the recipients to a group. You can also turn a message from a single person into an individual contact record by dragging the message to the People icon. But if you want to create contact records for a group of people, you have to create a contact record for every single person individually — no drag and drop and no copy and paste.

Track Time Zones for Meetings

It's not unusual to use Outlook to organize conference calls or video meetings between people in many different time zones. I've frequently had to set up calls between one person in London, another in Sydney, another in Chicago, and me in New York City. The scheduling tool in the Outlook Calendar does show each person's working hours — if they've set that up — but it doesn't actually show what time of day it is in each person's location. When you have to set up a call that will happen at an awful time for somebody, it's good to know exactly how awful. That way, you can make it slightly less awful. There are websites that help you understand the time in multiple time zones, but those don't include the availability information you get in Outlook. Thus, you have to guess at a time and then apologize when you guess wrong.

Back Up Outlook Data Easily

WARNING

Many people store their most critical business information in Outlook — information that's so valuable that losing it could practically close a business or end a career. It's no joke.

But after more than a quarter-century in the marketplace, Outlook has never been given a decent tool for safeguarding its own data from loss. Yes, everyone knows you should back up all the data on your computer regularly and you can make copies of your critical Outlook data (some of those tiny memory keys can do the job, and you can save Outlook data to a handheld computer if need be), but it's a little bit disturbing that no such feature has ever been added to Outlook itself. If you get your email service through Microsoft 365, though, all your Outlook data is stored safely in the cloud, so that's probably your best precaution.

Now that most people are using IMAP rather than POP for their mail accounts, the lack of backup is somewhat less critical than it used to be. That's because IMAP accounts store everything on the mail server, and just display it locally on your PC. With POP accounts, everything is stored in a .pst file; with IMAP accounts, a local copy of everything is stored in an .ost file. See Chapter 7 for more information about POP and IMAP.

Chapter **19**

Ten Things You Can Do After You're Comfy

I f Outlook offers an iceberg's worth of capabilities, I can only show you the tip in this book. You can already do some formidable tasks with Outlook. Time will tell (and pretty quickly at that) how much more you'll be able to do with future versions of Outlook.

You can't do much to really mess up Outlook, so feel free to experiment. Add new fields, new views, new icons — go wild. This chapter describes ten Outlook adventures to try out.

Take Notes

Outlook has a super-handy Notes module that allows you to type a quick note about any random thing and then get back to what you were doing. Press Ctrl+Shift+N to open a note, type some text, and then press Esc to make the note disappear. To read the notes you've created, press Ctrl+5 or open the Notes module from the navigation bar to see the full list of notes, and then double-click the note you want to read.

The Notes module is a rather primitive feature, dating back to the early days when Outlook emerged from the primordial ooze. Back then, the Notes module was a prominent feature of the product. I still prefer Notes for such simple things as instructions for filling out online forms or details about projects I want to remember later. Nowadays, Microsoft prefers that you keep freeform notes in Microsoft OneNote — a much richer and more capable member of the Microsoft Office family. But if you like your notes short, sweet, and simple, try Notes in Outlook.

WARNING

It might be tempting to store the usernames and passwords for various websites in the Notes module, but it's a risky security practice. Anyone who sits down at your computer and snoops your Outlook file can hit the motherlode and have all your passwords. There are safer ways to store passwords, like a password-management tool such as True Key.

Customize the Quick Access Toolbar

Office applications have an arrangement of controls (a *user interface*, as geeks like to say) that eliminates menus in favor of the Ribbon, tabs, and buttons. It's a good way of cramming a lot of different commands into a small space, but I often have trouble figuring out how to do many of the things I want to do. When I do finally locate the command I want, I forget how I got there when I need to use it again later.

However, there's hope. After you find the tool you need, you can right-click the tool and choose Add to Quick Access Toolbar. That adds a tiny icon to that thin strip of icons that sits just above the Ribbon. The Quick Access Toolbar is kind of like a bookmark bar for the commands you want to keep track of, just as you would bookmark websites in your web browser to return to them later.

TIP

The Quick Access Toolbar appears above the Ribbon tabs by default. However, if you click the down-arrow button at the right end of the Quick Access Toolbar and choose Show Below the Ribbon, it moves below the Ribbon.

Each Outlook form also features its own Quick Access Toolbar, with its customizations stored separately from the others. That's useful for speeding up tasks that you perform frequently using certain forms. If you like to print individual email messages from time to time, for example, you can add the Quick Print command when you're reading or composing a message. That way, the Print command is a couple clicks closer. The Quick Print command prints immediately to the default printer using the default settings, bypassing Backstage view.

TIP

You can also add more tools to the Quick Access Toolbar right from the toolbar itself. Simply click the down arrow to the right of the existing icons on the toolbar and choose any of the most popular commands to add. If you choose More Commands from this list, a much larger dialog box opens. From here, you can scroll through a longer list of commands. In this dialog box's Choose Commands field, you can display all commands. Add or remove commands from the Quick Access Toolbar to your heart's content.

Smarten Up Your Messages with Smart Art

I don't know whether art makes you smart, but design can make you look smart if you know what you're doing. If you don't know what you're doing, you can fall back on Smart Art — another intriguing feature on the Ribbon's Insert tab. Smart Art helps you create colorful, annotated infographics to add to your email.

TIP

An *infographic* is a graphic that conveys information, usually with a combination of text and shapes or pictures.

To get a better picture of what Smart Art can do, follow these steps:

1. **With a new message composition window open and the insertion point in the message body, click the Insert tab.**

2. **Click SmartArt.**

   If using the Simplified Ribbon, click the More Commands button to access the SmartArt command.

   If the SmartArt command is unavailable, click the Format Text tab and set the value in the Format group to either HTML or Rich Text.

3. **Try a few designs on for size.**

Translate Your Email Messages

If your incoming email messages are so confusing that they seem like they're written in a foreign language, maybe they are.

You can translate short bits of text in Outlook this way:

1. **Select some foreign-language text in a message.**

2. **Right-click on the selection and choose Translate.**

    A menu appears containing a possible translation.

For entire messages, here's an alternative method:

1. **On the Message tab, click Translate, and then choose Translate Message.**

    The translated version shows in the message window.

2. **(Optional) Return to the original by clicking Show Original.**

Add Charts for Impact

The Chart tool is just beneath or next to the SmartArt button on the Ribbon's Insert tab. The tool can make the thoughts you express in your email look positively orderly (no matter how disordered your mind may be).

Chart it up with these steps:

1. **From inside a new email message, with the insertion point in the message body, click the Insert tab and click Chart.**

    If using the Simplified Ribbon, click More Commands to access the Chart command.

    You see a two-part gallery: a list of general chart types on the left and specific examples of each type on the right.

    If the Chart button is unavailable, click the Format Text tab and set the value in the Format group to either HTML or Rich Text.

2. **Choose a general type from the list on the left.**

3. **Choose a specific type from the list on the right.**

4. **Click OK.**

    A grid opens, allowing you to enter numbers.

The mechanics of creating an Outlook chart are very similar to those for creating an Excel chart. If you need more detailed information about creating charts, pick up a copy of *Excel All-in-One For Dummies, Office 2021 Edition* by Paul McFedries and Greg Harvey.

Use Symbols in Email

If you frequently use symbols, such as the euro currency symbol, you can add those symbols to your email messages by clicking the Symbol button on the Insert tab while composing an email message; just choose the symbol you want. If you choose More Symbols, you can also insert such clever things as fractions, arrows, and strange hieroglyphics to baffle your recipients into complying with your wishes.

Open Multiple Calendars

You can create more than one calendar in Outlook. You might want to do so to track the activities of more than one person or to keep your business life separate from your personal life (which is always a good idea). The tricky part of keeping multiple calendars is dealing with schedule conflicts between the two. To see two calendars at a time, select the check box next to each calendar name in the navigation pane. See Chapter 9 to learn all about Outlook's Calendar feature.

Superimpose Calendars

An even slicker way to avoid conflicts on multiple calendars is to superimpose one calendar on top of another. When you have two cale ndars open, a small arrow appears next to the name of one. When you click that arrow, both calendars appear — one atop the other — with both sets of appointments showing. The appointments in the bottom calendar appear slightly opaque, while the top calendar items look clearer and bolder. When calendars are superimposed, you can see right away when time is available on both.

Select Dates as a Group

When you're viewing a range of dates, you don't have to limit yourself to fixed days, weeks, or months. Suppose you want to look at a range of dates from September 25 to October 5. On the To-Do bar, click September 25 and then (while pressing the Shift key) click October 5. All the dates in between are selected and appear in the Information Viewer.

Turn on the Folder pane to reveal the Date Navigator and then try it on the calendar that displays in the left corner. The Date Navigator is described in Chapter 9.

Pin a Contact Card

If you want to keep a person's contact information on-screen while you do something else, you can right-click on a person's email address in an email message (in the Reading pane or in the message's separate window) and choose Open Contact Card. Near the upper right corner of the contact card is a tiny picture of a pushpin. Click that pushpin to make the contact card float on the screen; click the pushpin again to make it go away. You can drag the card around so it doesn't cover whatever you are working on.

TIP

You've pinned a contact and it's not there anymore? Don't worry. That's probably because you're using Outlook in its default full-screen mode. When you click off the pinned contact, the full-screen Outlook screen hides it. Click the Restore Down or Minimize button in the upper right of the Outlook screen. See the contact now? Good.

Index

S

safe recipients, 118
safe senders, 118
Save As dialog box, 80
saving
  custom views, 300
  draft email, 79
  email copies, 89–90
  emails as files, 79–80
schedules, managing, 20
scheduling
  appointments, 196–206
  appointments from email messages, 48–49
  mobile emails, 278–281
screens
  forward, 76
  Inbox, 82
  reply, 72
screenshots, 98–99
ScreenTip, viewing, 36–37
Search, 38–40
searching
  area codes, 361
  contacts, 38–40, 181–183
  folders, 107–110
  Search, 38–40
  shortcut for, 354
security suite, 116
Select Attendees and Resources dialog box, 309–310
sender list, filtering junk mail with, 118–120
sending
  attachments, 93–97
  files, 16–18
  files from Microsoft Office Application shortcut, 353–354
  files from other applications, 95–97
  files to email recipient shortcut, 350–352
  links to files, 352–353

messages from different accounts, 153–154
messages on Outlook on the Web, 334–335
repeat emails, 356
replies, 72–74
status reports, 317
sensitivity
  of junk mail filter, 116–118
  setting, 66–67
Server Tasks view (tasks), 229
servers (email), 156–157
settings
  Conversation Clean Up, 135–136
  dialog box, 343
  forwarding, 90–91
  mail account modification of, 150–153
  message importance on Outlook on the Web, 335
  message options, 67–68
  on Outlook on the Web, 333, 342–346
  replying, 90–91
  sensitivity, 66–67
setup
  access permissions for calendars, 321–323
  Archive feature, 123–125
  email account in Outlook, 146–153
  flags for different days, 84–85
  forwarding options, 90–91
  junk mail sensitivity, 116–118
  Outlook to work with iCloud, 271–272
  priorities, 65–66
  replying options, 90–91
SharePoint, 26
sharing calendars, 212–217
shortcuts
  category, 303–304
  creating messages, 61
  Go to Date dialog box, 355

keyboard, 7–8
List view, adding items to, 355
module, 28
New Item button, 350
Quick Parts, 142
resending emails, 357
searching, 354
sending files, 350–352
sending links to files, 352–353
sending repeat emails, 356
turning message into meetings, 354
undoing mistakes, 354–355
signatures
  copying from existing, 100
  creating in emails, 99–101
  creating on Outlook on the Web, 345–346
Signatures and Stationary dialog box, 99–100
signing in/out, 330–331
Simple List view (tasks), 228–229
Smart Art, 367
smartphones
  mobile calendar use on, 282–283
  mobile email on, 275–282
  Pew research study of, 274
Sort dialog box, 298–299
sorting
  messages, 129–131
  from Sort dialog box, 298–299
  from table view, 98
  view of contacts, 175–176
spam
  defined, 116
  filtering, 116–121
  filters for, 104
  sensitivity setting, 116–118
status reports, sending, 317
subscribing to Google Calendar in Outlook, 262–264
suite (Office), 25

About the Author

Faithe Wempen, M.A., has been educating people about computers for nearly 40 years. She is a Microsoft Office Specialist Master Instructor, a CompTIA A+ certified PC repair technician, and the author of over 160 books on computer hardware and software, including *Office 2021 For Seniors For Dummies* and *Computers For Seniors For Dummies*. She also teaches Computer Hardware and Software Architectures at Indiana University/Purdue University at Indianapolis and designs custom online technology courses for several leading online schools. In her spare time, she's a fitness enthusiast, and you'll find her at the gym nearly every day having fun and staying healthy with her fellow gym rats.

Dedication

To Margaret, who has been making it possible all these years.

Author's Acknowledgments

Thanks so much to the extraordinary team at Wiley that made this edition about Outlook a reality: to Kelsey Baird for her assistance in getting the project started; to Lynn Northrup for her consistent and steady editorial guidance; and to Rod Stephens for his thorough and detailed technical editing.

Publisher's Acknowledgments

Executive Editor: Steven Hayes

Acquisitions Editor: Kelsey Baird

Project Editor: Lynn Northrup

Technical Editor: Rod Stephens

Editorial Assistant: Audrey Lee

Production Editor: Tamilmani Varadharaj

Cover Image: © rawf8/Shutterstock

CPSIA information can be obtained
at www.ICGtesting.com
Printed in the USA
LVHW061626040122
707840LV00010B/192